DEVELOPING BUSINESS SYSTEMS WITH CORBA

Managing Object Technology Series

Charles F. Bowman
Series Editor

and

President
SoftWright Solutions
Suffern, New York

Additional Volumes in Preparation

DEVELOPING
BUSINESS SYSTEMS
WITH CORBA

WAQAR SADIQ
FRED CUMMINS

 CAMBRIDGE
UNIVERSITY PRESS

 SIGS
BOOKS

PUBLISHED BY THE PRESS SYNDICATE OF THE UNIVERSITY OF CAMBRIDGE
The Pitt Building, Trumpington Street, Cambridge CB2 1RP, United Kingdom

CAMBRIDGE UNIVERSITY PRESS
The Edinburgh Building, Cambridge CB2 2RU, UK   http: //www.cup.cam.ac.uk
40 West 20th Street, New York, NY 10011-4211, USA   http: //www.cup.org
10 Stamford Road, Oakleigh, Melbourne 3166, Australia

Published in association with SIGS Books & Multimedia

First published in 1998

Design and composition by Kevin Callahan
Cover design by Yin Moy

Printed in the United States of America

A catalog record for this book is available from the British Library

Library of Congress Cataloging-in-Publication Data

Sadiq, Waqar.
    Building distributed, object-oriented business systems using CORBA
  / by Waqar Sadiq and Fred Cummins.
        p.   cm.
    Includes bibliographical references and index.
      ISBN 0-521-64650-2 (pbk.)
      1. Object-oriented methods (Computer science)   2. CORBA (Computer
architecture)   3. Business—Data processing.   I. Cummins, Fred.
II. Title.
QA76.9.035S23   1998
005.2'76—dc21   98-12758
                                                           CIP

ISBN 0-521-64999-4 paperback

*T*his book is dedicated to my wife, Talat, and to my children, Zan and Marium, for their continuing support and understanding while I was writing this book.

Waqar Sadiq

I want to express my appreciation to my wife, Hope, for her continuing support during the many hours I spent writing and revising the text of this book.

Fred Cummins

Contents

Legal Notice

This book contains a discussion of various computer software technologies including but not limited to methods, systems, algorithms, techniques, etc. (collectively, the "technology"), that are the property of Electronic Data Systems, Corp ("EDS"). Some or all of this technology may be protected by patents, trademarks, copyrights, or other intellectual property rights (collectively, the "intellectual property"). EDS may have patents pending on certain aspects of the technology and may apply for patents on other aspects of the technology in the future. No license of any kind, either express or implied, is granted to any party as to any intellectual property except as expressly set forth herein or in the EDS software license provided in connection with software included with this book.

No liability for patent infringement is assumed with respect to the use of the information contained herein. The user of any information provided herein is liable for patent infringement or any other cause of action arising out of the use of information in this book.

EDS assumes no liability for any damages resulting from the use of the information contained herein. While the authors have sought to provide correct information in this book, EDS assumes no responsibility for errors or omissions. EDS makes no warranty of any kind, express or implied, with regard to the information contained in this book. EDS shall not be liable in any event for incidental or consequential damages in connection with, or arising out of the furnishing or use of the information contained in this book.

About the Authors

Waqar Sadiq is an enterprise architect at EDS and is the lead architect and developer for a business object facility. He has been building distributed business systems for over 13 years and has been actively using object technology for the last 8 years. He has been involved with CORBA standard and products since 1991 and has applied CORBA technology to solve business problems successfully. Waqar has successfully led the development of several CORBA-based projects with EDS and is recognized as a source of distributed technology expertise.

Fred Cummins, BSEE, JD, is an engineering consultant with Electronic Data Systems (EDS) and is a member of the corporate Leading Technologies and Methods organization. As such, he participates and consults on the development of computer systems and applications. He is the EDS representative to the Object Management Group (OMG) and the principal author of the Business Objects Facility standards specification proposed by EDS and others. Throughout his information-technology career (over 30 years), he has been in the forefront of technology, from the development of advanced data-communication systems to the development of a reflective, object-oriented language and environment with integrated artificial-intelligence facilities, and, most recently, he has had a role with OMG. He has authored a number of papers on object technology, chaired a number of conference workshops, obtained several patents (both issued and pending) related to object technology, and led the development of a comprehensive process for development of commercial applications of object technology within EDS. Fred has participated in the development of a wide range of business applications including manufacturing, sales, finance, transportation, and engineering.

For the past 15 years, he has led a team engaged in the development of advanced programming tools and has worked with artificial-intelligence and object-oriented technologies. He is recognized as a source of insights and strategic perspective on computing-technology trends and opportunities.

Foreword

When we started the Object Management Group in 1989, we could see the future. Not clearly, mind you; viewing the future is always dicey. Besides the fog that besets you there's the worry of what filters, mirrors, and prisms lie along the image path! There were, nevertheless, two definite ideas: object technology would lead the way to building component-based systems; and distributed systems would be the norm rather than the exception. As we wrote back then in the *Object Management Architecture Guide,* the model of individual "islands" of computing would die in the nineties.

As the title of this book directly suggests, we were right. As the nineties draw to a close, books outlining how to build distributed, object-oriented systems abound. However, what about the several trillion dollars worth of information-technology equipment and software already installed around the world? This tremendous legacy of hardware, software, and (most importantly) people has to be integrated, not replaced.

Let me give you a personal perspective. In 1996, after living in our house for three years, my family decided together that we needed about 60 square meters (roughly 600 square feet) more living space. We had the following options to fulfill this need:

- Demolish the house and build a new, larger one.
- Move to a larger house.
- Add on to the existing house.

The first option I think would have qualified us for serious psychological support. Even the second option would have required an enormous investment for a rather small return. We chose the third and final option, which was cost-effective, rapidly accomplished, and successful.

You wonder what this has to do with objects? Think about how IT vendors introduce new technologies and approaches every year, and suggest that you take up those technologies. Which option do they suggest you take? Well, naturally, the first option! If you think about it, just as in expanding a house, this option is almost never the effective option for integrating new technology.

This book not only introduces distributed-object systems using CORBA, it does so with sensitivity to the legacy problem. By relying on CORBA, which spans computing platforms and networking platforms, the authors chose a technology that has found its way into daily use at Wells Fargo Bank, Federal Express, British Aerospace, CNN, and hundreds of other world-spanning operations. More importantly, they have explored directly how such systems can integrate the existing systems and experience already found in those organizations. Examples and the use of object-modelling clarify the subject well.

Most interestingly, the authors give an overview of an approach to what is likely the most important trend of the late nineties: business object modeling and application development by composition of business objects. With a rigorous approach to modeling, timing, and developing business models with direct mappings to the CORBA implementation technology, this book gives a solid overview with a clear grounding in CORBA. This alone is worth the price of admission.

One does not always see the future clearly. I can promise the reader, however, that distributed object-oriented computing solutions are here to stay, and a CORBA-based approach is so deeply embedded in the international IT community now that every enterprise developer will need to know something about it. This book is an excellent way to build that experience. It even provides its own peek at the future of business-application development. The wealth of detail and examples make it a pleasure to read. So why are you still reading the Foreword?

Richard Mark Soley, Ph.D.
Chairman and Chief Executive Officer
Object Management Group, Inc.

Preface

We intend for this book to open the door to development of the next generation of computer-based business systems. It will do this by providing a conceptual model for future systems that is based on emerging technologies, and by demonstrating to the reader how to develop systems that are implementations of this conceptual model.

Object technology first emerged as a programming paradigm for simulation. The paradigm enables developers to structure their programs in ways that cluster data and functionality into units that represent the real-world elements of the problem being solved. The benefits of this clustering of data and functionality and the modeling characteristics of the software structure led to the growth of this paradigm for solving complex problems. These capabilities also led to the development of powerful graphical user interfaces. Computational overhead and the tendency of these systems to require substantial amounts of computer memory initially limited the scope of applications.

With the emergence of microprocessors and continued improvements in the cost-performance capabilities of computers, object technology has gained popularity. Initially, a demand for graphical user interfaces drove this popularity. However, as the advantages of the object-oriented paradigm have gained recognition, this technology has been increasingly used for the development of application programs.

The advantages of object technology arise from the definition of objects as the computational representation of real-world concepts; from the ability to create new, specialized objects incorporating the functionality of existing objects; and from computational mechanisms that enable the easy interchange of objects representing variations on a basic concept. These advantages yield opportunities to evolve and adapt solutions and to reuse objects in the solution of different problems that involve the same concepts.

The marriage of object technology and client-server architectures creates the opportunity to provide powerful applications with sophisticated user interfaces. The client-server architecture greatly expands the computational resources available to each user. The object-oriented structure of the software makes these applications more adaptable. Also, the reuse of objects improves the quality, cost, and speed of delivery of the applications. There are substantial libraries of objects that provide commonly used computational and user interface mechanisms. The industry is still struggling to develop techniques for effective reuse of objects that model the enterprise—the business objects.

While the adaptation and reuse of objects offers substantial improvements in development productivity and responsiveness, the run-time sharing of objects enables the seamless integration of applications to achieve more comprehensive and timely models of the enterprise. This leads us to the next generation of business computing systems—systems where many applications are built on shared objects in a distributed computing environment. The development of CORBA (Common Object Request Broker Architecture) standards for interoperability by the Object Management Group (OMG) has allowed multiple vendors to provide compatible components for implementation of these systems in heterogeneous environments involving multiple operating systems and programming languages.

We, the authors, have worked with this evolving technology and have a deep appreciation of both the potential and current limitations. We have worked with different languages, tools, and environments; have experienced the challenges of developing business applications; and have participated in the development of a comprehensive systems engineering process. We have a vision of the future, but we also recognize the practical realities of today's technical environment.

Available products and standards are moving in the right direction, but shortcomings remain that must be overcome by application developers. The design of objects for sharing is still an art, and there are challenges in scaling up the technology for enterprise-level integration. Nevertheless, the technology offers substantial benefit for limited-scope systems today, and proper design of these applications will enable them to evolve into the enterprise computing systems of tomorrow.

Object technology is still the realm of a limited number of application developers. Fewer still have the opportunity to learn about distributed object architectures. There are books on CORBA standards and related technology.

However, they do not provide the concrete information and examples needed to build practical applications.

This book provides insight into the architecture of the future and practical guidance for the development of current applications consistent with that architecture. It also illustrates, with a meaningful application of current products, how the technology can be used now to deliver practical business solutions. Based on our experience as developers, trainers, and mentors, we believe the best way to provide a solid understanding of this technology is by examining a realistic example system. We have selected a system problem that we believe will illustrate not only the nature of business systems in this technology, but also how such systems can be developed. We hope that this book will fulfill a need and help application developers exploit the potential of CORBA technology.

Acknowledgments

This book brings together the results of experience over many years with many different people, too numerous to mention. The ideas developed for the Business Objects Facility are a particularly important part of this book. The depth of understanding and functionality of the demonstration software would not have been possible without the vision and support of the following people at Electronic Data Systems: Tim McGowan provided early support in the initiation of the project; Jay Hyun established the Business Objects Facility as a key element of the strategic architecture; and John Meyer, President of the EDS Diversified Financial Services business unit, recognized the business opportunity and funded the effort to make it a reality. Through their commitment, we were able to flesh out our technical solutions and make an insightful contribution to the development of the Object Management Group specifications for Business Objects Facilities. The functionality and quality of the initial production system would not have been possible without the skills and dedication of Steve Marney and Bill Swift, who helped us refine the ideas and translate them into code. Osman Minkara provided domain knowledge that gave us system requirements for a meaningful stock brokerage application problem. And Shahzad Sadiq provided a constant source of encouragement throughout the writing of this book.

Introduction

This book is about how to develop business solutions using distributed-objects technology. Systems of this type have been enabled by Common Object Request Broker Architecture (CORBA) standards established by the Object Management Group (OMG) and products that implement those standards. This technology will radically change the nature, scope, quality, and flexibility of computer systems in the future. Through understanding the nature of this change and the capabilities of current products and methods, application developers can start to deliver business solutions that will eventually evolve into the large-scale integrated systems of the future.

The change will bring many challenges and risks as we develop new components, implement new methodologies, and learn new techniques. Why should we be working toward distributed-objects systems?

This new architecture will yield major business benefits. Businesses need systems that are more integrated and provide more timely and consistent information about the business. Systems must be more adaptable so that they respond more quickly to changes in the business. Additional levels of integration are needed to exploit the capabilities of work-flow management and intelligent agents. The cost of systems development and maintenance must be reduced. We must stop developing systems from scratch and start building them from compatible, reliable components. Finally, we cannot be burdened with major conversion efforts whenever there is a need to adopt new computing, communications, or database technology. The manner in which distributed-object computing addresses these challenges is discussed in Chapter 1.

This material is intended for managers, designers, and programmers. Managers will be interested only in the higher level concepts and develop-

ment process. Designers will also be interested in the more detailed technical information and design issues, and they should find some of the programming examples useful. Programmers will want to go from the concepts
and development process down to the details of the example implementation. All are expected to have prior knowledge and a level of comfort with
object technology that is appropriate to their level of responsibility.

The focus of this book is on the development of business systems. These
systems use objects to represent business concepts and their attributes and
relationships. Record-keeping and solutions to business problems are
achieved by updating objects and invoking their functionality to perform
business processes and computations. Integration of multiple applications is
achieved through the sharing of run-time business objects.

This book is not intended to teach C++ nor object-oriented programming.
We are not concerned about developing an object request broker (ORB). The
prime objective is to teach how to put CORBA to work for you. To this purpose,
we spend most of our time in this book discussing and resolving pragmatic
issues that arise during planning, design, and programming of CORBA-based
systems. In support of the text we provide a prototype system to illustrate
important concepts and to show how to implement those concepts. The application, although limited in functionality, is an executable system and incorporates a prototype Business Object Facility that is discussed in Chapter 5.

The first part of the book describes concepts and methods. This begins
with a conceptual model of enterprise computing in the future and the
opportunities and challenges this represents. It then moves to a discussion of
the underlying technology; finally, it focuses on the development process and
methods that are needed to develop distributed-objects applications.

Part 2 discusses the technical issues faced by developers during design
and implementation of CORBA-based systems. It begins with a discussion of
a Business Object Facility (BOF) to support application development, discusses a number of design issues, and explores specific problems of implementation in C++.

Part 3 describes the tools and components employed for development of
the prototype application included with the book. These are leading products
in the industry and represent the state of the art. The discussion is not included as an endorsement but to support understanding of the capabilities offered
by available tools and the approach taken in the prototype application.

The Appendix includes a glossary and a discussion of the prototype application problem, including implementation, code examples, and references.
Complete source code for the prototype application is provided on a diskette.

PART 1

Concepts and Methods

This book describes the development of distributed, object-oriented business systems. Part 1 sets the technological context by defining the nature of these systems, a target architecture, and development approach. Chapter 1 defines distributed-objects technology. Chapter 2 describes architectural models of distributed object-oriented systems. It begins with background on its development leading to the model we envision as the appropriate goal for technology still under development. It closes with an approach to current development with available technology. Chapter 3 discusses components of the OMG distributed-objects architecture as a reference for discussions that incorporate these components. Chapter 4 describes considerations for the application-development process for projects using this technology. The reader should read Part 1 to understand the meanings attached to terms, our assumptions about the capabilities and direction of evolution of the technology, and the manner in which business requirements are expected to translate into an operational system.

CHAPTER 1

Introduction to Distributed-Objects Technology

Although object technology originated in the mid-1960s, it did not become an important part of contemporary technology until recently. As it has grown in importance, it also gained popular attention in the technical press and is used in product promotions. Since object technology requires a significant shift in the way of thinking about systems, there are many misconceptions and abuses of the terminology. Many products are now touted as "object-oriented" even though they lack critical characteristics and important capabilities. Because there are no standard definitions for object-oriented and related terms, it is difficult to dispute their claims. As these products gain market share, users adopt misconceptions and spread ill-founded conclusions about the technology and its potential.

It is important to understand what we mean when we refer to object technology in general, and distributed-objects technology in particular. This chapter presents definitions as a basis for understanding the material that follows. This is the object technology that has been refined and holds great promise for the development of large-scale, distributed business systems in the future.

We begin with elementary object concepts, then discuss how these concepts extend to databases and distributed systems. Finally, we discuss concepts of particular importance in a distributed-object system design.

1.1 BASIC CONCEPTS

The basics of object-oriented programming involve the nature of objects and classes, the concept of encapsulation, the mechanism of inheritance, and the nature of polymorphism. We discuss these in the sections that follow.

1.1.1 Objects and Classes

An *object* is a unit of software representing a concept in the domain of a problem being solved. It incorporates both the data (sometimes called the *attributes* or *state* of the object) and the functionality associated with the concept for computational purposes (usually called *methods*). Figure 1.1 illustrates an Account object where the outer ring represents the interface—the requests the object will honor. The data elements Number, Customer, and Balance are stored within the object and accessed through corresponding methods. The other methods—Interest, Credit, and Debit—may use or update the data elements in performing their functions. There are different ways of implementing this clustering of data and functionality. The most common approach, which we assume here, is by using *classes*.

A class is a specification that applies to all objects sharing the same data structure and functionality. An object described by a class is called an *instance* of that class. When a request is sent to an instance of a class, the class defines what functionality is provided and how the data is structured. Without the class specification, the object would merely be a collection of meaningless bits. The data elements are called *instance variables* to identify them as variables within an instance of a class.

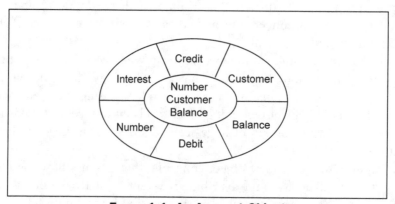

FIGURE 1.1. An Account Object

1.1.2 Encapsulation

The data of well-designed objects is *encapsulated*. This means the only way the data may be accessed from outside the object is by calling the object's methods. This achieves a separation of the interface of the object—the facilities it presents to the outside world—from its implementation—the way its methods are programmed and its data is stored. Encapsulation allows the implementation of an object to be changed without affecting how other parts of a system use the object. The methods made available for access to the object are often called its *public interface*. The public interface of an object will usually not include all of its methods.

Methods are invoked by sending messages. A *message* looks very similar to a function call, but there is a fundamental difference. The method executed in response to a message depends on the object to which the message was sent. The context of the message or one of its arguments identifies the target object (depending on the language). This selection of the appropriate method completes the separation of the interface—the external view of a target object—from the implementation—the actual functionality implemented for the object. In Figure 1.1, the methods for Credit, Debit, and Interest computations can be implemented differently on different types of Account.

The hiding of data is part of our concept of encapsulation. The instance variables of objects should not be directly accessible; they should be accessed only by methods for that purpose. "Accesser methods" should always be used to get and put instance variable values, even for methods on the same object. In the figure, the instance variables Number, Customer, and Balance will be accessed by sending messages to invoke the corresponding accesser methods.

1.1.3 Inheritance

Inheritance is a mechanism for defining classes in terms of other classes. When a new class is defined, it may be defined as a specialization of an existing class. This means that as a starting point it inherits the data structure and methods of the class it is specializing. Figure 1.2 depicts an inheritance relationship where SavingsAccount and CheckingAccount are defined as *specializations* of Account. The original class is the *superclass* of the new object. A specialized class may be called a *subclass* of the original object. New data elements may be defined on the specialized class, methods defined on the

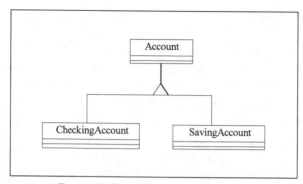

FIGURE 1.2. Class Inheritance

specialized class may be new additions, or they may override inherited methods. This allows programmers to extend and refine an application by building on existing class definitions.

Where classes have common methods and data, an abstract superclass may be created so that the common components can be defined in one place and inherited by multiple subclasses. Objects with a common superclass are considered members of that superclass since (in most languages) they will all respond to the messages defined on the superclass. In typed languages, like C++, the common superclass is used as the definition of the *type* of objects of that class and its subclasses. The type of an object usually identifies the set of messages an object will honor regardless of their implementation. Messages that are targeted for the common superclass will be valid for instances of any of its subclasses.

Some environments provide *multiple inheritance*, meaning that a class may inherit data definitions and methods from multiple superclasses. Multiple inheritance can complicate a system by making it difficult to extend or maintain. However, multiple inheritance is essential where the language is strongly typed (e.g., C++) in order to support polymorphism (discussed below).

Typed languages require that variables containing references to objects be defined as referencing a particular type of object. The type specification determines the messages that may be sent by reference to the associated variable. Smalltalk and Java support single inheritance. Java, which is a typed language, provides a separate interface specification that supports multiple inheritance to define types (more about interface specifications below).

1.1.4 Polymorphism

The last key feature of object-oriented programming environments is *polymorphism*. The separation of interface from implementation supports polymorphism, the ability to interchange different classes of objects. For example, in a banking system, accounts would be represented by account objects (objects of the Account class). There will be different subclasses of accounts (e.g., checking and savings) where the computations and data storage may differ. As long as all classes of accounts support a common interface, they may be interchanged for purposes of participating in various banking processes. For example, the three types of accounts may all respond to an Interest message, but they will compute interest differently. Polymorphism greatly improves the ability to represent complex problems and to evolve and extend a system by introducing new classes of objects.

Message-sending supports polymorphism because when a message is directed to an object, the function it invokes depends on the class of the target object. For example, the interest computation on a bank-account object may be different for a checking account than it is for a savings account. When a message is sent, the message-processing mechanism must determine the class of the target object and then invoke the appropriate method.

1.2 OTHER OBJECT CONCEPTS

There are three other object concepts to support our discussion of business applications and distributed computing. They are: interface specifications, object granularity, and business objects.

1.2.1 Interface Specifications

In Java and distributed computing based on CORBA, interfaces are defined separately from classes. The interface definition only includes specifications for the *method signatures* (name and parameters) of the objects' public methods. The same interface may be implemented by different classes. For CORBA, object interfaces are defined using *IDL* (Interface Definition Language). These interface definitions are *object types*. By conforming to the interface specification, objects of different classes implemented in different languages may be the same type. This expands the potential scope of polymorphism and facilitates the independent development of products that conform to standard interfaces.

Both CORBA and Java support multiple inheritance of interface specifications. This allows interfaces to be defined for certain *protocols* (sets of methods used for a particular activity) and combined as appropriate to define interfaces to objects that participate in multiple protocols.

1.2.2 Object Granularity

Object concepts can be used to represent each of the elements of a problem domain and their interrelationships. Object concepts can also be used to interface large components that conceal complex, fairly self-contained solutions. These are referred to as *fine-grained* and *large-grained* objects, respectively.

A large-grained object can have an identity and respond to messages like other objects without revealing its internal structure. A-word processing system operating on a document can be characterized as a large-grained object. Generally, large-grained objects exist in their own address spaces as distinct processes. The internal elements of these objects might be affected by messages to the primary object, but the internal elements cannot be directly addressed as distinct objects. The large-grained objects can be integrated into larger systems, but the level of integration is restricted. If concepts represented within a large-grained object occur again elsewhere in the system, they must be represented again. This can create inconsistencies and increases the overall complexity of the system. There will usually be no shared code where the same concept occurs in multiple, large-grained objects.

With fine-grained objects, solutions are implemented using objects to represent all elements of the problem situation. Applications are integrated by sharing objects representing shared concepts. For example, multiple applications that examine or change information about a particular employee can operate on the same object so they all share the same information and much of the same functionality. Fine-grained objects often share the same address space.

1.2.3 Business Objects

We are primarily concerned with the objects used to represent concepts in the domain of the problem to be solved. These objects will contain the instance variables and methods involved in the application functionality. We refer to these as *business objects* since they implement "business solutions" to distinguish them from other objects used to implement applications.

Objects can be used in many different ways in computer systems. Objects are used to implement *graphical user interfaces*. These objects correspond to the graphical elements appearing on the screen such as windows, buttons, circles, and lines. They also respond to other internal elements that manage inputs, outputs, and the relationships between the graphical elements and the objects implementing an application's functionality.

Objects can also be used to implement operating system components such as ports, collections, and transactions as well as facilities for manipulation of elementary data such as integers and strings. In some languages, values such as numbers and character strings are implemented as objects. We refer to these as *elementary objects* or *elementary values*. We refer to other objects that support applications, such as the user interfaces, the computing services, and the operating system objects as *computational objects*. There are objects containing groups or arrays of objects for various purposes and we refer to these as *collections* unless there is a particular reason to be more specific.

We are concerned with applications using fine-grained objects that represent business concepts to implement business solutions. Applications will be integrated by sharing business objects. These shared business objects will ultimately represent a shared model of the business—an enterprise model.

1.3 A CONCEPTUAL MODEL

To develop business solutions one must capture the nature of relevant business concepts as objects. This analysis should produce a *conceptual model* independent of programming languages and operating environments. It must provide a consistent framework for applications in a distributed heterogeneous environment. This will enable the sharing of common concepts as well as common implementations among multiple applications.

Our conceptual model focuses on the interfaces and semantics of objects without exposing the details of their implementations. The conceptual model reinforces encapsulation and polymorphism, and is independent of the implementation language.

Figure 1.3 provides a graphical representation of the conceptual model of the object in Figure 1.1. From this conceptual perspective we see only the public methods of objects. The methods define the public interface. The

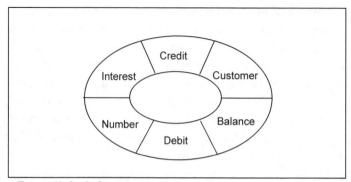

FIGURE 1.3. A Conceptual Model for an Account Object

internal data structure is not visible nor directly accessible. There are two basic types of methods: aspects and operations

1.3.1 Aspects

We define an *aspect* as a data characteristic such as Number, Balance, Customer, or Interest in the figure. Aspect access methods either return a value or assign a new value to the aspect. Only aspect update methods will have a parameter—the new value to be assigned. As an interface specification, an aspect does not specify if the value to be returned or assigned is actually stored in the object. The value could be stored in another, related object, it could be computed, or it could be a shared by all members of the class. In the figure, the value of Interest could be obtained from another reference object. The value of Balance could be computed, based on a series of credit and debit transactions.

There are two types of aspects: *attributes* and *relationships*. Attributes return elementary values that express a characteristic of the object such as Number or Balance in Figure 1.3. *Relationships* return references to related objects such as Customer in the figure. Relationships are often implemented so that the object referenced has a complementary reference back to the original object.

Relationships have cardinality: A relationship may be restricted to referencing only a single object or may be capable of referencing many objects. For example, the Account in Figure 1.3 will have one customer, but the customer could have many accounts. When a relationship cardinality is "many," the aspect provides access to a collection. For purposes of the conceptual model, we refer to the cardinality of the relationship aspect as "one" or "many." If referring to the full relationship, we refer to the cardinality as "one-to-many" or "many-to-many," etc.

1.3.2 Operations

Operations perform a computation related to the object and often involve its aspects in the computation. The computation may alter the state of the object by assigning new aspect values. An operation is performed by a method designed for that purpose. Operations often have associated parameters that further define or qualify the operation to be performed. In Figure 1.3, Credit and Debit are operations. For our purposes, operations on business objects will only access instance variables of objects through their aspect methods.

Operations implement the object interactions that create and modify the business model, and perform the computations necessary to develop problem solutions. An application operation will begin with a message to a primary object; the object will send messages to other objects participating in the completion of the desired action. Each contributes the functionality and data relevant to its role in the problem situation.

1.3.3 Architectural Implications

The application language, architecture, and environment should minimize the amount of translation and programming necessary to implement objects of the conceptual model as functioning software elements. In addition, the interfaces between processes in a distributed-objects environment should support interactions between objects executing in different languages and environments without special programming by application developers. This is called *interoperability*. The extent to which a distributed computing environment supports this conceptual abstraction will be a key factor in the value it brings to the enterprise.

1.4 DATABASES

Object technology is fundamentally a programming and software-design technology. However, as the scope of object-oriented applications has expanded, the design of databases has been effected as well. Since object-oriented programs operate in computer main memory, databases are necessary to preserve the state (i.e., the data) of an application when the computer is shut off.

Objects preserved in a database are *persistent objects*. Objects not preserved when the machine is turned off are called *transient objects*. To make applications more reliable and computer failures less devastating, it is important that the state of the application is captured in a database whenever significant changes have been applied. In addition, databases provide a mechanism by which multiple users can share data; the database-management system prevents updates by multiple users from conflicting.

1.4.1 Data-Storage Structures

Relevant business data is already in databases. Many object technology applications must interface to conventional, *relational databases*. Unfortunately, the relationships stored in objects do not map directly to conventional databases. In addition, objects may include unconventional data types such as images and sounds.

In a relational table, a foreign key reference is specified as a reference to a particular table. For example, if each customer entry has a foreign key reference to an account, then all accounts must be in the same table. Figure 1.4 shows a relational table on the left containing both a checking and a savings account. The checking account has a fee and the savings account has interest; the table has columns to accommodate both types, since they will both be referenced as accounts. In an object-oriented application, different types of accounts will have different structures and would be more appropriately stored in different tables. On the right in Figure 1.4 are the equivalent objects containing only the relevant instance variables. It is possible to map object-oriented structures to relational databases. This mapping increases complexity and restricts the flexibility of the applications, which places an additional burden on development and maintenance activities.

As object technology gained popularity, relational database vendors rushed to avoid the negative publicity that relational databases did not support objects. Most of their effort was devoted to accommodating non-standard data types, e.g., images and sound. While this eliminated an absolute barrier to objects with non-standard data types, it did little to solve the more fundamental incompatibility problem: Relational databases do not support polymorphism.

Object-oriented databases are designed to accommodate object-oriented data structures, including the diversity created with specialized subclasses. A relationship can be with different classes (polymorphic), unlike relational databases, which restrict a relationship (foreign key reference) to a specific table. Some object-oriented databases also store object methods and the database server will execute those methods in response to messages. The class definitions of the programming environment are used directly as database specifications. This direct mapping of program structures to object-oriented databases eliminates development and maintenance overhead. Object relationships are implemented as direct references within the database structures. This results in improved performance in the retrieval of complex structures. On the other hand, the tabular structure of relational databases yields better performance for ad hoc queries used to retrieve records meeting specified search criteria

1.4.2 Transparency of Persistence

From a conceptual perspective, the primary purpose of a database is to provide persistence—to preserve the state of objects when the computer is turned off. Not all objects in an application need to be persistent. User-interface objects are not usually stored in the database. The user interface is reconstructed based on the application objects when the user starts up his or her computer. On the other hand, objects representing the state of the enterprise should be persistent so that updates are preserved when the computer is turned off.

In an ideal programming environment, the environment will determine when a persistent object should be retrieved for use or stored to preserve its state. Queries, or searches for objects that meet certain search criteria,

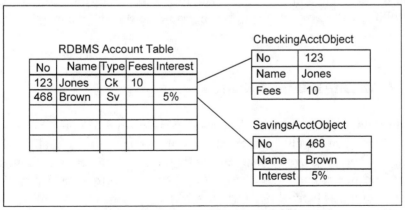

FIGURE **1.4. Relational Mapping of Objects**

should be performed in the same manner for transient objects as they are for persistent objects. They should be the same whether a persistent object is *active* (in memory) or *inactive* (only available from the database). This level of database transparency should be a goal for object-oriented computing environments.

1.4.3 Concurrency

Databases also provide *concurrency control* where two or more application processes may operate on some of the same objects. When application operations are performed on objects, the states of the objects may be inconsistent at certain points in the process. A *transaction* is defined as the processing that takes affected objects from one consistent state to a new consistent state reflecting the completion of a particular unit of work. If the transaction fails to go to completion, then all changes must be rolled back.

If multiple transactions are updating some of the same objects and their operations are interleaved, some transactions could be operating on information that is inconsistent as a result of the actions of other transactions. This could yield invalid results. Database-management systems provide concurrency control when multiple applications operate on some of the same data. Only one transaction at a time is allowed to retrieve, update, and store any particular object.

The concurrency control of database-management systems is used by many current object-oriented applications to support multiple users. Each user has a copy of the application program that retrieves the objects it needs from the database and puts them back in the database when they are done. If multiple users attempt to access the same object, the database causes all but one to wait.

1.5 DISTRIBUTED-OBJECT SYSTEMS

Applications based on shared databases open the door to multi-user systems and insure recoverability, but the applications remain functionally isolated. Users cannot concurrently interact with the same objects for cooperative work, and processing cannot easily be distributed across diverse databases and computers. The goal of distributed object systems is to allow objects on multiple computers to interoperate as if they were in a single computing

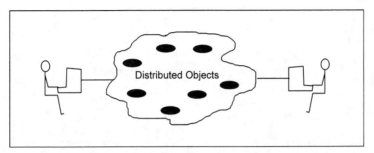

FIGURE 1.5. A Distributed-Objects System

environment as suggested by Figure 1.5. Such environments allow the scope of applications to be expanded. They also increase the potential for integration. In addition, active objects (those in computer memory) may be shared by multiple users. This level of sharing supports a great degree of integration of operations and collaboration among users. The CORBA (Common Object Request Broker Architecture) specification from the Object Management Group (OMG) was developed to support the implementation of distributed-object systems.

In a CORBA-based system, processes executing on the same or different computers are linked by *object request brokers* (ORBs), shown in Figure 1.6. The ORB facility allows objects in these different processes to interact as if they were in a single environment on a single computer (except, of course, for communication delays). If one object in a process has an object reference for an object in another process, that reference is indirect. The remote object will be represented by a proxy object, as illustrated in the figure. If the Customer object sends a message to the Account object, it goes to the proxy object first. The proxy object invokes the object request broker, which forwards the message to the remote object and returns the result.

In each process or ORB domain, every reference to an object in another domain is represented with a proxy object. Each domain may send and receive messages from all other domains—they are peers. However, they need not be used as peers. Each domain "knows about" the external objects through their proxies and the proxies contain sufficient information to locate the associated domain and object within that domain.

The interactions between objects, from an application programming perspective, are the same as in a single environment even though the objects are being executed on different computers. The objects may also be implemented in different languages. The target object may be a facade—often called a *wrapper object*. The object wrapper can be an adapter interface to a legacy

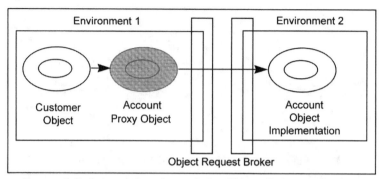

FIGURE 1.6. Integration through an Object Request Broker

application, which is then incorporated as a component, i.e., a large-grained object. The integration of objects operating in multiple environments is defined as *interoperation* by OMG.

For an object request broker to provide its message-forwarding service, the interfaces to target objects must be defined to the object request broker. This is accomplished by specifications in IDL (Interface Definition Language) as mentioned earlier. IDL is also defined by OMG. All objects represented by proxies must have associated IDL type specifications. The proxy objects also provide the information necessary to identify the type of a target object.

The CORBA specification supports the interoperation of fine-grained objects and large-grained objects. An ORB domain can expose the interfaces of many objects within that domain. If the domain is a large-grained object, then only one object interface will be exposed. The Enterprise Computing Model defined in Chapter 2 of this book focuses on integration of fine-grained objects. Nevertheless, integration of large-grained objects will also play a role in the development of practical solutions, particularly in computations and visualizations confined to desktop computing. Some legacy applications may also be integrated as large-grained objects. Integration of large-grained objects is a necessary part of the overall architecture.

1.6 IMPLEMENTATION ISSUES

Several supporting services not inherent in object-oriented technology become important in distributed-object systems. These services must be implemented with consistent interfaces and mechanisms in all participating environments for the overall integration to be reliable and maintainable. They are described briefly in this section as a foundation for later discussions.

A number of these issues are addressed by the Business Object Facility (BOF) design in Chapter 5.

1.6.1 Garbage Collection

Some object-oriented environments provide automatic *garbage collection* or *memory management*. When objects are no longer in use, they are eliminated from the environment and the memory space they occupied is reclaimed for other uses. In applications of limited scope, explicit release of object memory (destruction of objects) can be managed explicitly. This is often a source of program errors because the developer may not keep track of all the ways an object is being used. In large systems, which incorporate independently developed components, appropriate release of unused objects can become very complex. This is further compounded in distributed-object systems. C++ does not provide garbage collection. Smalltalk and Java do provide garbage collection, but it does not extend across distributed environments.

Automatic garbage collection is a very valuable feature. It should be provided to manage the release of objects referenced in multiple computing environments. Reclamation of objects must be coordinated with deletion and deactivation, discussed below. Objects still referenced elsewhere in a system should not be reclaimed unless they can be restored when needed to respond to a message. This tracking of references should not be the responsibility of individual programmers.

1.6.2 Life Cycle Services

Life cycle services are the operations by which instances of objects are created and destroyed. There are six operations to be considered: *create, delete, copy, move, activate,* and *deactivate.*

When an object is created, it must be created in an appropriate address space in the distributed environment. This should be determined through a flexible mechanism supporting reconfiguration of the network. Creation of an object may include creation of a corresponding persistent object in a database.

Deletion of an object is the converse of creation and may include propagation of the delete to related objects. Deletion implies that the concept being represented is no longer valid in the problem domain. Deletion should be linked to the garbage-collection mechanism so that an object is not deleted if there are outstanding references to it. Deletion is expected to remove the concept from the problem space. It must include deletion of the corresponding entry in the database if the object being deleted is persistent.

The copy operation duplicates the target object. It may cause related objects to be copied, such as when copy of an order object includes a copy of its order items. The copy might be created in the same address space or another address space. The move operation relocates the object to another address space, and like the copy operation, this may propagate to related objects.

The activate operation brings a persistent object into an address space so it can participate in computations. This may involve translating rows of relational tables into objects if a relational database is used. Deactivation causes the active instance of a persistent object to be removed from memory. This should not be done if the object is currently participating in computations and might be deferred if the object is used frequently. When an object is deactivated, it can restored from its persistent state.

1.6.3 Naming Service

The *naming service* provides a mechanism for finding objects of interest in the distributed environment based on a permanent identifier, usually a meaningful identifier to system users such as a Social Security number or a city name. The naming service "binds" the identifier of the object to its object reference. This is normally requested when an object is created. When an end user requests an action involving such an object, the user provides the external identifier and the naming service obtains the object reference. The implementation of the naming service must be coordinated with life cycle services and persistent storage facilities. This coordination insures that the object reference for an object of interest is found if it is currently active, the object is activated if it is not, and the activated object reference is returned.

1.6.4 Change Notification

Change notification is a service whereby one object provides notices whenever an aspect of it (usually an instance variable value) changes. For example, if attributes of an account are being displayed and one of the values changes, the display should be updated to reflect the change. This capability is sometimes called a *dependency mechanism* because actions of one object are dependent on notification of events on another object.

To serve a wide variety of services, you need a consistent change-notification mechanism is that works across heterogeneous languages and computing environments. Any object should accept a standard request for notification of change in one of its aspects. Whenever a change occurs, a standard message should be sent to the designated recipient. Another standard message should be accepted to turn the request off. The generalized mechanism then allows one or multiple displays to be updated for the same object without explicit programming of the object being displayed. The same mechanism may be used to initiate pending processes or activate rules. A consistent change-notification mechanism is required for all business objects in a distributed-objects environment. The mechanism should work across domains regardless of the language or platform.

1.6.5 Concurrent Transaction Management

A *transaction* is a process that takes a system from one consistent state to another. A transaction may be a user-initiated process to add, change, or delete information about a particular situation or to perform a related series of computations. In the midst of processing a transaction, some objects are changed while other related changes have yet to be made. If the transaction is stopped without being completed, the system is left in an inconsistent state. Consequently, transactions must either be completed successfully, or the incomplete changes they have made must be rolled back. This is fundamental transaction management.

Transactions are conventionally associated with database-management applications because it is important that what is stored in the database is consistent. Transactions either *commit* and the database is updated, or they are *rolled back* and the database is left unchanged.

In an environment where objects are actively shared, the database no longer provides concurrency controls. If, while a transaction is still active, another transaction becomes active and operates on some of the same objects, then the second transaction may be acting on inconsistent information. It could be modifying information that the first transaction is relying on. Read-only transactions can be allowed to access the values in objects in use, particularly if the new values are not assigned until the active transaction commits. The generally accepted solution to concurrency control is to force the transactions to be executed so that the result is the same as if they were executed serially—this is called *serialization*. This facility must be implemented in the distributed-objects environment.

Transaction management and concurrency control are essential for multi-user, distributed-object systems. CORBA specifications provide elementary facilities, but application programmers must understand how to incorporate them. These facilities are discussed in greater detail in Chapters 3 and 5.

1.6.6 Query

In relational-database systems, all records for a particular entity type are stored in the same table. For example, all parts are in one table, all customers are in another table, and all employees are in yet another table. This makes queries or searches for information straightforward. The query simply looks in the tables of interest for records that meet the query criteria.

In object-oriented systems and databases, objects of a particular type are not stored in tables. In fact, objects that are similar for one purpose may be a mix of classes. For example, a bank may wish to search accounts, but there may be several different classes of accounts. Instead, objects are accessed through relationships to other objects. These meaningful relationships frequently involve collections of objects such as all the employees of a corporation. While this collection might be valid conceptually, the implementation is that the employees are all assigned to departments within the corporation and are not directly accessible from the corporation object.

This is further complicated in a distributed-object system when the objects of interest or some of the objects that must be accessed to find these objects are not in a database, but are active in computer memory. Queries must be programmed to trace the relationships and iterate over the collections to find the objects of interest regardless of whether they are active in the computer or stored in databases. The OMG Query Service specification defines a mechanism where queries are applied to collections that may be collections of active objects or logical collections of object stored in databases.

A specialized search mechanism, the *Trader Service*, is also defined by the OMG. A trader service will accept registration of services to be made available in the distributed environment. Clients may request the identity of registered services meeting certain criteria and the trader service provides a collection of those meeting the criteria from those registered. This is a useful facility for a limited set of problems. It is discussed further in Chapter 3.

1.6.7 Object Relationships

Relationships between objects must be consistently implemented to complement related services. Relationships should be encapsulated so that changes in relationships can be coordinated and controlled to be consistent with the object model. Generally, relationships between objects are complementary— each object references the other. The continued integrity of such relationships requires that when one object changes a relationship, the related object makes a corresponding change to its relationship.

The implementation of relationships should also capture information about the nature of the relationship as it affects other operations. A complex business concept such as an organization, an order, or a mechanical design may be comprised of many objects. The overall concept is represented by a single object and its components are represented by other objects related to it directly or indirectly. Such a composite structure, for example, the order object in Figure 1.7, should be treated as a unit. However, the primary object and its components may reference other objects that should not be considered part of the unit. If an organization's structure is to be copied so that changes can be made without disturbing the original structure, the organizational elements should be replicated. The employees, buildings, and job descriptions, etc., should not be duplicated with the organizational elements. The implementation of relationships should provide a generalized mechanism to define the bounds of the composite structure for such operations. The existing CORBA mechanism, the combination of life cycle and relationship services, is discussed in Chapter 3.

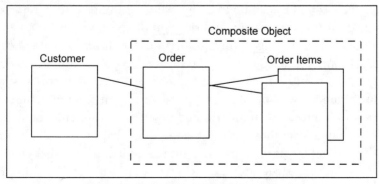

FIGURE 1.7. Composite Object Bounds

1.6.8 Exception Handling

Exceptions are situations where the intended action cannot be completed or an irreconcilable inconsistency is encountered. Common exceptions occur when an iterative operation reaches the end of a collection or a relationship is null. These are usually handled programmatically within normal application processing because they are expected to occur and associated methods are expected to return special values indicating that the exception has occurred. These are defined in normal object-interface specifications.

Unanticipated exceptions or those that cannot be handled within normal application processing present a different kind of challenge. In real-time or fault-tolerant systems, and even normal operating systems, developers may go to great lengths to resolve these exceptions without terminating system operation. However, such exceptions should be expected to cause the current transaction to terminate with an appropriate error message in most business applications. In this manner, the system will at least be left in the same state the transaction found it in.

1.7 SUMMARY

The above discussion is not a comprehensive treatment of concepts and features provided by object-oriented languages, databases, and environments. A variety of facilities, particularly in different languages, have not been included because they have limited applicability or are not relevant to the design of distributed computing applications. In general, the unique characteristics of certain languages, databases, and environments should not be visible in the object interfaces accessible through an object request broker.

Object technology has come to mean different things to different people. To fully exploit this technology and develop distributed-object systems, we need a clear understanding of the basic requirements and extended capabilities in these environments. To develop business object components that can be shared across enterprises, we must develop those components with a common understanding of the conceptual model they should implement. For objects to interoperate in distributed-object environments there must be consistent support facilities and protocols. This chapter provided a consistent definition of objects and the capabilities needed. In the next chapter we describe the broader structure of distributed-object systems and the nature of the business systems they will support.

CHAPTER 2

Distributed-Objects Strategy

This chapter develops a strategy for the application of distributed-objects technology. It describes the relationship between current client-server implementations of object technology and future implementations of distributed objects. This discussion leads to a conceptual model for distributed-objects systems for the enterprise. The chapter closes with a discussion of an application architecture utilizing current technology that anticipates the architecture of the future. The architecture and components discussed provide a framework for the more detailed discussions in the chapters that follow.

2.1 BACKGROUND

Object technology began as a programming paradigm. It emerged from efforts to develop improved simulation techniques. The goal was to model real-world entities and their interactions to better understand the behavior of real-world systems and explore the impact of alternate situations and processes. As a programming paradigm, it is supported by specialized languages and environments. Simula was the first recognized object-oriented language, developed for simulation in the mid-1960s [Dahl & Nygaard].

Object technology gained widespread acceptance in two primary domains: graphical user interfaces and artificial intelligence (AI). The Smalltalk language and environment represents the dominant force in early development of the graphical user interface domain. For graphical user interfaces, objects represent the elements that appear on the screen. These are often complex models that would be difficult if not impossible to implement with conventional techniques. Objects implement these display elements as configurable and adaptable components that can be used in many applications.

In the AI domain the representation of complex problems and knowledge are key concerns. Objects make this complexity manageable and allow the solutions to evolve through rapid prototyping and iteration. There are a number of languages and object-implementation variations developed for AI. A common theme of these applications is the structuring of systems and applications to reflect the problem being solved. Along with specialized languages, there are special tools and environments to support the abstraction and facilitate the management of complexity.

Object technology was focused on single-user systems for many years. As applications grew and client-server technology emerged, there was a need to enable multiple users to interact with a shared model. This was addressed through the use of databases. The state of objects (i.e., data) could be stored in a database, retrieved for processing in a single-user, object-oriented environment, and stored back in the database for another user to access.

Because the object models did not map well to existing database structures, object-oriented databases were developed. However, the need to interact with legacy systems and support more conventional functions resulted in a requirement for object-oriented applications to interface with relational databases. Relational databases have been adapted to provide improved support to object-oriented systems, particularly storage of unconventional data types such as images and sounds.

An alternate approach to providing a shared object model was slower to emerge. That alternate is distributed objects, where objects executing on multiple computers interact over the network to participate in application processes. This architecture allows the workload to be distributed and presents the potential for large-scale integration. It opens the door to integration of independently developed solutions implemented with different languages executing in diverse computing environments. Furthermore, the information used by multiple users is actively shared because the users are interacting with the same objects. Support for these distributed-object systems running in heterogeneous computing environments was the goal for which the Object Management Group (OMG) was formed. The architecture being developed by the OMG, CORBA (Common Object Request Broker Architecture) and related specifications is discussed in greater detail in Chapter 3.

2.2 Object-Oriented Client-Server Applications

At the same time that OMG was developing a distributed-objects architecture, object-oriented applications were being developed in client-server environments. The design of these applications, associated tools, and components evolved and it became apparent that they should be organized into three tiers, as illustrated in Figure 2.1. The objects representing and implementing the user interface are in the top tier. Those representing the relevant business concepts and implementing the business solutions are in the middle tier. The database and objects implementing the interface to the database are in the bottom tier.

Actions by the user are recognized as events by the user-interface objects, which then send appropriate messages to the business objects to initiate application processing. The user interface could include graphical objects, keyboard inputs, audio input and output, video, and other device interfaces. When relevant changes occur in the state of the business objects, messages are sent to the user interface objects to change their state. These are seen as updates to the display or generation of other outputs. The control of a particular display often centers on a "view" object. This object defines the mechanisms of access to the application. It provides an abstraction of the business objects appropriate to the particular user interface display.

The business objects perform the application processing in response to messages from the user-interface view. This processing may cause values being displayed by the user interface to change. In some environments, changes to individual values are communicated to the user interface, causing it to update the display. In other environments, the view object causes the display to be updated when the action initiated by the view is completed.

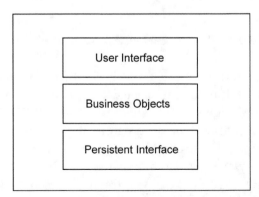

Figure 2.1. The Three-Tiered Object Application Architecture

The bottom layer links the application to a database or other persistent storage. Objects in this layer along with the underlying software provide persistence—the mechanism for storage and retrieval of objects in a database. When an object is required from the database, an appropriate request message is sent to a database object. The requested object (along with related objects if appropriate) is retrieved from the database and instantiated (constructed as members of the appropriate classes) in the computing environment. If the database is object-oriented, this process may be straightforward; if the database is relational, the relational data structures must be converted to object structures.

In the three-tiered architecture, business applications exist independent of each other, with shared persistent data managed by the database. The database resolves potential concurrency conflicts that might arise from two users of the same or different applications attempting to operate on the same objects. Actions by one user are not directly communicated to another user unless the second user's application examines the database to see if any changes have occurred. Users do not concurrently share a model of the business: they share information by exchanging the state of objects of common interest through the database.

The three-tiered architecture suggests appropriate layers for partitioning systems in a distributed computing environment. The interactions between layers are usually less frequent than the interactions that would occur across arbitrary partitions of the application elements. Thus the user interface may be in a client environment and the business objects and persistent storage may be in a server environment—a "thin client" configuration. Or the user interface and business objects may be on a client if there is high user interaction and only persistent storage might be on the server—a "fat client" configuration.

2.3 LESSONS FROM THE THREE-TIERED ARCHITECTURE

The three-tiered architecture does not achieve the potential of a distributed-objects environment. It represents a stage in the evolution of object-oriented applications from which useful insights may be gained. Each of these layers represents a different level of abstraction of the business model. They exchange messages to effect changes and coordinate their representations. The level of activity across these boundaries may be relatively low and the interfaces should be well defined. As a result, these boundaries are the primary candidates for the physical partitioning of the application in a distributed computing environment. This design also offers other advantages to the flexibility and manageability of the application.

2.3.1 The User-Interface Layer

User interface objects and business objects represent fundamentally different concepts. While the user interface presents information about the business objects, its objects represent graphical and other interface elements used to achieve visualization or other forms of communication. Graphical elements are used in many applications where their position, size, color, etc. is determined as appropriate to achieve the desired presentation. They are built into frameworks and may be manipulated with special tools to allow developers to paint user interfaces.

The user-interface separation is also important for support of multiple views. Different aspects of an application, often the same business objects, may be presented with different displays to provide different perspectives. For example, in simple business graphics, aspects of a set of business objects may be presented in bar graphs, pie charts, or line graphs. If these were not separated from the business objects, each new application of a bar graph, pie chart, or line graph would need to be programmed again. This separation supports the development of reusable user interface components and greatly improves development productivity.

The user-interface layer has no direct connection to the database layer. This is because the user interface is implemented as transient objects—objects that disappear when the system is turned off. The user interface is typically reconstructed each time it is activated to reflect the current state of the objects being represented. There is no need to be concerned with a connection between the user interface and the database.

2.3.2 The Business-Objects Layer

Keeping the user-interface facilities separate from the business objects allows the independent development of presentation techniques or graphical mechanisms. The applications are more portable and are not affected if new types of user interface are developed. If multiple displays were implemented directly in the business-application objects, the application would become extremely complex.

The separation of application objects into a different layer from the per-sistent-storage management objects also keeps the application simpler. The persistent-storage layer must deal with retrieval of the appropriate objects and it must properly translate the database structures to objects and vice versa. These are not business problems, but computational problems and should be separate from the business solution. The business-objects layer is focused on solving the business problem. The objects used in one application may be reused on other related applications to reduce development, maintenance time and costs, and improve the quality and consistency of solutions.

2.3.3 The Persistent-Storage Layer

The separation of the business-objects layer from the persistent-storage layer provides flexibility. This layer can accommodate diverse data storage facilities. It will limit the effects of changes in the data-storage facilities on the rest of the application. It can also absorb changes to the shared-data model. As new applications are developed, additional attributes and rela-tionships may be added to the database. Since these were not required by the existing applications, their persistent-storage interfaces can continue to ignore them, and the applications are not affected. The persistent-storage layer can also perform the mapping of application objects to a legacy data-base implementation.

Data structure translation can be eliminated by using an object-oriented database. There is a need to interface individual applications to larger and more complex structures required to support a global view of the shared objects used by many applications. This will be similar to the use of views in conventional databases. A local view used by one application is a simplifica-tion of the underlying database structures that combine related records and exclude unneeded attributes and relationships. There needs to be restricted access to widely shared objects to meet system security requirements.

2.4 VIEWS

An important concept of the three-tiered architecture is that of view objects. As noted earlier, the application incorporates an abstraction of the shared model implemented in the database to solve a particular problem. The user interface displays incorporate abstractions of the application model to provide visualizations of particular aspects of the application problem. They provide an orderly and flexible way of implementing these interfaces and the associated abstractions.

A view represents an abstraction of the business model that is consistent with the user-interface perspective. It communicates commands to the application and communicates display updates to the components of the display. This clarifies the interface and limits the propagation of application changes from one layer to the other. It also makes it easier to define the display as an ad hoc, plugable component that is only attached to those objects that are currently of interest.

To minimize the programmatic impact of displays on the application, an appropriate implementation of views will enable attachment of a display without explicit programming in the application-layer objects. To accomplish this, the views should use a generalized change-notification mechanism to obtain notice of changes to relevant aspects in the application objects being "viewed." This approach to linking user interfaces to application models has been well established among Smalltalk developers for many years [Goldberg].

In summary, views are objects that provide an abstraction between layers in the computing model. Views send messages to the model being viewed to effect changes or initiate processes. They request notification of changes so that these can be incorporated in the dependent abstraction. For example, the displays are updated when the application objects change. At each layer, views—one, many, or none—can be attached to the model being viewed with no explicit programming in the layer being viewed.

2.5 INTEGRATION OF ARTIFICIAL INTELLIGENCE

Object technology has been used for AI applications for many years. In AI applications, objects are used to represent complex problem situations and may also represent knowledge about the interactions and relationships between objects. The AI applications of particular interest here are often called *knowledge-based systems*. These systems incorporate business knowledge to provide automated advice and sometimes business decision-making. They are used to make scarce expertise more widely available, improve the reliability of decision-making, or to more efficiently extract and apply knowledge from experiences. These applications often utilize specialized languages and programming paradigms: techniques in which concepts and computations are expressed in unconventional ways. These applications used the three-tiered architecture as well. A knowledge-based system has a user interface, objects representing the problem situation, and persistent storage, which often provides the link to relevant business information. However, knowledge-based systems have additional implications for the design of future large-scale integrated systems.

Knowledge-based systems are often ancillary to the primary business problem. They may provide assistance to a user to perform a complex task, to find a desired solution, or to guide the user's actions. They may also be used to monitor system activities and initiate actions when particular situations arise. Such ancillary processes may be called *intelligent agents*.

These applications have three characteristics with implications for future business systems models:

1. They introduce another need for views.
2. They often require the ability of a program to access information about and modify itself (*reflection*).
3. They may require specialized language expressions such as predicates or rules.

The views may be abstractions of shared business objects, the business objects used by a particular application, or a user interface. Reflection and specialized expressions create a need for specialized languages such as Prolog and CLOS (Common Lisp Object System). Thus, these applications may execute in separate environments linked to relevant user interfaces and business objects through their own specialized views.

2.6 THE ENTERPRISE COMPUTING MODEL

While the architectures discussed above support graphical user interfaces and solutions to complex problems, the support of multiple users leaves something to be desired. Each application extracts what it needs from the database, performs its activity, then places the results back in the database to be accessible to others. There is no active sharing of the information, so different users and applications can incorporate the same information concurrently. There is no straightforward way for actions taken by one user to be immediately reflected in the information being used by another. The applications are sharing data, not objects. A fully functional distributed objects architecture provides the opportunity to actively share objects.

At the same time, insights gained from experiences with client-server and knowledge-based systems suggest we should not simply enable multiple users to interact directly with a single set of shared objects, particularly if those objects are shared across the entire enterprise. There is a need for applications to be built on abstractions that differ from the global model of the enterprise. The global model is more complex and must resolve conflicting terminology used in different areas of the enterprise. The enterprise model must continue to evolve as the scope of applications expands and the business changes. Individual applications must be insulated from this continuing change. There is a need to encapsulate legacy applications to incorporate their enterprise information in a way that is transparent to other, distributed-objects applications.

Individual users and applications should not have access to all of the information incorporated in an enterprise model. The protected information should not be contained in objects that are instantiated in local servers or desktop computers that provide inadequate information protection.

The Enterprise Computing Model presented in Figure 2.2 exploits these insights and enables large-scale integration of applications. The model describes an abstraction for the design of future business systems. It describes the future application developer's view of enterprise computing and conceals the underlying mechanisms by which the system executes in a heterogeneous, distributed computing environment. The Enterprise Computing Model shows four different groupings of objects and their relationships. Underlying

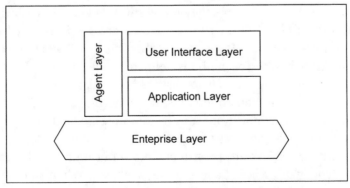

FIGURE 2.2. The Enterprise Computing Model

the model is the distributed computing environment, which includes the computers, communications facilities, databases, and supporting software needed by distributed, interoperating objects. Unlike the three-tiered model, data storage is not defined as a distinct layer. It is a quality of objects that must continue to exist when the system fails or is turned off. The partitioning represents a partitioning of objects.

The boundaries between the groupings are logically separate processing domains that may be aligned with physical separations of processing because interactions are generally less frequent at these boundaries. Interoperation across these boundaries is supported by object request brokers. Each layer may be further partitioned into clusters of objects that work together. This allows the different groupings to be implemented in different languages, computing environments, or geographical locations. Components in these different groupings may be developed by different specialists supporting reuse and addressing specialized objectives. The boundaries will support the implementation of security controls.

Objects in each of the layers have different characteristics and different roles in the enterprise system. Each of the boundaries introduces an abstraction. The Application Objects use abstractions of the Enterprise objects. The User Interface objects are visual abstractions of the Application Objects. The Agent Objects are abstractions of one or more of the other components.

2.6.1 The Enterprise Layer

At the bottom level are the *enterprise objects*. These business objects, taken together, model the current state of the shared aspects of the enterprise. They have many relationships and attributes because they contain all the shared information about the concepts they represent. In some ways, they are similar in concept to the corporate database. However, as objects they have functional interfaces—their attributes and relationships are not accessed directly as data but through accessor methods defined by their public interface specification. They are programmed to insure that updates are consistent and comply with business constraints. As the enterprise model evolves, the impact on individual applications may be minimized by extending the object interfaces while preserving existing methods.

The enterprise objects are persistent, but application developers should not be burdened with reading and writing databases. When an object in this environment is declared as persistent, the environment assures that updates will not be lost. Because these objects are the source of all information about the business, they must be contained in a secure environment and only accessed for authorized purposes. Access by individual users should be restricted to certain objects and even certain aspects of those objects. The enterprise objects should only be accessed through authorized views.

Since the enterprise objects have functional interfaces, they may be implemented in a heterogeneous environment. They may be accessed from distributed systems and may be stored in different types of databases. Some of them may be implemented as interfaces to legacy applications. Some, which appear as single objects with many attributes and relationships, may actually be composites of information located in scattered locations. Over time the legacy applications and scattered information can be replaced with more consistent and efficient implementations without necessitating changes in related applications.

While interfaces of the enterprise objects must comply with a global enterprise model, that does not mean that they are necessarily developed by a single, centralized organization. Just as certain enterprise information is owned by particular departments or divisions, the objects that implement these concepts may also be owned and implemented by particular organizations in different languages and computing environments. The crucial requirement is that all of the enterprise objects comply with the enterprise interfaces and information-protection requirements, and that changes to these objects and their interfaces be closely controlled.

2.6.2 The Application Layer

In the middle layer are application objects. These are the business objects used to solve specific business problems. A single business entity such as a customer or account can be represented only once in the enterprise level. However, many applications could independently represent the same customer or account for different purposes using different subsets or views of the information. These objects are local views of the corresponding enterprise objects. Applications will also have other objects needed only to support computations for the specific business problem, which will not be represented in enterprise objects.

This separation of application objects from enterprise objects allows specific problems to be solved without burdening the developer with the complexity of the full enterprise model. It provides security by restricting application access to only those views authorized for the particular application and user. In addition, changes to the enterprise model will be less likely to have an impact on the application. The application view can also be adapted to different enterprise implementations as long as the business concepts are compatible and sufficiently represented.

For on-line applications, updates to the enterprise objects should be reflected in each application's local view, so that the user is always working with current information. To achieve this, the business-application views must be actively linked to the associated enterprise objects for propagation of changes. This is equivalent to the linkage of user interface views driven by application objects.

2.6.3 The User-Interface Layer

At the top level is the user interface. This is equivalent to the user-interface facilities of current object-oriented applications. Alternative displays may be linked to the business-application objects through different views. Since the user interface is linked through an object request broker, it may be executed in a different environment and written in a different language from the environment and language of the business-application objects.

Sometimes it is appropriate for multiple user interfaces to be linked to the same business-application objects. This allows multiple users to collaborate in the solution of the same problem. The user interfaces could be implemented at widely scattered locations interacting through an object request broker to display a shared business application. For multinational corporations, specialized user interfaces or components may be incorporated to support local language and cultural requirements independent of the business objects.

2.6.4 The Agents Layer

The last layer of the Enterprise Computing Model contains agents. Agents are components that analyze and sometimes affect the way mainstream business processes are being performed. They perform *meta processes* because they observe and act on the actions and results of mainstream processes.

Agents may be linked to any of the other domains through views. They may monitor the enterprise objects and perform routine tasks or alert appropriate persons to situations requiring some action. Workflow management should be implemented as agents so rules for routing and authorization of work are not embedded in applications. Agents may be linked to business application objects to provide assistance in the solution of complex problems. These agents may notify the user of inconsistencies or incompleteness of the solution being developed. They can also help the user evaluate alternatives. Agents may be linked to the user interface to provide help, automate tedious tasks, or function independently as an intermediary to make the computer appear more human.

In the past it was necessary to implement agents in the same language and environment as the subject information or to develop mechanisms to access it indirectly. This limited the solutions and increased the complexity of the combined applications. It tended to discourage significant investment in sophisticated solutions. The linkage of agents through an object request broker allows these functions to be implemented in specialized languages supporting unconventional programming paradigms. As greater consistency and stability are achieved in the other system components, it becomes more practical to invest in the development of sophisticated agents for a variety of purposes. In addition, the use of views helps insulate and adapt these "meta" systems to changes in the mainstream systems.

2.6.5 Views and Adapters

The foregoing discussion of the Enterprise Model layers has alluded to the use of views to provide the linkage between these layers. Views are an essential element of this architecture and their architectural requirements should be well understood. Local views have been used for many years in conventional databases. They function primarily as a security measure to restrict applications to the data they are authorized to access. They can also provide an abstraction from a complex data structure to a simpler structure representing the way the complex structure can be viewed for a particular application. This mapping between the two abstractions limits the effects of changes to the database or the application. The same basic concepts are incorporated here.

We separated views into two components: views and adapters. These two components exist on opposite sides of a boundary between layers. They work together to achieve the conventional purposes of views and provide some additional capabilities. The roles of views and adapters are illustrated in Figure 2.3.

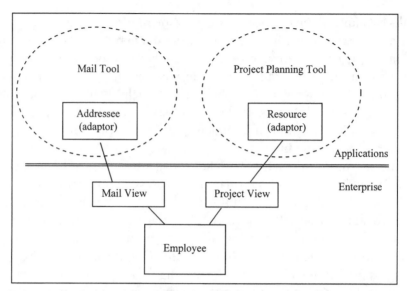

FIGURE 2.3. Views Interfacing an Application to an Enterprise Object

A view provides an abstraction of a subject object or structure. However, the view in this model exists to restrict access to the subject object. Only those messages authorized for the particular user and application are allowed to pass through the view. The view exists in the same environment as the object it protects and is given the same level of security. Different applications will obtain access to the same object through different views.

Adapters exist on the client side of the boundary and represent the subject object in the context of the application. Applications and local organizations may think of certain aspects of an enterprise object in different ways and use different terminology. Adapters can provide for this translation. An adapter may also add methods and instance variables to those incorporated from the subject object in the remote environment. There will frequently be methods and variables needed to support local computations that are not relevant to other applications. In addition, the adapter can incorporate caching capabilities so instance data that would be retrieved from the remote subject object can be held locally to improve performance.

In Figure 2.3 two local applications are linked to an employee object in the enterprise layer: a mail system and a project-planning system. The views in the enterprise layer restrict access to the employee object so that the employee salary and other private information is not available. On the application side, each application has an adapter to represent the employee object for its respective purpose. The mail system sees the employee as an addressee. It may reveal certain information to the user so that the addressee can be properly identified. The project planning system, on the other hand, provides a different representation of an employee since it sees the employee as a resource much like a computer or an office space. The resource adapter may present a different set of methods in its interface and translate messages to those methods into appropriate messages to the employee object. The resource adapter is also more likely to have local methods and instance variables that do not have any equivalent on the employee object.

Views are stateless and need not be persistent; they simply filter methods. For example, a view might allow an employee to access certain information about other employees, but it might also allow the employee to access additional information about himself or herself. This suggests the use of two views, but that depends upon the specific implementation. Views can be created when needed and destroyed when no longer in use.

An adapter provides for adapting the interface of an enterprise object (or other model being abstracted) to the requirements of the particular application. The adapter object might automatically forward all messages it does not understand. It will intercept some application messages to change the message name or parameters to conform with the interface of the enterprise object. If the adapter contains local state information, it may be desirable for it to be persistent, if for no other reason than to allow the application to be restarted if it fails.

Change notification can be used to keep the cache current with changes in the state of the target object. Changes in the adapter state performed by the application would be forwarded to the target object. Caching could provide a substantial performance improvement if the application makes frequent accesses to the state of the target object.

2.7 AN ARCHITECTURE FOR CURRENT APPLICATIONS

The Enterprise Computing Model is a strategic vision for the large-scale integration of systems in a distributed-objects environment. In the current state of technology, there is considerable risk and expense associated with the development of a supporting architecture for such systems. In addition, the development of industry standards and commercial products will outdate any proprietary solutions within a few years. Consequently, it is impractical for most individual users of the technology to develop their own supporting architecture.

The long-term success of this model depends on the availability of software components that implement standard interfaces. These standards are being developed by the OMG and other organizations such as IEEE (Institute of Electrical and Electronics Engineers), ISO (International Standards Organization), IEC (International Electrotechnical Commission), and The Open Group (consolidation of X/Open and the Opens Systems Foundation). These efforts will yield software products within the next couple years. Application developers should start taking advantage of available technology to build applications that exploit the advantages of distributed objects technology so that they can be adapted to the Enterprise Computing Model. Here we consider how such applications should be architected.

The three-tiered architecture should be the foundation for current applications. However, current technology can allow this architecture to be extended in important ways.

1. By interfacing the layers with an ORB, they can be implemented on different machines in different languages.
2. Business solutions can be implemented on different servers and can be more accessible to users.
3. Multiple users can share the same application over intranet connections allowing widespread access and support for collaborative computing.

These are important capabilities that can be achieved with a modest investment in the development of a distributed-objects architecture. The following sections describe a general approach.

2.7.1 Separation of Layers

Fundamental to this architecture is the separation of business objects and their functionality from objects and functionality for the user interface and persistent storage. If business objects represent only the business concepts and interactions of those concepts to solve the business problem, this layer remains the same as the architecture evolves to the Enterprise Computing Model. Many of these business objects will eventually become adapters on the enterprise objects. Conversion of these objects to adapters should not require significant change to the application structure or logic unless the business concepts are inconsistent with the enterprise model.

All application operations on the business objects initiated through the user interface must be performed by methods on the business objects. For example, when a button is pressed on the user interface, it should activate a single method on a business object to perform the desired operation. For a single display, the actions and linkages to obtain field values should all be managed by a single adapter object that connects the display to the business objects. The logic to perform the actions should not be on user-interface objects nor on the user-interface adapter object. It must be delegated to the business objects. With this design, a new user interface can be developed for a different operating environment. It may also provide a different visualization and will be able to access all the same application functionality.

2.7.2 Business Objects Encapsulation

To insure the easy conversion of business objects to adapters, encapsulation of the business objects must be preserved. The public interface should be clearly defined, used consistently, and there should be no direct access to the instance variables. Even the methods defined on a business objects should use the accesser methods to access the instance variables of the same business object. The standard forms associated with CORBA language bindings should be used for the attribute get and set methods. These methods will remain functional even when the instance variables may be implemented in a remote enterprise object.

2.7.3 Persistence and Queries

The implementation of database access and queries should be separated from the business objects. Commercial products are available to help with the implementation of a generic database interface and the mapping of objects to relational databases. An approach to implementing this separation is shown in the Business Object Facility discussed in Chapter 5. The business objects should contain no programming that relates to database accesses or queries. These should be encapsulated in the database layer.

2.7.4 Transactions and Concurrency

Along with the separation of persistence and query processing, transactions and concurrency control should be separated from the programming of the business objects. As with current three-tiered applications, most solutions rely on the database for concurrency control. Consequently, the application transactions are essentially database transactions. A transaction service should be implemented as the focus of transaction control and to perform transaction *commit* or *abort* operations. This provides an implementation that is consistent with the future architecture.

The use of the database to control concurrency is the primary difference between this short-term architecture and a full implementation of distributed objects. Objects to be used within a transaction will be retrieved with locks for that purpose and released when the transaction is completed. Concurrency control for those shared objects would not utilize the generalized solution envisioned for the Enterprise Computing Model.

2.7.5 Life Cycle Services

Create, activate, and *copy* operations should be performed in a manner consistent with the life cycle services discussed later in this book. For the most part this means these operations are performed by life cycle manager (factory) objects determining where the business objects are instantiated. Delete operations must be linked to transaction and persistence processing to cause deletions to occur in the database at transaction commit. Deactivate operations will be implicit at the end of each transaction, Move operations are not necessary in this architecture.

2.7.6 Naming Service

Applications should obtain access to business objects through a naming service. The implementation of this naming service may be quite different from that to be used in the future, but the interface should be fundamentally the same. The naming service should return an object reference to an active business object. The naming service should utilize the life cycle service and the persistence service to instantiate objects and retrieve their current state from the database.

2.7.7 Enterprise Modeling

The business objects should be designed with the enterprise viewpoint in mind. As applications are developed, an enterprise-level conceptual model should also be developed. This model evolves as each new application is undertaken. If incompatibilities with existing applications emerge, try to revise the existing applications to make them compatible. This does not mean that they must use the same model, but that a mapping can be defined. This insures that the existing applications can eventually be interfaced to the enterprise objects.

2.8 Summary

This chapter provided a vision of the future architecture of business systems and a strategy for the transition. The Enterprise Computing Model describes how applications can be partitioned and integrated, and shows how natural partitioning of the objects can be mapped onto a distributed computing environment. It exploits a computing abstraction that insulates business-system developers from computational details. Most importantly, it defines an architecture in which object technology can achieve large-scale integration of business systems while preserving flexibility and modularity of implementation. This large-scale integration is needed for improved management of the enterprise as well as for improvements in individual productivity and quality of work. It facilitates independent development of applications and components of applications. It also aids the rapid adaptation of systems to changing business needs. It supports the development of an integrated model of the enterprise which insures that computer-based decisions and operations throughout the enterprise are timely and consistent. It provides the foundation for a higher level of enterprise automation, including the integration of intelligence and workflow management.

The full realization of this future architecture requires the development of standards and commercial products embodying those standards so that systems can be built on a stable foundation. While it is impractical for each user of the technology to develop the needed environment, current efforts to develop standards should yield limited availability of products in the next year. Meanwhile users of the technology can implement more limited solutions to enable a transition to the Enterprise Computing Model when supporting products become available. We described a general approach to implementation of current applications consistent with the long-term strategy. The remainder of this book describes in more detail the elements of a distributed-objects architecture and provides insight into the nature and challenges of this next-generation architecture.

REFERENCES

Dahl, O., and K. Nygaard. "SIMULA— An ALGOL-Based Simulation Language," *Communications of the Association for Computing Machinery*, Vol. 9, No. 9 (1966): 671-678.

Goldberg, A. and D. Robson. *Smalltalk-80: The Language and Its Implementation*, Reading, MA: Addison-Wesley, 1983.

WEB SITES

OMG (Object Management Group)
　　http://www.omg.org/

IEEE (Institute of Electrical and Electronics Engineers)
　　http://www.ieee.org/

ANSI (American National Standards Institute)
　　http://www.ansi.org/

ISO (International Standards Organization)
　　http://www.iso.ch/

IEC (International Electrotechnical Commission)
　　http://www.iec.ch/home-e.htm

The Open Group (consolidation of X/Open and the Opens Systems Foundation)
　　http://www.xopen.org/

CHAPTER 3

CORBA—An Overview

The Common Object Request Broker Architecture (CORBA) and related specifications developed by the Object Management Group are central to a distributed-object environment. There are other books and papers that describe these specifications and implementations in detail. This chapter provides a general understanding and ready reference to the architecture and terminology. It puts the architecture in perspective for development of applications based on the enterprise-computing model discussed in Chapter 2.

Figure 3.1 illustrates the Object Management Architecture (OMA) defined by the Object Management Group as the context for CORBA specifications. This architecture provides a basis for partitioning the specifications development efforts. The diagram depicts objects in three different roles interacting through an object request broker. The circles represent object-oriented implementations, while the rectangles with semicircle faces represent conventional implementations with object-oriented interfaces, or *wrappers*. The environment supports object-oriented interactions, but recognizes that this includes the encapsulation of conventional components.

The architecture exists to support the interoperation of objects in a distributed computing environment. Interoperation means that objects interact with each other, performing *operations* or *services* for each other to accomplish local and system objectives. While objects may be sometimes characterized as clients or servers, these relationships are not designed into the physical computing network. Objects may be clients or servers or both, and

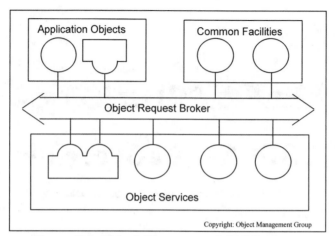

FIGURE 3.1. Object Management Architecture

their location in the network is based on external interfaces and workload distribution.

The *Object Request Broker* (ORB) provides the mechanism by which messages may be exchanged by objects existing in different address spaces. These may be on the same or different computers. Each address space will be served by an ORB, which will communicate with other ORBs to relay messages. We refer to these object address spaces as ORB domains since each is served by an ORB.

When objects are distributed across a heterogeneous network, some operations that were quite simple in a single computing environment become inherently more complex. For example, to invoke a service involves not only sending a message, but first finding the service in the distributed environment. The location should not be pre-programmed for a specific computer. In addition, the network is expected to be heterogeneous (i.e., the objects will be running on different computing platforms, written in different languages, and stored in different databases). This requires that certain operating environment services be provided with standard interfaces. *CORBA object services* are the supporting components and services necessary for the development of consistent applications in this heterogeneous environment. These include specifications for managing transactions, for life cycle operations (create, delete, copy, and move) for object relationships, for concurrency control, and so on. In a non-distributed environment, the language compiler, development environment, and operating system provide most of these services. The OMG object services specifications define the interfaces to objects that will implement these services in a way that supports integration across multiple computers.

Common Facilities are application components that provide functionality occurring frequently in application requirements such as facilities for rendering displays, managing change, and system administration. When these application components are available as products, they will substantially reduce the effort to develop applications, the consistency of applications will be improved, and the portability of applications will be enhanced through reduced dependence on any particular platform or technology.

The applications segment represents the actual business applications that operate in this environment. OMG efforts are addressing this area with industry-specific task forces and a Business Objects Domain Task Force (BODTF). For example, significant efforts are under way to define standard business objects for financial services, for telecommunications, for manufacturing, and for health care. See the OMG Web page—www.omg.org—for current information. Specifications for abstract business objects will provide a consistent base for development of applications specific to a particular business or organization. This will promote the development of business-application component products that provide functionality that is fundamentally the same for all organizations in an industry. Each enterprise can then specialize the components for their competitive advantage while avoiding the effort required in developing the systems from scratch. The economies of scale achieved with these products will result in an overall improved quality of systems.

The OMG architecture is still under development. Key components are already standardized and available as products in the marketplace. For some of the remaining components, standards have been adopted but products are still under development, and for still other less critical components, standards remain to be developed. One of the key components for business-application development is the Business Objects Facility (BOF). The BOF standard is currently under development, but key characteristics and an initial implementation of a BOF are discussed in Chapter 5.

In the following pages, we describe the OMG architectural components, as they are understood at the writing of this book. Some of these components are still being defined, particularly those in Common Facilities, so the reader is advised to refer to the OMG web page for details on current specifications (www.omg.org). The following sections first briefly discuss terminology associated with the CORBA object model and then discuss each of the architecture components and their implications for development of business applications.

3.1 THE CORBA OBJECT MODEL

OMG defines an object as "an identifiable, encapsulated entity that provides one or more services that can be requested by a client." Objects may be large-grained or fine-grained. An ORB domain, i.e., an executing process with an ORB connection, may have one or more objects visible to the rest of the environment—typically, many objects will be visible through the ORB.

The above definition references *services* and *requests*. This is because the client and/or the server may not be object-oriented software. For object-oriented implementations of client and server, a request is a *message* and a service is a *method* on an object.

To send a request, a client must have the identity of an object implementation. This identity is an *object reference*. The request must be directed to an object of a specified type defined with the Interface Definition Language (IDL). The object reference is not a globally unique identifier, but only an identifier that will enable the ORB to route the message to the intended recipient based on the specified interface. The fact that two references to the same object are not equal can cause problems with operations that check to see if two variables are referencing the same object. Operations are provided to perform comparisons on the actual objects in a remote environment when required.

OMG describes object implementations as performing services, but also refers to these services as operations. The form of an operation request is the *operation's signature*. The signature specification appears within the IDL of an interface specification. An operation may have different implementations on different objects that conform to the same interface specification. An operation implementation is called a *method*. The semantics of the operation are expected to be the same for the different implementations. However, except for comments, IDL does not include expressions to define semantics. Consequently, supplemental text or comments provide such information as the specific meanings associated with method and attribute names, the valid relationships of objects to the values in method arguments, and the expected valid state of an object or the rest of a system when a message is sent or the result is returned.

A request must conform to a service specification within the interface type designated for the target object. A request may have arguments and a return value defined by the specification. Those arguments and return values have type specifications as well. There are two general categories of types: *basic* and *constructed*. *Basic* types are elementary data values such as numbers and strings. *Constructed* types are data structures. Objects *per se* are not currently passed to an ORB; objects are passed by reference. Object references are constructed types where the type specification identifies the interface of the object referenced.

An extension to IDL interface specifications is under consideration to support passing by value. Note that passing by value would require that the receiving domain have an implementation for the same class of object that would accept the same instance variable values, and objects would be continually moving around the network, potentially creating workload-management difficulties. Consequently, selection of objects to be passed by value will require careful consideration.

An operation may return an exception that must be a constructed type defined in IDL. OMG defines a number of standard exceptions.

3.2 THE OBJECT REQUEST BROKER

The Object Request Broker (ORB) makes an application interface accessible to the distributed-objects network. Each participating ORB domain has an ORB implementation. ORBs from different vendors can interoperate in a distributed-object environment if they are compliant with the CORBA 2.0 specification. However, OMG specifications do not yet establish ORB interfaces that allow applications to be portable to different ORBs. Generally, the specifications define interfaces to objects that are remotely accessible. Many of the interfaces to the object request broker and other services and facilities may be within the same address space and therefore are not included in the standard. The uniqueness of these local interfaces is not a problem for interoperability, but it is a problem for application portability—where an application is to use a different vendor's ORB.

Figure 3.2 illustrates the basic structure of an ORB. A client may be an object or a conventional program that wants to request a service from an object implementation in another ORB domain. The client sends a request through the ORB. The request is delivered to the ORB in the receiving environment and to the object implementation. Generally, both *clients* and object implementations function in both roles. Figure 3.2 depicts the partitions in functionality for specification of interfaces and for interfaces to different languages and modes of communication.

In addition to the ORB structure and application interfaces, other specifications are required for ORBs from multiple vendors to inter-operate in a

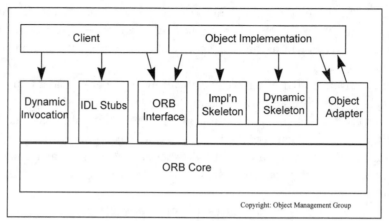

FIGURE 3.2. ORB Structure

heterogeneous environment. The interfaces of object implementations are defined with the Interface Definition Language (IDL). The mapping of IDL expressions to different programming languages is defined by OMG language bindings. Finally, the protocol between ORBs is defined so they can inter-operate. The following sections briefly describe the Interface Definition Language, the ORB structure, language bindings, and the inter-operability protocol.

3.2.1 Interface Definition Language

The Interface Definition Language (IDL) is a specialized language designed to specify object interfaces accessible through an ORB. IDL looks much like a programming language, but it does not provide terms or syntax for the expression of executable instructions. It defines types of objects and the forms of messages that can be sent to those objects.

Object types are different from classes. Types define interfaces while classes define implementations that support interfaces. IDL supports inheritance, but the inheritance of interface specifications need not parallel the inheritance of the classes that implement those interfaces.

IDL specifications are maintained in an ORB run-time repository, often called the *interface repository*, to support compatibility checking and language binding of messages. Some development tools will process IDL to generate skeletal classes in a programming language. These mechanisms help achieve consistency in the application components and databases. Developers

```
interface Client;
typedef sequence<Client> Clients;
interface Client : BusinessObject{
/*
** Business operations.
*/
  Account OpenNewAccount(in string description,
           in string accountType,
           in string invObjective,
           in double startingBalance);
  Accounts GetAccounts() raises(BOException);
};
```

FIGURE 3.3. IDL Example

may be required to write IDL, although some object modeling tools will generate IDL from class models. Figure 3.3 illustrates IDL for a brokerage Client object which has Accounts.

3.2.2 ORB Structure

The ORB structure in Figure 3.2 shows six local interfaces. One application may use several of these interfaces. In the diagram, the *client* represents an application sending a request to an *object implementation* in another ORB domain. A single application or ORB domain may have both clients and object implementations. Cooperating ORBs provide the mechanism that delivers a message from a client in one ORB domain to an object implementation in another ORB domain and returns the result.

The application systems need not be implemented as object-oriented applications as long as they observe appropriate protocols and send or receive messages. The client may be a non-object-oriented application that sends messages to request actions, and the object implementation may have an object-oriented interface but be implemented as a conventional program. The applications may also be written in different languages since messages are exchanged in a common form. IDL bindings determine the translations to and from the common form.

Although it does not appear in the diagram, an interface repository is an important component of the ORB implementation. The repository contains the interface specifications defined in IDL. Various ORB functions will refer to the interface repository to obtain the interface definitions required to perform their functions. The interface repository is not generally visible to applications. The interfaces through which these interactions occur and are managed are discussed below.

3.2.2.1 IDL Stubs

IDL stubs are code generated from IDL specifications to define proxy objects in a client ORB domain. A proxy object is the local representation of a remote object A proxy object functions like other objects in an object-oriented environment, except that messages to it are relayed through the ORB to the object implementation in another ORB domain. The IDL stubs provide the necessary code to receive messages and route them through the ORB. IDL stub code must be generated for all object types that may be remotely referenced.

3.2.2.2 Dynamic Invocation Interface

The Dynamic Invocation Interface (DII) allows the client to dynamically construct a message to be sent rather than generating IDL stubs ahead of time. This mechanism is useful for applications that do not know the interfaces they will be using at the time they are written. For example, development tools such as browsers and debuggers must work with any interface the user may specify during testing. The run-time repository will typically be used as a source of interface specifications. This is not the mechanism normally used by applications since it is less efficient and more subject to programming errors. The DII also provides more control over the message-sending processes than IDL stubs, for example, for asynchronous communication.

3.2.2.3 ORB Interface

The ORB interface provides direct access to ORB functions. It provides operations to obtain initial references to fundamental object services, and it provides functions for checking object references for object equivalence or nonexistence. It also provides access to lower level ORB functions such as those needed to utilize the dynamic invocation interface. For example, object references can be converted to strings used to identify objects in persistent storage or for passing references as request variables. In general, most application operations will be performed through the interfaces discussed earlier.

3.2.2.4 Object Adapter

The object adapter is responsible for the generation and interpretation of object references for the objects in its associated ORB domain. The object adapter provides the mechanisms for (1) activation of an ORB domain (if the application containing a target object is not running), (2) activation or creation of a target object in the domain, and (3) invocation of methods through the implementation skeleton or the dynamic skeleton interfaces. There may be various implementations of object adapters, but currently, the Basic Object Adapter (BOA) is standard.

3.2.2.5 Implementation Skeleton

The implementation skeleton performs message sends to objects for requests received from remote clients through the ORB. The object adapter invokes the appropriate skeleton code based on the type of the target object. This code is generated from IDL and reflects the IDL language bindings that define the expression of messages and argument values in the particular language. The skeleton code is essential for typed languages where a message must be directed to a particular object type. Essentially, the skeleton code invokes a method locally as a surrogate for a requester that is remote.

3.2.2.6 Dynamic Skeleton Interface

The Dynamic Skeleton Interface (DSI) provides for the dynamic creation of message sends to objects in the receiving environment. This functionality will typically use the ORB run-time repository to generate the appropriate message form. The DSI is to object implementations what the DII is to clients. The DSI is used for environments where the object implementation is unknown at compile time and the interface specification must be dynamically applied. The primary application of the DSI is for gateways for inter-ORB communication. It is generally of little interest to application programmers.

3.2.3 Language Bindings

IDL specifications include bindings (i.e., interpretations) for various programming languages. These bindings determine the compatibility of messages exchanged between components written in different languages. The ORB implementation of these bindings provides the interoperability between different languages. For example, if a message is sent from a C++ environment, the bindings for C++ will determine how the message is translated for communication. When the message is received by the destination ORB, bindings for the language of that environment, e.g., Smalltalk, will determine how the message and its parameters are expressed to invoke a method on the target object. Of particular concern is the equivalence defined for elementary values (character strings and integers), which will be converted from their form in the sending environment to a corresponding form in the receiving environment when they appear as message parameters.

3.2.4 Inter-ORB Protocol

OMG defines two primary mechanisms for achieving interoperability between different ORB implementations: inter-ORB bridges and the General Inter-Orb Protocol (GIOP). The interface for communication between CORBA ORBs and Microsoft's COM (Common Object Model) is a bridge—a conversion mechanism. Bridges may also be used to implement administrative boundaries between ORB networks. The GIOP is a connection-oriented protocol that allows ORBs to exchange information without a bridge because they talk the same language. The GIOP must be implemented on a communications transport layer. The Internet InterORB Protocol (IIOP) defines how the GIOP is to be implemented for a TCP/IP transport layer. Other transport protocols may be used, but ORBs are required to support the IIOP to comply with the CORBA 2.0 specification. The application developer will generally be unaware of the inter-ORB protocol except as it may determine the compatibility and security of inter-ORB communications. ORBs may also incorporate Environment Specific Inter-ORB Protocols (ESIOPs) instead of the GIOP to incorporate other modes of communication. An ESIOP is defined for the use of OSF DCE known as the DCE-CIOP (Common Inter-ORB Protocol).

3.3 OBJECT SERVICES

Object Services provide functionality that enables applications or assists in the operation of a distributed-object environment. The following sections describe a number of object services that have been defined by the OMG and discuss their use for applications.

3.3.1 Event-Notification Service

The event-notification service specification defines a protocol by which a *consumer* may obtain notices of events from a *supplier* elsewhere in the distributed environment. This protocol may be used directly between a supplier and consumer or it may be used with *event channels*. The service is designed so that the supplier need not know what consumers, if any, will be interested in its events, and the consumer may be designed not knowing what suppliers might provide events.

Events may be communicated in *push* or *pull* mode. In *push* mode, the supplier communicates an event when it occurs. In *pull* mode, the consumer asks for events that have occurred. These protocols provide a generic capability that can be adapted to various requirements.

An *event channel* can be used to provide a service to decouple suppliers and consumers of events. Suppliers can communicate events to the event channel and the event channel will redistribute the events to interested consumers. If a consumer needs to receive notice of certain events, it registers with the event channel. This allows applications to monitor the activities of other applications or system services in a generalized, application-independent manner. In addition, the monitoring application need not have explicit awareness of all sources of events and any new sources will be automatically included when they become active. For example, a service might be designed to route printouts to printers. It might request the event-notification service to provide notice whenever a printer becomes active or inactive. Thus, when a print job is to be assigned, the service is aware of all active printers, and if a printer becomes inactive, it may re-route jobs that have not yet been completed.

The OMG event-notification service is very generic. It does not define quality of service, but leaves this for particular implementations. It also does not define a standard protocol for initiating event notification from a supplier.

As we will see later, a mechanism for ad hoc change notification from business objects will be very important for the implementation of the Enterprise Computing Model. While there is similarity, the change-notification mechanism requires the ability to activate notification on individual instances for specified aspects and the ability to communicate the new values of changed aspects. This will be discussed further in Chapter 5.

3.3.2 Life Cycle Services

The *life cycle services* specification defines interfaces for creating, deleting, copying, and moving objects in a distributed computing environment. For example, if a client wishes to create an instance of an object, there must be a mechanism to determine the environment where it should be instantiated and where the request is to be directed. In many cases, it may be inappropriate for the client to determine or even know where the instance is to be created. Similarly, a copy of an object may be created in another environment or an object may be moved from one environment to another. Often object structures, such as a customer order or an employee record, should be treated as a unit for *retrieval, copy,* and *move* operations. The bounds of such compound objects (i.e., objects containing other objects) are determined by the relationship service (see below).

3.3.3 Name Service

The *name service* keeps track of *name bindings*—associations of names in a context to their corresponding object references. Generally speaking, a *name* or *identifier* only has meaning within a particular *context*. For example, if you are given a nine-digit number, it has no particular meaning on its own. If you are told that it is a Social Security number, you know the context and thus the meaning. Contexts may be nested like a file-directory structure. They essentially define categories of identifiers or *name spaces*.

A name binding may be added to a context, deleted from a context, or requested from a context. Contexts may also have name bindings in other contexts forming a context hierarchy. The name binding for an object might be expressed as a sequence of names reflecting a name binding within several levels of contexts. The name service should be utilized to bind external identifiers like part numbers and department names to object references. In many cases, external identifiers will be qualified by the role of the application user (i.e., organization and job function).

The name service associates identifiers with object references. When a user enters an identifier, the associated object may be active or it may exist only in a database. The mechanism by which inactive, persistent objects become activated is not defined in the specification. There is an assumption that the ORB will resolve this when a message is sent to the object, and ORB vendors have implemented facilities of this type. However, this will not be sufficient under all circumstances.

The name service is also designed to be federated. This means that different name services may be integrated to function as a single name service. This federation should function much the same as directories in a distributed file system.

3.3.4 Persistent-Object Service

The persistent-object service provides a standard interface to data-storage facilities. Conceptually, the data storage may be in a flat file, but as a practical matter, persistence will normally be achieved with a database. The persistent-object service has several interfaces to provide mechanisms for identifying the appropriate data store, for translating the object data structure between the internal form, and the external storage form and for managing *storage* and *retrieval* operations.

The original persistent-object service did not gain acceptance and at the time of this writing a new *persistent-state service* is being defined. An alternative *persistence-management facility* is discussed with the Business-Object Facility in Chapter 5.

3.3.5 Concurrency-Control Service

The *concurrency-control service* provides a mechanism to control concurrent operations on a shared resource to coordinate the interaction of multiple users or independent application processing. The service supports a locking protocol. When a resource is accessed, a lock must be requested from the concurrency-control service. If the resource is already locked, then the requester must wait until the lock is released. The lock may be in the context of a transaction such that when the transaction is completed, it and all associated locks will be removed.

This service is useful for managing resources that do not provide their own concurrency control. Generally, it is desirable for resources to encapsulate concurrency control so that a user of the resource does not need to deal with this issue explicitly. Resources that do provide their own concurrency control could use the service; however, it does add overhead. When a lock is requested, the concurrency service must search its list of current locks to determine if the resource already has a lock outstanding. If there is a lock outstanding, there is still a need to determine if a deadlock would occur if the requester of the lock were to wait (e.g., the requester would be waiting on a process that is already waiting on the requester).

In the implementation discussed in Chapter 5, each object is responsible for its own concurrency control, but the concurrency service could still be used for other resources.

3.3.6 Externalization Service

The *externalization service* externalizes an object to a data stream that may later be *internalized* to create an object that is equivalent to a copy of the original object. The service may externalize to a variety of external formats, but there is a *Standard Externalization Format* that must be supported in order for externalized objects to be internalized by compliant vendor products.

One very useful application of the externalization service is testing. A complex object structure that implements a test situation can be externalized for future use. Whenever the test is to be rerun in the same or a different environment, the test situation can be recreated by internalizing the externalized objects. Similarly, internalization might be used to initialize an application environment.

3.3.7 Relationships Service

The *relationship service* provides a mechanism by which associations of objects can be defined in a distributed environment. A relationship is defined by a *relationship object*. Each participating object is linked to the relationship object through a *role object*. The role object defines how its participating object or objects participate in the relationship. For example, a role object would define a *contains* participation. The general assumption is that in containment relationships, operations such as *copy* and *delete* should traverse the relationships, while for reference relationships these operations would be bounded by the relationship.

Figure 3.3 illustrates some relationships. Each relationship is implemented with a relationship, object depicted by the diamond, and two role objects, depicted by small circles. The role objects are specialized to indicate the types of participation they represent. Here there are reference relationships, that may be many-to-many, and there is a containment relationship where a Portfolio contains multiple Holdings. Containment relationships are one-to-many.

The relationship service allows relationships to be established independent of the objects being related (the relationships are not known to the related objects) by using node objects in the relationship network that have references to the primary objects. This allows relationships to be created and operated on without activating or modifying the related objects. Essentially

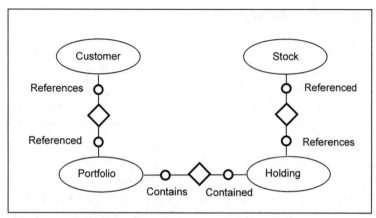

FIGURE 3.4. Example Relationship

these relationships provide a mechanism for contemplating and associating objects without their active participation, as in the case wherein a phonebook associates people with phone numbers without their direct involvement.

However, for relationships inherent to the concepts being represented, the relationship service violates encapsulation. Relationships are required to be created, accessible, and modifiable without respect for any constraints or dependencies of the related objects. The model does not recognize a relationship that is implicit, i.e., one that is computed by the participating objects.

For example, suppose a father object has a relationship with children objects. The father's relationship with his daughters, exclusive of his sons, can be computed. Relationships should be accessed in the same manner whether they are stored or computed. Furthermore, with the relationship service, a child can be added to the relationship without the participation of the father object; thus a related update based on number of children might not be performed. A consistent and encapsulated relationship would only be accessed through methods on the related objects and the members of the relationship might either be stored (implemented with explicit references) or computed.

Encapsulated relationships would have implicit concurrency control by virtue of being accessed through the associated objects. The relationships defined by the OMG specification will require independent concurrency control since they may be independently accessed and updated. The relationship and life cycle services are closely coupled because, for example, relationships determine the scope of *delete, move* and *copy* operations and the *move* and *copy* operations must replicate the relationship structure.

3.3.8 Transaction Service

The *transaction service* provides support for transaction management. A transaction object represents a transaction, and its object reference is carried by operations performed for that transaction. The transaction object implements *begin*, *commit*, and *rollback* operations for the transaction. *Commit* and *rollback* will remove locks created for the transaction with the concurrency control service. These actions will also be propagated to objects changed by the transaction processing (if they have registered with the transaction service). Typically, these objects are persistent objects and their state should be stored in persistent storage if the transaction commits, or should be restored if the transaction is rolled back. The Business-Object Facility discussed in Chapter 5 implements the linkage to persistence.

The current transaction-service specification defines no interface for deadlock detection. When a transaction attempts to use a resource that is already in use by another transaction, the transaction could be suspended to wait until the resource becomes available. Under some circumstances the two transactions could be waiting for each other, resulting in a deadlock. The transaction service should have the necessary information and provide the mechanism to detect such a deadlock.

3.3.9 Security Service

The *security service* provides mechanisms to authenticate the identity of a user, to restrict user access to data and functionality, to provide security audit information, to support administration of security authorizations and policies, and to support non-repudiation, i.e., proof of origin and proof of delivery of information. Generally, security should be implemented at ORB domain boundaries to minimize the risk of unauthorized access to protected objects. Protected objects should remain in secure environments. Access to these objects should only be through interfaces authorized for particular users on particular objects. These restrictions can be more reliably enforced at the ORB boundary where messages will not be forwarded if the senders do not meet with the interface security restrictions.

The OMG security service provides for *access decision functions* to be invoked at the ORB boundary. These functions may authorize access depending on such factors as characteristics of the target object, the time, and the operation to be performed.

In general, implementation and control of security should be achieved independently of the application development. In some cases, however, the scope of access to a type of objects may depend on the relationship of the user and the particular instance. For example, an employee may be able to view only certain information about other employees but all information about him or her self. The employee's manager may be able to change information that the employee cannot change.

3.3.10 Time Service

The *time service* provides a consistent definition of the current time throughout a distributed system. The time service is a key element of the security service and can be important to applications for support of audits.

3.3.11 Licensing Service

The *licensing service* provides mechanisms for monitoring and controlling usage of system components and for support of billing. For business applications, this may be important for managing licensed application components or supporting software, or for allocating costs of information services. For example, a component might implement a robot simulation. The objects for the robot components, the workpiece the robot operates on, etc. could be integrated into a production model. The license fees for each component could be based on usage. The licensing service might be used to capture this usage data.

3.3.12 Properties Service

The property service allows attributes to be dynamically associated with objects. This service is of interest primarily for support of system services or system administration functions. Additional attributes and relationships can be associated with specific objects without affecting their implementation.

These attributes and relationships, of course, are not accessible through the defined (IDL) interface. These properties are not encapsulated so that the associated object has no control over their values or relationships with other aspects of the object. Like the relationship service, they should only be used where information is to be associated with an object for an independent purpose in which the object is an "un-knowing" participant.

3.3.13 Query Service

The *query service* provides a mechanism for applying selection criteria to a collection of objects. The query service may return a new collection of objects that meet the criteria or it may update or delete selected objects. Selection criteria may be applied to attributes, relationships, and computed values. The collection queried may be a collection of active objects or it may be an implicit collection of persistent objects, some or all of which may be inactive. The query service does not perform logical searches or pattern matching in the manner of logic programming (e.g., Prolog).

3.3.14 Change Management

Change management provides mechanisms for coordinated changes to versions of system elements including changes to the structure or functionality of existing object instances and interface definitions (IDL). Change management provides mechanisms for the creation and access of versions of objects. Creation of a new version may be triggered when a transaction commits. Mechanisms also provide for authorization of the creation of new versions and for checkout and check-in control of the application of changes. Change management may be very valuable for applications that utilize versions such as for plans, diagrams, drawings, or product configurations. Change management is also important for the management of change to components of distributed object systems.

3.3.15 Collections

The *collection service* defines a robust set of collection classes for general use in applications. The standard defines consistent interfaces and operations on these collections to support consistency of a distributed application design in a heterogeneous environment. Collections can be persistent. A variety of collection types are defined in the OMG standard, providing various protocols such as preventing duplicates, returning members in a defined sequence, providing keyed access, etc.

3.3.16 Trader Service

The *trader service* operates like yellow pages for advertising in a distributed environment. It might be implemented as a generally accessible process on the network to which requests for identification of services can be directed. Services register with the trader service using attributes to characterize the service. A client requests references to services with certain selection criteria. The trader service will return a collection of references to those registered services that meet the selection criteria. Distributed facilities can become dynamically linked without restriction of the network node in which they are executed. In addition, clients can establish ad hoc links with new services.

A typical application of the trader service might be to identify available printers. When a printer is activated, the object representing it would register with the trader service with appropriate attributes designating features of interest. When an application needs to print, it may ask the trader for available printers possibly using user profile information to select the appropriate one or presenting the available list to the user.

3.4 COMMON FACILITIES

Common facilities are applications or components of applications that are for general use. The following sections describe a number of common facilities that have been defined or are under consideration by OMG and discuss their relevance to development of applications. These common facilities are discussed in three categories: (1) user interface, (2) information management, (3) system management, and (4) task management.

3.4.1 User Interface Common Facilities

This group of common facilities focuses on the user interface.

3.4.1.1 Rendering Management
Rendering management provides facilities for presenting objects and their associated concepts graphically or audibly. It also provides facilities for the

interpretation of input from various devices such as the keyboard, a mouse, a speech-recognition facility, or a scanner. Most applications will utilize such a facility within the interface facilities provided by a library or programming environment. Consequently, the existence of this facility may be transparent. However, the use of an interface facility that complies with industry standards will make the application more portable.

3.4.1.2 Compound-Presentation Facility

The *Compound-Presentation Facility* manages the basic windowing, menuing, and command components of a graphical display. Like rendering management, these facilities will usually be provided by a library or environment and will require little attention at the application programming level.

3.4.1.3 User-Support Facilities

These facilities are expected to expand over time. At the moment there are two: the *Help Facility* and the *Text-Checking Facility*. These are both stand-alone components that should be incorporated in applications where applicable.

The Help Facility specification defines an interface for interactive help that will be context sensitive and accommodate internationalized text and multimedia. The *Text-Checking Facility* specification provides an interface for a text-checking service that will perform spelling checks, hyphenation, grammar checks, and a thesaurus lookup. The service will operate on text strings or files of text. These facilities can be very useful for providing a rich user environment that is consistent across applications and platforms while, at the same time, avoiding the time and cost to develop it.

3.4.1.4 Desktop Management Facilities

Desktop-Management Facilities provide the user with a visualization of the computing environment. This may be an extension to desktop displays such as provided by the Windows or Macintosh environment, but expanded in scope to reflect the distributed-object environment. The desktop provides the user with the mechanisms to access components and services that are of interest and to utilize them to accomplish business functions.

These facilities will be important for providing a user interface to the environment, but for the most part they will be invisible to applications. It will be possible to implement applications without these facilities and to later install the applications in environments that provide these facilities.

3.4.1.5 Scripting

The *scripting* standard is for a common interpreted language that can be transmitted to different computing nodes on the network and executed. The purpose is to support dynamically portable functions and mobile agents. The primary candidate for this language appears to be Java; it has been designed to be platform independent and an interpreter has been designed with the explicit purpose of being able to receive and execute Java code without jeopardizing security. Java is supported by at least one ORB in the marketplace, and an OMG standard should be adopted by the time this book is published.

This opens the door for applications that run at ad hoc locations. The mobile code could be transmitted to a previously non-participating computer and it could become a participant in a distributed-object environment at a moment's notice. Implementation of mobile agents with this facility, however, assumes that the recipient is prepared to provide access to local information and has adequate protection against security violations.

In an open network, it is only appropriate to use the scripting language for the user-interface layer since access to local files and the ease with which users might modify applications could threaten security. However, if the application can be given controlled access to authorized files and other system facilities, then a full application could be installed ad hoc with a user interface and local agents to assist the user.

3.4.2 Information-Management Common Facilities

This section focuses on the modeling and exchange of information.

3.4.2.1 Information-Modeling Facility

The *Information-Modeling Facility* specifies interfaces of tools for modeling objects, related information about the system, and integration of existing components and legacy systems, as well as tools for the generation of diagrams and IDL and other application specifications. It is not particularly important that this be done with a standards-compliant facility at this time, particularly since there is still considerable diversity and instability in the available tools and techniques. Nevertheless, an appropriate tool or tools should be chosen and it should provide outputs that will drive the implementation of a system in a distributed-objects environment.

At this writing, a standard meta-model is under consideration by OMG. The adoption of this standard meta-model will allow modeling tools to share information, and it will also provide a standard representation of the results of modeling for use in other facilities. Standard meta-model interfaces (a meta-object facility specification) are also being defined for access to the meta-model.

3.4.2.2 Information Storage and Retrieval Facility

This facility comprehends all forms of information-storage facilities. This level of facility when used for database access should not be visible to the normal business-application developer since this should be incorporated into the persistence service. It is important, in general, for system flexibility and compatibility that a consistent data-storage abstraction be defined. Systems programmers should use it for implementation of databases, and it should be used by application developers for other forms of data storage such as diskette files. Developers will need to look into the availability of standard interfaces for other storage media if and when they are needed for particular applications.

3.4.2.3 Data Encoding and Representation Facility

This specification defines interfaces for facilities for the creation and interpretation of data exchanged in a common encoding and/or compression format or formats. This provides for the exchange of data using various media between heterogeneous computers. The availability of this facility may determine the limit of heterogeneity of the application environment if there is a requirement for exchange of data between computers. Note that there are several levels of standards for exchange of information. This is the lowest level. The following paragraphs describe higher levels.

3.4.2.4 Data-Interchange Facility

The *Data-Interchange Facility* is a fairly low-level standard that supports the transfer of data in different formats. The facility should be able to generate and recognize various data-stream labels and formats and incorporate appropriate facilities specific to the data types. Typically, these data types will be image, audio, text, or binary objects. The need for such facilities will depend on the application.

3.4.2.5 Compound-Interchange Facility

The *Compound-Interchange Facility* provides a mechanism for externalizing and internalizing compound-object structures such as compound documents where the compound structure must be extracted from or linked into an associated application environment. For example, consider the case in which a document exists within a word-processing application where objects considered external to the document provide the user interface and various tools to operate on the document. This facility might be employed for storing and transporting complex models such as engineering designs, cost models, machine-tool programs, or production schedules. The need for such facilities will depend on the application.

3.4.2.6 Information-Exchange Facility
The *Information-Exchange Facility* addresses the exchange of expressions representing data and operations. These expressions may incorporate a common reference model to give them context and meaning. Such a facility would be required to support the transport of mobile agents (see below) where referenced classes and interfaces must be based on a common reference model supported at all affected sites. The need for such a facility is not currently commonplace and will depend on the application.

3.4.2.7 Time-Operations Facility
This standard defines objects that represent date/time information and associated operations. Specialized objects represent an instance in time, a duration of time, and a window of time (a period between two instances in time). The objects are capable of expressing this information in various forms at various levels of specificity and of performing various computations such as determining the overlap between two time windows. These standards should be incorporated in all applications for greatest adaptability and longevity, particularly if the applications share time information with other applications.

3.4.3 System-Management Common Facilities

The *System-Management Facilities* support system administration. The standard defines consistent interfaces for organizing managed objects into libraries and defining policies for the creation, deletion, modification, and grouping of instances of managed objects. The facility also allows context and implementation specific instances of objects to be created and managed through a generic factory interface. This is a core standard for the implementation of system-administration facilities that span heterogeneous networks. Applications are not likely to be affected by these facilities except for utilizing factory objects for the creation of instances in order to enable the generalized system-management capabilities. If a system-management facility implementation is not available, it should be possible to extend factory objects with these standard interfaces when implementations become available.

3.4.4 Task Management Common Facilities

Task Management Facilities operate on the mainstream applications to search, monitor, or control activities.

3.4.4.1 Workflow Facility
The *Workflow Facility* provides for the coordination and monitoring of the flow of work through organizations and between knowledge workers and computer operations as a result of the creation or modification of objects by business-process activities. Workflow may be based on predefined business processes and policies, or it may be ad hoc as in a project plan or job-shop routing. It will be important that applications comprehend workflow interfaces if they involve work that may be managed or coordinated by a workflow process.

3.4.4.2 Mobile Agent Facility
This facility enables executable units to be deployed to remote sites to interoperate with authorized resources at the remote site as well as at the point of origin. This can be a very powerful facility for distributing workload and minimizing network activity where the majority of the operations involve resources at a remote site. Java applets are a potential form of this capability. In the CORBA context these applets would communicate with external resources and servers through an ORB.

3.4.4.3 Rule-Management Facility
The *Rule-Management Facility* definition calls for an expert system shell with standard interfaces, rule language, activation mechanism, inferencing mechanism, and federation mechanism (interoperation of rule facilities). It is not clear that this technology has evolved to the point where users of the technology would accept a standard language and inferencing mechanism.

3.4.4.4 Automation Facility
The *Automation Facility* applies to large-grained objects such as documents or spreadsheets and defines a protocol by which they inter-operate. This sup-

ports the embedding of such objects within each other (e.g., a spreadsheet in a text document) and operations on these objects with scripts and macros. The facility also supports access to component objects by contextual specification (e.g., spreadsheet cell B3). This facility may be particularly important for the integration of an application with other packaged desktop applications. For such applications it may be appropriate for the application to support Microsoft COM protocols.

3.5 THE BUSINESS OBJECTS FACILITY

The objective of the *Business Objects Facility* (BOF) is to provide a higher level of abstraction of CORBA services and facilities in order to make the implementation and interoperation of business objects more straightforward. Business objects are objects that represent concepts in the business domain of the application and interact to represent the problem and compute solutions. Using this abstraction, application developers should be able to concentrate on solving the business problem with minimal concern about computational mechanisms.

The functionality and interfaces of a BOF are a central aspect of this book. The OMG specifications are currently under development. Chapter 5 contains a description of an initial BOF implementation by EDS.

3.6 SUMMARY

There are many components in the OMG architecture and many interactions between them. Utilization of these components can be a major challenge. Fortunately, the development of a Business Objects Facility will simplify and encapsulate important aspects of the architecture for application developers. In the short term the application developer should understand the nature and roles of these components and either obtain products that implement these facilities or implement similar interfaces to minimize conversion efforts when the application is eventually integrated into a large-scale distributed environment. In the long term, the application developer will still need to be aware of many of these components and specifications so that they are incorporated as appropriate and applications achieve optimum portability, interoperability, and flexibility.

CHAPTER 4

Planning and Managing Development Projects

In this chapter we discuss the planning and management of distributed-objects system development. There are several fundamental factors that affect these projects:

1. The use of iterative development rather than waterfall, analysis-design-construction.
2. The sharing of objects, both as software and as shared elements of production systems.
3. The extensive use of graphical user interfaces.
4. The integration of heterogeneous network components.
5. The distribution of processing and interactions across a network.
6. The potential for large-scale integration.

These factors are not all unique to the development of distributed-object systems, but they occur together and all contribute to the complexity of the undertaking.

This chapter does not attempt to define a model process. Nor does it attempt to address basic project-management techniques and processes. It is assumed that the reader is familiar with project management and the basic principles for requirements tracking, change control, verification, and validation, etc. There are other sources of such material that address these topics more rigorously than is appropriate here. Extensive work has been conducted by standards organizations such as IEEE (Institute of Electrical and Electronics Engineers), ANSI (American National Standards Institute), ISO (International Organization for Standardization), and IEC (International Electrotechnical Commission). We focus attention on ways the software-development effort is changed by object technology, and, in particular, a distributed-objects architecture.

Most systems-development organizations already have a basic process they follow for software development. The fundamentals of these disciplines still apply. The material that follows suggests ways in which those processes and disciplines should be adapted to address the requirements of distributed-objects system development. We discuss considerations for project planning and management from several perspectives: modeling, object sharing, tools and components, system architecture, and the development process.

4.1 MODELING

Objects are used to represent concepts that occur in the conduct of the user's business. Both the data about the concept and actions associated with the concept are implemented in the associated object. This reduces the conceptual gap and the translation effort to take business processes and implement them in the computer system. It also means that when the business situation changes it will be easier to relate the change occurring in the business to the change required in the software. The basic business concepts seldom change, but at least some of the associated data and functions often do, and there are often special cases that can be represented by specializations of the existing objects.

4.1.1 Business-Process Modeling

It is very important that the business itself be well modeled. The accuracy of the model will directly affect the simplicity of the solution and the adaptability of the resulting system. This may take considerable effort, but it must be done early in the development process. The modeling effort requires user participation and definition of *use cases* [Jacobson] to assure deep understanding of the business concepts and interactions.

Use cases are derived from analysis of business processes. The application-process developer should understand the business processes, be aware of common elements of related business processes, and understand the implications to the portions of the business processes to be automated. A use case defines a specific situation as a basis for determining the actions to be taken by the system to resolve that situation. Typically, use cases can be identified through consideration of business events and variations in the surrounding circumstances. The design of the application is then evolved through the examination of multiple use cases and generalization of the solution. It is much easier to discuss and define examples and follow them through, than to always work with generalizations.

The application-process developer uses objects to represent the business concepts and implement these processes. Elements of the business process must be associated with different objects according to the impact that variations in those elements have on the process. For example, different kinds of bank accounts will require different computations for interest or different penalties for not maintaining a minimum balance. These differences should be embodied in the associated methods on the different classes of accounts.

As the business processes are analyzed in increasing detail, variations in the business concepts as well as new, less obvious business concepts will be discovered. To assure consistency, this ongoing process should be managed by specialists in object modeling.

4.1.2 Object Modeling

As processes are analyzed top down, objects tend to be developed bottom up. The concepts represented by objects are discovered through analysis of the processes. The data and functionality of the objects are then discovered and refined as the roles of the objects in various processes are analyzed. The same objects are often used in many processes. They will support many different users.

The designs of shared objects must be consistent across the enterprise in order to function properly in a variety of contexts. The development of a model shared by multiple applications facilitates the sharing of information, potential operational integration of the applications, and the reuse of object implementations.

However, different users in an enterprise have different conceptual views of some of the same entities within the business. For example, the project planner sees employees as people with skill levels and travel constraints while the payroll clerk sees them as people with salaries and bonuses. While the core concept is the same, each user should be presented with a view appropriate to his or her role. At the same time, the coordination of activities and sharing of information across departments requires that there be a common model that reconciles these different views. This requires object modeling to have two dimensions. Each application must be modeled to represent the perspective of the particular business activity. At the same time, an enterprise model should be developed and maintained that supports the entire enterprise. The development of these two models must include a mapping between them. Most often, the application model will be a simplification where enterprise concepts with one-to-one relationships may be represented as a single concept in the local application and only certain attributes and relationships are visible. The application development process should recognize the need for reconciliation of the application model with the enterprise model.

Object modeling has similarities with data modeling. The entities of data modeling have a close correlation to the classes of object modeling. This is probably the basis for wide acceptance of Rumbaugh's approach [Rumbaugh], which bears a close resemblance to relational modeling. Figure 4.1 shows a typical class diagram taken from the example application in the Appendix. However, unlike relational databases, objects exhibit inheritance and polymorphism. The modeling notation often has a limiting affect on the robustness of the model, and many models fail to fully utilize inheritance and polymorphism.

Nevertheless, a relational-like model can be a good starting point for an object model, particularly for the more fundamental entities and relationships. As the model grows in complexity, however, a tool will be needed to capture and manage the complexity of polymorphism and inheritance. It will not be possible to view or manage the model as a drawing or set of drawings. The tool should enable the developer to examine a consistent repository of information from different perspectives. Current tools are evolving in this direction.

Perhaps the most important analytical technique is CRC (Class Responsibility-Collaboration) analysis [Wirfs-Brock]. This technique treats the objects as active participants that have responsibilities and use collaboration with other objects to fulfill these responsibilities. This technique reinforces polymorphism and inheritance, and is easy for both developers and users to comprehend.

Another technique is the use of *roles* [Reenskaug]. Rather than attempt to define all of the functionality of objects from the outset, Reenskaug suggests

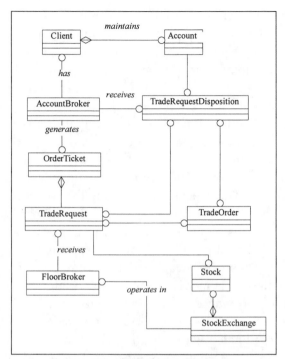

FIGURE 4.1. OMT Class Diagram

that the analyst only be concerned with the role of an object in the implementation of a process or set of related processes. A role may apply to different classes, thus defining polymorphism, and the composite of roles associated with a class determines the functionality to be supported by the class. This has particular merit in the development of *enterprise objects*—objects that are shared across the enterprise rather than designed to meet the needs of only one application perspective. Views and adapters, discussed in Chapter 2, provide an implementation of the concept of roles with a separation of the localized representation of a limited perspective from the shared, enterprise-level implementation.

Fusion promotes the use of object interaction graphs [Coleman] and Booch [Booch] uses object-interaction diagrams (see Figure 4.2). These support CRC analysis of use cases. Fusion also integrates a number of techniques and notations with an analysis and design process. It provides a more complete approach to the development of applications, but leaves out many aspects of a complete development effort. For example, the greatest source of object-technology project overruns and failures are delayed and inadequate attention to the supporting technology: the application architecture and its integration with the enterprise-computing infrastructure.

Object modeling requires expertise and dedicated effort. The required expertise goes beyond proficiency in modeling techniques. It requires understanding of both business and technical terminology and concepts, the ability to conceptualize the allocation of functionality to objects and their interactions to perform system functions, and skills in human communication and conflict resolution. The goal of modeling is the definition of a complex set of elements and their interrelationships that reflect the concepts of the business domain, use appropriate terminology, and reflect a consensus of the developers involved. The dependencies among the components and the terminology make it difficult to partition the work. The need to achieve consistency and consensus requires dedicated effort. The responsibility cannot be shared by a number of people with other responsibilities.

The smaller the modeling team and the more devoted they are to the development of the object model, the better the results. The size of the modeling team must be balanced against the amount of effort required and the timetable of related activities. At the same time the efforts of the modeling team must be coordinated with related efforts. The structure of the model must be resolved with the analysis of processes, the design of the user interface and the cost, security, and performance implications of the architecture.

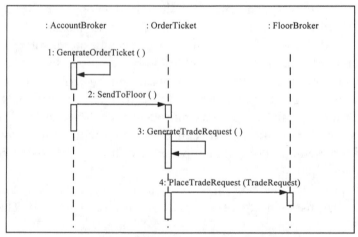

FIGURE **4.2. Object Interaction Diagram**

4.1.3 User-Interface Design

While business objects model business concepts inside the computer, the user-interface objects provide the visualization and mechanisms by which users interact with business objects. The development of user interfaces requires special skills and perspective. The user-interface designer must observe standards and design techniques that achieve a common look and feel and help the typical user quickly adapt to new displays. Please refer to the efforts of standards organizations such as ANSI for assistance in achieving an effective and compatible design. The user-interface designer must understand the business perspective of individual users so that the presentation of relevant business concepts will be consistent with that perspective. Finally, the user-interface designer must understand how the user does his or her job so that the job activity is efficient and navigation among different displays is natural and supportive of the user activity. User-interface designers should work closely with end users, and to be efficient, the development work should be organized so that an end user works consistently with the same designer.

Generally speaking, user-interface designers need not be skilled in object-oriented programming. As the tools improve, the time spent programming user interfaces is decreasing. Developers use graphical user-interface design tools—implemented with objects—to lay out displays, incorporate display component functionality, provide facilities for display navigation, and map fields and buttons to application-object attributes and methods.

A user-interface display should be linked to the application objects through an adapter, as discussed in Chapter 2. The adapter object has the responsibility for relaying display actions as messages to the application. It also has responsibility for relaying changes in the application model to the display. The connection between the user interface and the application model should be such that multiple displays may be connected, ad hoc, to the application model. The application model should have no programming specific to the displays. The displays should have logic for visualization and acceptance of inputs, but should not include any application-specific logic. This separation is key to flexibility in both the user interface and the application. For example, internationalization may be achieved by implementing multiple sets of displays for the same application. This should be reflected as well in the separation of responsibility between the user-interface developer and the business-process developer.

4.2 SHARING OBJECTS

An important promise of object technology is the ability to share objects. This should occur at four levels. First, code is shared within an application through inheritance and the consistent use of each class to represent its associated application concept. Second, software components can be shared across applications based on a consistent object model. Third, objects can be shared in production systems; run-time sharing of objects assures that all applications are working with the same information and users are making decisions based on timely and consistent data. Finally, legacy systems can be integrated—another form of shared production objects.

4.2.1 Basic Requirements

Fundamental to sharing is effective use of encapsulation and polymorphism. Encapsulation is achieved by definition of the public, functional interface of an object to conceal the details of its implementation. This means that the implementation may be changed without requiring corresponding changes in the processes that use the object. Polymorphism is implemented through message sending. Different classes of objects may participate in the same processes and message sending will cause the appropriate functionality to be invoked for each. This improves the management of complexity and supports the development of more generalized processes in which the polymorphic components participate.

To achieve the goals of encapsulation and polymorphism, the public interfaces of objects must be carefully designed. The interface protocols and message forms must conceal potential variations in implementation, and they must be consistent throughout the system for equivalent interface semantics. Each method signature should be documented to include the semantics of the method functionality, definition of parameters, the expected return value, required pre-conditions, and exceptions that may result. All methods with the same name should comply with this interface specification. For example, a message that causes an object to produce printable output for a particular purpose must be of the same form for all objects that might service a similar request. This means method names must be chosen carefully and controlled, and the meanings and types of message parameters must be consistent.

Attention to interface specifications and separation of interface from implementation are reinforced by the use of IDL (Interface Definition Language) for distributed-object systems using the OMG architecture. Java also requires interfaces to be designed as distinct from implementations. This separation encourages more flexible design. Unfortunately, current analysis and design tools do not provide facilities to exploit this.

Encapsulation and polymorphism also cause the implementation of business processes to be difficult to analyze because the processes are implemented in multiple objects. The method that is invoked to perform an automated process may be very brief. The actions performed are, for the most part, delegated to other objects. The other objects involved, and therefore the actual methods invoked, may be very dependent on the particular situation—polymorphism may allow many different objects to participate in the process. This makes it all the more important that the semantics of messages and their parameters are clearly defined and consistent for all objects that support them.

4.2.2 Organizational Implications

The development team should have motivation and discipline to exploit the reuse of software components. Reuse must occur within the project through inheritance of class structure and functionality, and through incorporation of the same object code wherever the concept is used within the system. This should also occur across projects through the utilization of common components in the form of classes, or, more often, in the form of complex components involving a number of objects. We discuss these briefly as intraproject and interproject modes of reuse.

Intraproject reuse occurs as a result of a well-defined object model and continuing coordination and control by the object modeler. The model must appropriately represent business concepts and provide a class hierarchy that uses abstract classes to cluster common functionality for inheritance. The model must also identify and consistently define the name, form, protocol, and semantics of interfaces for similar object functions. Since the designs of objects will continue to evolve throughout the project, this is an ongoing effort. Because of the need for global consistency, the effort is best done by a small number of people who are skilled object designers and understand the business domain.

Interproject reuse presents additional challenges. In general, the objects developed for a single application are not immediately suitable for use in others. The demands of the initial project will prevent developers from devoting the time needed to develop objects that will have multiple application utility without refinement. By the end of the initial project, there will be new insights on how the objects should be designed for greater utility, and the initial application funding usually does not include the opportunity to do the necessary rework.

Objects reused from other projects will represent a level of risk. Good documentation and an accessible, reliable support staff that can assist in the proper use of the objects and respond quickly to needs to further refine or extend the objects can minimize this risk.

The challenge of reuse increases with the size of the organization. It is relatively simple for small teams. For large projects, it requires close coordination and control. Cross-project sharing for a single department or small enterprise can be managed with management motivation, technical reviews, and standards efforts. In large organizations, there must be standards for interoperability and mechanisms for cost recovery or profit making by the supporting organization. There should also be mechanisms to assure that support needs and revisions will be addressed promptly and appropriately for all "customer" organizations. These reuse management issues are the real challenge.

The application-development process must recognize the effort required to identify and evaluate reusable components from other projects or outside vendors. In addition to the quality of the components and the level of support provided, this evaluation activity must assess the impact of the design of these objects on the rest of the project. The shared components will necessarily establish a starting point for the definition of business concepts (classes) and their functional interfaces (method signatures). They will also incorporate computational objects, collections being the prime example, which should be consistent throughout the application to avoid unnecessary complexity and constraints on polymorphism.

If objects are also shared in a production environment, additional complexities arise. While the environment should support management of concurrent access to shared objects, there will be issues related to the coordination of changes across applications and organizations. In addition, installation of production changes will need to be coordinated between applications and their local adapters and views as well as with multiple computers and architectural components.

In summary, there are eight key elements to successful reuse:

1. Effective use of encapsulation and polymorphism.
2. A robust object model.
3. Re-engineering of application-specific implementations.
4. Standards for object interfaces.
5. Support and documentation for the reusable components.
6. Cost-recovery mechanisms for development and support.
7. Change control.
8. Interoperability support such as standard protocols and a Business Objects Facility (see Chapter 5).

4.2.3 Legacy Integration

It is desirable to replace conventional systems with object-oriented systems in stages, and object-oriented applications often use business data from existing applications. These factors require the integration of legacy and object-oriented systems. To achieve this from a distributed-objects perspective, the legacy system or a portion of it, must become an object or set of objects incorporated into the distributed-objects environment.

In most cases, integration is achieved through a shared database. This requires a mapping of the conventional data structures to objects. If the legacy system is wrapped with an object-oriented interface to incorporate its functionality, it is likely that the undertaking will be more complex—problems can arise with respect to both concurrency and the consistency of interface protocols. In addition, interactions with legacy system processes and retrieval of structures from legacy databases will compound application-performance concerns. This activity may be a major drain on project resources and the implementation may present significant risk of poor system reliability and performance.

These are problems that should be separated from the object-oriented design of the application; they are not problems of representing the business, but are computational, implementation problems. The legacy system must be represented by appropriate, consistent objects whether they are implemented through a functional interface to the legacy application or constructed from data retrieved from the legacy database. The design of this interface, and its performance impact on the application(s) under development must be addressed early in the development process so that alternatives can be considered and adequate time is allowed for the implementation of solutions.

4.3 TOOLS AND COMPONENTS

There are a number of tools and components that assist application developers in their work. These should be selected early in a project because some of them are needed at early stages and there are often interdependencies to be considered in the selections. The following sections briefly discuss some of the key facilities.

4.3.1 Analysis and Design Tools

Tools are needed to help application developers capture and integrate requirements, develop consistent and robust object models, and produce effective designs. It is particularly important to have an integrated object-modeling tool. There are various techniques for visualizing such models, but the most important tool capability is that the various views must be driven by a common model. As the scope of applications increases, as components are shared by multiple applications and as shared enterprise models are developed, it will be impossible to manage this information as independent drawings. At a minimum, an analysis tool should support class models illustrating classes and relationships, interaction diagrams, and displays to capture and view textual descriptions for method signatures, classes, attributes, and relationships.

The OMG is in the process of defining specifications for a common analysis and design meta-model and specifications for interfaces to a meta-model (the meta-object facility), which will provide the common denominator for sharing models between tools. It will be important to select tools that comply with that standard to maintain flexibility and accommodate future specialized tools. The availability of a common model will also foster development of additional tools with specialized views.

Design considerations tend to be language dependent. Some languages, such as Smalltalk, come with robust development environments and much of the design work can be done in the programming environment if guided by good design standards, patterns, and techniques. In other languages, such as C++, it is necessary to do more design work before starting to program. However, programming environments for C++ are becoming increasingly supportive of interactive development.

4.3.2 User-Interface Tools

Effective tools can dramatically reduce the programming effort required for user-interface development. Most user interfaces should require little programming. Layouts should be "painted" interactively. Interactive tools enable developers to assemble graphical components and link them to the application objects. The user interface is designed, often with user participation, using such tools. The user interface developer can then concentrate on efficient human–machine communications and effective support of the tasks to be performed by the user.

Some tools provide the capability to define portions of a display as a sharable component. This reduces the development effort and promotes consistency. General design of the user interface coupled with a recognition of recurrent operations and visualizations should be leveraged to utilize sharable components.

4.3.3 Language and Programming Environment

The selection of language and programming environment will depend on a number of factors relating to the characteristics of the application, the computing environment, related applications and components, and the skills of the development staff. The choice will have an impact on development productivity and the frequency and complexity of defects.

An interactive development environment is a must. Developers should be able to quickly program, test, analyze, and modify their code. It is essential to be able to trace or step through malfunctioning code, examining variables to identify the source of problems. It is also key to the ability to quickly make a change, recreate the test situation, and validate the result.

4.3.4 Class Libraries

Class libraries containing computational components are very important for developer productivity. Many classes are built into programming environments provided with Smalltalk. Substantial libraries of classes are now available for C++. Some of these libraries are discussed in more detail in Chapter 8. There is also a growing body of Java components available in the marketplace. Selection of libraries must consider potential incompatibilities with other components. The scope, documentation, and reliability of these libraries will have a significant impact on development effort and system quality.

4.3.5 Configuration Management

Configuration management requires special tools and clear definition of responsibilities, particularly for large projects. Integration of the work of multiple developers must be managed so that they all have a reliable base to work on. Once a component is shared with others, further changes must be carefully validated and controlled. Interdependencies between components are more complex for object-oriented systems because of the extensive sharing of code. Control must be based on versions of both the components and the integrated system. When the system is deployed, it may be necessary to combine different components to configure specific nodes in the network because of the functionality to be supported or the requirements of the platform. The configuration-management system is key to providing such capabilities.

4.3.6 Database Tools

Tools are needed for implementing and tuning databases. Object-modeling tools often have the capability to generate the data-definition language for object-oriented databases. Tools are also available to capture the mappings of objects to relational tables and generate associated code. Once the database is implemented, tools will be needed to identify and analyze performance problems. It is also important to look at the quality and completeness of operational tools for monitoring database performance, managing failed transactions, backup and recovery, and garbage collection—removal of deleted objects and consolidation of available space. Some object-oriented database products are weak in this area. The availability and effectiveness of database tools can have a significant impact on the cost and time required to complete a development project and the ability to provide quality service once it goes into production.

4.3.7 Distributed Objects Supporting Software

Earlier discussions were devoted to defining the requirements of supporting software for a distributed-objects system. The long-term benefits of the distributed-objects architecture will depend on the implementation of a stable and robust architecture that incorporates standard components and protocols. A business-object facility must be either developed or purchased to address this need. Chapter 5 outlines the requirements and describes an initial implementation of a business-object facility. Without such a facility, the effort and risk associated with each application development project will be unacceptable. In addition, the potential for large-scale integration will be severely limited.

The testing and debugging of distributed-object systems is a significant challenge, particularly when problems are a consequence of concurrent processing or interoperation errors. Tools are needed to capture and analyze the state of the system when an error is detected and to trace processing, assist in the examination of trace information, generate timing data, help identify bottlenecks, and display system activity for monitoring of workload distribution. There is currently an absence of commercially available tools to provide these capabilities. Some of these capabilities should be integrated with a Business Objects Facility.

4.4 SYSTEM ARCHITECTURE

The system architecture is the network of computers and software that enables applications, servers, and databases to interact to achieve business objectives. This architecture should not be developed for a single application, but should be designed to evolve to the enterprise computing model discussed in Chapter 2. For the most part, the architecture will be constructed from purchased components that application developers must assemble, configure, and program to appropriately distribute the processing, establish the communications, implement the databases, and provide a network that is manageable, reliable, responsive, and efficient.

Given a system architecture designed for the integration of applications, the architecture of each application must be designed to specialize, and if necessary extend, the system architecture to meet the specific application requirements. Since each new application will incorporate many components shared by other applications, the impact of the application must be carefully assessed and addressed.

In designing a system architecture for many applications, a wide range of possibilities should be considered and a consistent approach defined. This design will be extended and partially validated through the implementation of the first application. With each subsequent application development, many of the factors will be revisited and potentially modified due to new insights, new requirements, or new supporting products. Like the development of shared objects, development of the system architecture will be iterative.

The following are primary aspects to be considered:

- **Database design**. The design of databases requires attention to consistency with the object model and good storage and retrieval performance. Both retrieval of specific objects and patterns of generalized queries should be considered.

- **Object-to-relational mapping**. Most applications will continue to use relational databases and the mapping of objects to relational tables must reflect both polymorphism and the need to support queries.

- **Database query and retrieval optimization**. If applications simply retrieve individual objects when they are needed, performance will be unacceptable. Mechanisms must be implemented to utilize optimization techniques.

- **Data distribution and network layout**. The distribution of databases, processing, and network links must reflect the composite processing patterns of multiple applications. This configuration may change for each application and may need to be dynamically adjusted for workload shifts. Simulations will be needed to predict network loading and to devise adjustments before performance is impacted.

- **External system interfaces**. Applications may require interactions or communication of data with external systems. Each of these may require unique interfacing mechanisms and protocols. Of particular interest are linkages to client systems or other servers over an intranet or the public Internet.

- **Legacy-system integration.** A strategy for legacy-system integration and phase-out should be defined and adapted as required for particular legacy systems and application dependencies.

- **Network protocols and communication.** Different network protocols and communication facilities may be required as the scope of the integrated system expands. These may involve gateways and differing system-management and performance considerations.

- **Integration of network services.** Network services (e.g., object services such as the transaction, name, trader, and query services) must be integrated for consistent operation and management of the distributed-objects environment. As the scope of the system expands, the heterogeneity of the service components will increase, creating integration problems.

- **Information protection and system security.** Security in a distributed-objects environment presents new challenges both because of the risk of exposure in communications and the widespread sharing at a fine level of granularity.

- **System failure containment and recovery.** A distributed-objects system has many potential points of failure. The system should be designed to limit the propagation of failures and assure the prompt and reliable recovery of system services, sometimes through redistribution of work.

- **Configuration management.** As the scope of the system expands, the diversity of components and number of changes will expand as well. Strategies and mechanisms must be in place to coordinate changes where there are dependencies and allow changes to be withdrawn in an orderly fashion if a serious problem is encountered.

- **System administration.** The management of system operation will be increasingly complex as the scope of the integrated system expands. Integrated tools will be needed to quickly identify and resolve poor performance, security threats or component failure problems.

These are all important considerations for both the development of an integrated system and the successful implementation of each application. The level of attention required for each will vary considerably from one project to the next, and will certainly be affected by the level to which the systems infrastructure already supports the application architecture.

Many of these topics are addressed further in later chapters, particularly in Chapter 6. The first level of system architectural development is the selection of components. The OMG standards will improve the potential for configuring solutions from multiple vendors integrating heterogeneous platforms, languages, and databases. Nevertheless, selection of components and configuration of the architecture should be addressed by a team of specialists. Beyond selection of components, there remain many design issues involved in achieving a reliable, cost-effective, high-performance, and secure architecture. The architecture should be designed to eventually support the enterprise, not for the requirements of a single application. The work to design, prototype, validate, and implement the architecture should start well in advance of application design and programming.

Even though they may start as homogeneous configurations, over time the networks of computers supporting distributed systems will most likely involve different types of hardware, operating systems, languages, and databases. This may not be true for early, small-scale systems, but diversity will develop as the scope of integration is expanded, independent systems become integrated, and new products offer cost, performance, and functionality advantages. The goal is to be able to accommodate diversity, incorporate new technology, and continue to improve the systems without large-scale redevelopment efforts, and without jeopardizing system integrity and performance.

The distributed-objects architecture should lead to large-scale integration that exceeds current capabilities. As the scope of integration increases, there is a risk that management of change will become a major challenge. Integration of new applications and changes to existing applications will need to be compatible with multiple computers, operating systems, languages, and related applications. Different versions of software may be in production on different computers due to timing of installations or upgrade incompatibilities. The solution is to establish an appropriate level of standards and change control. Even though it may be distributed and heterogeneous, the autonomy exercised over changes to the configuration and acceptance of changes must be limited. Tools will be needed for remote installation of changes, remote validation of configurations, and remote diagnosis of problems.

Most of the architectural considerations are not unique to object-oriented application development. However, since object-oriented applications are often implemented with new architectures, there is a high risk that they will fail due to inattention to architectural issues. Architecture design must be addressed early in the project. Ideally, the basic architecture should be determined by an enterprise infrastructure specification that is designed before individual application development efforts are undertaken and that reflects the strategic direction of the enterprise.

4.5 DEVELOPMENT PROCESS

The primary reason that project management for object-oriented application development differs from conventional project management is that the design can be incrementally developed. However, typical object-oriented applications also include new business processes, graphical user interfaces, and distributed computing architectures. The combination can be very challenging. It is difficult to separate the project-management requirements of object-oriented programming from the requirements introduced by these other factors. The following sections provide suggestions for planning a distributed-objects system-development project.

4.5.1 Iterative Development

The structure of object-oriented software allows a solution to be developed somewhat incrementally. If the basic concepts are well defined, then there is a good foundation for the definition of data and functionality. When an object is initially designed, it will be impossible to anticipate all of the data elements and functionality associated with it and to envision all of the processes in which it will eventually participate. As each new process is implemented, the participating objects may undergo modification or extension.

The detailed design of an object will evolve throughout a project and beyond. The nature of objects makes it both possible and necessary. The development process should reflect this. Initial efforts should focus on mainstream processes. Once these stabilize, the design can be extended to resolve exception conditions and special cases. Later, the functionality can be extended to address issues that arise through the interaction of processes of other users and systems.

Iterative development refers to the practice of developing part of the solution, then revising or extending it in a repetitive cycle. The developer will first implement a fairly simplistic solution and demonstrate it to validate requirements and identify further refinements. The solution can then be revised with relative ease to reflect new insights and extend its capabilities. The result is early feedback to the user regarding the interpretation of requirements and the development of solutions that are more appropriate to the business need.

A concern is that the iterative process might go on endlessly, with the user asking for more and more improvements. One part of the solution is to control the scope of functionality and focus attention on getting the included functionality right. Along with this, the number of iterations in which the user participates can be controlled so that the user only has a certain number of opportunities to come up with new ideas. While the resulting application might not exhibit the ultimate in capabilities, it will, nevertheless, be adaptable. Enhancements and extensions can be incorporated in subsequent efforts.

4.5.2 Stages of Development

Although iterative development can be very effective, the activity must be structured into stages where results are reviewed, decisions are made, and progress is assessed. The review and acceptance of various work products will define the degree of completion of these stages of development. Earlier stages should not be viewed as prerequisites for later stages, but rather as a basis for assigning priorities to various activities. Work on tasks of later stages may be started while tasks of earlier stages are still in process. Figure 4.3 depicts the overlap of stages.

In addition to the overlap, each of these stages includes some analysis,

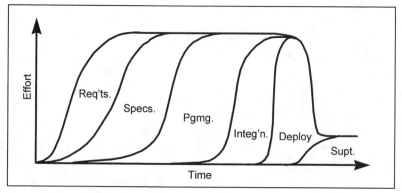

FIGURE 4.3. Potential Overlap of Stages of Development

design, and implementation. The earlier stages are heavier on analysis and the latter on implementation, but in iterative development the entire process—analysis, design-implementation—is applied repetitively, each time extending the functionality and moving the application closer to completion.

The development stages that provide a basic framework are as follows:

- **Requirements determination.** This stage concentrates on determining what the system owner wants. There are several dimensions to be considered, among them are the business processes supported, the scope of automation, characteristics of user interfaces, existing and planned system architecture, performance expectations, interfaces to other systems, and applicable standards. At the end of this stage, these factors should be documented. In addition, solutions to challenging problems should be prototyped, an initial object model should be defined for the business concepts to be represented, the basic application architecture should be defined, and scripts should be completed for the business processes to be automated.

- **Specification.** The specification stage should focus on the detail of how the system will be implemented. Specifics of the architecture, networks, computers, databases, etc., should be defined and performance factors should be analyzed. The databases should be designed and mappings should be defined if relational databases are being used. Classes should be designed with accesser methods and basic operational methods based on responsibility-collaboration analysis. User interfaces should be prototyped to determine layout and identify functionality. Testing plans should be developed based on requirements and design. Complex user interfaces and business processes should be prototyped if they have significant impact on the architecture, the object model, or the business operation.

- **Programming.** This stage is where the mainstream programming is completed. The user interfaces should be integrated with the application objects and automated processes so that users can validate the solutions on a single-user basis. Testing of components should be completed and user acceptance test plans should be used to evaluate results within the single-user scope. Initial user documentation should be completed.

- **Integration.** All the pieces are brought together in this stage. The single-user solutions are integrated. The network and database facilities are incorporated. A test configuration of the completed system must be implemented and used for integration testing and performance tuning. During this stage, performance problems must be resolved, exception handling facilities implemented, recovery facilities and procedures completed, and both user and system documentation finished.

Beyond the integration stage, the system must go through verification, validation, and user-acceptance testing before being deployed in the business environment. The above stages are similar to those of conventional development processes, but they should not be viewed as a "waterfall" solution. They are a means to prioritize activities and assess progress. As individual work products are completed they should be reviewed. When some aspects of the project are completed for one stage, the participants may move into the next stage. At the same time, if there is a significant variance in the stages completed in different activities, then there is a risk that developments in the delayed activities will impact the validity of activities that appear to be completed. In such cases it may be appropriate to reassign personnel to bring the project back into balance.

The significance to developers of completing a stage for a particular work product is that the free-wheeling iterations stop. Further requirements for changes to the work products must be evaluated and approved before they are undertaken. It is participation in reviews and evaluation of change requests that keeps the project manager in charge of the project

4.5.3 Change Control

Change control is not new and for most work products there are no new issues. However, change control for object-oriented systems source code is particularly challenging because of the extensive sharing of code. While a new system requirement can often be implemented with localized changes, by the same token, a change to a few objects can impact many processes. Implementation of a new business process will often involve many objects, and it is inappropriate to define a changed component as consisting of all of the participating objects.

If the system is small, change control may be exercised at the level of versions of the entire system. A base system is configured as soon as there is an elementary working set of objects. This base can then be used by individual programmers as an environment to test their changes. Additions of new classes, instance variables, and methods (excluding specializations of existing methods) can be allowed with minimal control since they should not affect functionality already implemented. Updates to the base must be controlled.

The problem is that an update of the base system will probably involve the work products of a number of programmers and the changes will not have independent effects. Consequently, each time a new base system is configured, there will be problems to resolve, and the work of individual programmers using the base system for testing may suffer.

For large projects it is essential that *components* be defined. A component in this context is a collection of elements that give the system a certain extended capability. A component should be the work product of a small number of programmers, preferably one or two. The definition of a component should be meaningful in terms of the capability it adds to the system, but the scope will also be affected by the language and available tools.

A component will depend on the existence of other components that implement the classes, instance variables, and methods used by the new component. Configuration management must include management of the dependencies between components and the relationships of their versions.

While the enterprise model will provide flexibility, there is still be a need to manage changes at different levels. In particular, when an application introduces new aspects or operations that should be shared across the enterprise, both the application and the affected enterprise objects will need to be changed. These need to be changed together, however, the change should not affect other applications that do not use the new aspects or operations.

4.5.4 Team Organization

Like most system-development undertakings, the required formality of the plan and staff organization will depend on the particular undertaking—the scope, problem complexity, integration requirements, team experience, etc. If the effort is small, the team is experienced, and the duration is short, then the plan and staff organization may be relatively informal. If the effort is large, formal planning and organization will be crucial. In distributed-object development efforts, there is a need for more coordination and communication than in conventional development projects. This is a consequence of the extensive sharing of code, scope of integration, and potential interactions among various components both functionally and in contention for resources. The development effort cannot simply be partitioned based on high-level system functions. Instead, if the team is large, the work should be partitioned according to the type of activity and disciplines involved.

The organization of the project team should recognize the need for specialists. In particular, there should be people who specialize in user interfaces, business processes, object design, and architecture. Within architecture there may be a need for additional specialists, as discussed earlier, if there is not already a supportive infrastructure. Additional specialists may also be required for system testing, user training, and documentation.

If the project is large, these specialties should be organized into teams of specialists. The teams must be coordinated through exchange of documents, joint participation in reviews, and ad hoc committees to address particular issues.

4.5.5 Verification and Validation

Testing of object-oriented programs is not as simple as testing conventional programs. In conventional systems, the major components are usually processes, where each process is the work product of a single developer with minimal sharing of code. In object-oriented systems, most of the major processes will be performed by invoking code developed by others. With polymorphism, the code invoked in a single call will have the possibility of invoking a variety of different object classes that are the work of different developers.

Development and testing generally use a bottom-up approach. Objects are implemented with elementary methods based on the business concepts represented and typical actions expected to perform. These can be tested fairly easily. The scope and complexity of processes is then incrementally expanded, incorporating the elementary processes already tested. The test cases use some of the elementary methods and polymorphic alternatives, but not necessarily all possible combinations. Testing of all possible call paths is not practical. The assumption is that the objects and their methods are true to their interface specifications and therefore, polymorphic exchanges will not have ill effects. Developers must consider the validity of this assumption and incorporate test cases to create conditions where different implementations of the lower-level methods or different combinations of component objects might cause inappropriate results. By the time the major processes are being developed and tested, most of the lower level methods will have been validated in several different contexts. However, to assure thorough testing, independent tests should be conducted.

Because of the limitations of testing and the potential impact of malfunctions in shared objects, the validation and verification of application code cannot be left to testing. Design reviews and code walkthroughs should be used extensively throughout the development process. Design documents should be reviewed, then revised and re-reviewed if changes occur. A single developer cannot anticipate all of the contexts in which an object may be used. Likewise, code should be reviewed in walkthroughs after it has passed unit-level tests and again when integration is near completion.

Testing and reviews require planning, an understanding of the business requirements, and a knowledge of the design being implemented. Use cases should be captured along the way, used in reviews, to define test cases, and refined as the objects and business processes are refined. Test cases can be automated to execute a series of messages with a set of objects representing the test situation, independent of the user interface, and with minimal human intervention. However, code walkthroughs will still be required to consider circumstances that might not be covered in the tests.

4.5.6 Documentation

Development of documents should be an integral part of the development process. Both technical and user documents are essential for effective communication among team members and users. This communication provides the opportunity for user feedback on application functionality and for peer feedback on design.

Development of user documents should progress along with user-interface development so that the user understands how the system is supposed to work as it unfolds. The completed user documents must be available when it is time for user acceptance testing. System documents should also be developed as the business processes, object model, and architecture are developed. They are essential for developing a consensus on design and achieving a consistent object model.

Technical documents will be important to the long life of the system and control of maintenance costs. Once the system is completed, the level of maintenance may be very low. As a result, the developers who understand the intricacies of the business problem and the system design will move on to other challenges. When a change is eventually required, the maintenance programmer must be able to quickly discover how the system works and recognize the design patterns to implement the change in a consistent fashion. In an object-oriented system, how it works will not be apparent from looking at the code of individual methods.

Conventional structured programs provide levels of abstraction directly—major processes are successively broken down into lower level sub-processes. Object-oriented processes, on the other hand, are scattered across the participating classes. Consequently, overview documents are very important for the maintenance programmer. The application process scripts from analysis should provide overviews and descriptions of call patterns, and example object-relationship structures should facilitate understanding of the detailed operations. Documents should include descriptions of processing for representative cases with discussion of boundary conditions and major variations.

Classes and their primary attributes and relationships should be initially documented during systems analysis. Method descriptions and definitions of parameters should be documented as the methods are defined. These should be incorporated in the code of classes and methods. It may be useful to programmatically extract and format this into documents for reference outside of program code. The code of methods should also be annotated to assist in understanding; this is particularly important for C++. For languages like C++, without memory management, the scheme for creation and destruction of objects should be documented.

At the same time, method interfaces should be documented independent of the various implementations. Each method name should have a specification that is independent of different implementations. This must include a generic description of the action to be performed, the definitions and types of parameters, the expected return value(s), and possible exception conditions. Relevant pre- and post-conditions should also be documented. These documents form the basis for message sends. This is consistent with the separation of interface from implementation supported by IDL and Java. The sender of a message should rely on nothing more about the implementation. Implementations must be consistent with this interface specification to ensure that polymorphic variations in processing will produce desired results.

Class-inheritance information should be accessible from the application code with appropriate development tools. Tools should provide searches to find all implementations of a method name and all message sends to a particular method name. Programming environments should also provide the ability to step execution, to generate traces, and to access the stack to obtain call paths. These mechanisms will provide access to how an application works at a detailed level. Understanding how it works will be more difficult for distributed-object systems. To the extent testing is not done in a single address space, the developer will need traces that cross address spaces and tools to monitor the state of remote objects. Tools are also needed to identify where interfaces are implemented or referenced in multiple executable systems.

Documentation should not be viewed as overhead. Documentation is key to successful design and communication within a development project, to cost-effective maintenance of the application after development is completed, and for reuse of components across multiple applications.

4.6 SUMMARY

The most fundamental impact of distributed-object technology on the planning and management of development projects arises from the use of iterative development and sharing of software. However, this impact is also intertwined with implications arising from the associated reengineering of business processes, the use of graphical user interfaces, and implementation of the computing architecture. The development projects are more complex than traditional projects and may require the involvement of multiple specialists.

The project manager must organize for iteration and specialization, set milestones for stages of completion of a multitude of activities, formalize completion of work products with reviews, and control subsequent changes.

One of the major difficulties experienced by object-oriented projects is a result of delayed attention to architecture and technical design. Ideally, key aspects of the architecture should be established by an enterprise infrastructure strategy before any application development is undertaken. Unfortunately, this seldom happens. The challenge is further complicated by the continuing rapid evolution of the technology, standards, and products. The standards emerging from efforts of the Object Management Group should help bring some order to the field.

The adoption of distributed-object technology should not be undertaken as a solution to a single business problem, but as an adoption of a new paradigm and information systems infrastructure. It should be planned in that context and auxiliary activities should be established to manage both the enterprise infrastructure and component reuse, independent of individual applications.

REFERENCES

Booch, G. *Object-Oriented Design with Applications*. Redwood City, CA: Benjamin Cummings, 1991.

Coleman, Derek, P. Arnold, S. Bodoff, C. Dollin, H. Gilchrist, F. Hayes, and P. Jeremaes. *Object-Oriented Development: The Fusion Method*. Englewood Cliffs, NJ: Prentice Hall, 1994.

Jacobson, I., M. Christerson, P. Jonsson, and G. Overgaard. *Object-Oriented Systems Engineering: A Use-Case Drive Approach*. Reading, MA: Addison-Wesley, 1992.

Reenskaug, W. and L. Reenskaug. *Working with Objects: The OOram Software Engineering Method*. Englewood Cliffs, NJ: Manning Publications/Prentice Hall, 1996.

Rumbaugh, J, M. Blaha, W. Premerlani, F. Eddy, and W. Lorensen. *Object-Oriented Modeling and Design*. Englewood Cliffs, NJ: Prentice Hall, 1991.

Wirfs-Brock, R., B. Wilkerson, and L. Wiener. *Designing Object-Oriented Software*. Englewood Cliffs, NJ: Prentice Hall, 1990.

PART 2

Architecture, Design, and Programming

This part presents a specific approach to implementation of business applications using distributed-object technology. The foundation of this approach is the development of a Business Objects Facility (BOF) based on requirements defined by the OMG. A BOF provides a level of abstraction of distributed objects services and facilities that make it much easier for application developers to focus on solving business problems.

Chapter 5 describes the general requirements of a BOF and discusses its implementation. Chapter 6 examines a number of design issues that must be addressed for development of applications using this architecture. Chapter 7 discusses the implementation issues that must be addressed in programming such an application in C++. Examples of programming techniques can be found in the prototype application included in Appendix B and on the diskette that comes with this book.

CHAPTER 5

The Business Objects Facility

The development of CORBA-based applications is supported by services and facilities defined by OMG, and discussed in Chapter 3. These services and facilities complement the object request broker and address fundamental capabilities required for implementation of a distributed-object architecture. These facilities are defined in terms of standard interfaces so they can be implemented in innovative ways by different vendors, which may lead to further advances in the technology. However, when an application developer is faced with using these generic components, it is not clear how they should best be integrated to meet the application requirements. In addition, there are a number of decisions left to the component vendors and application developers that may significantly impact on performance, flexibility, and large-scale integration of the system.

This integration of CORBA components is a major technological hurdle for most application developers. It substantially increases the duration and risk of projects that attempt to apply CORBA technology. Those that succeed are still faced with the problem of their solution not being compatible with the solutions of others. Therefore they can only achieve interoperation of business objects if those business objects are implemented in their particular architecture.

In 1995, as more application developers became active participants in OMG, the challenges of application development and interoperability of sharable business objects came into focus. The result was an effort by the

Business Objects Domain Task Force to develop specifications for a Business Objects Facility. Figure 5.1 illustrates the roles of Common Business Objects and the Business Objects Facility (BOF) as defined by the Business-Objects Domain Task Force (BODTF). The ORB and other OMG services form the CORBA infrastructure. From the application developer perspective, the BOF incorporates these CORBA components and provides a higher level of abstraction for development of business applications. This abstraction makes certain assumptions about the nature of the applications to be developed in order to remove some of the degrees of freedom of the base architecture. This greatly simplifies the task of application developers. Specifications for the BOF along with a set of consistent protocols provides a level of consistency that will enable the interoperation of business objects developed with BOFs from different vendors.

The BOF then sets the stage for development of standard business objects to be marketed and incorporated in various applications. Figure 5.1 illustrates how common business objects can provide a base to be complemented by industry-specific objects, and further extended and specialized to implement particular applications. The definition of common business objects is beyond the scope of this book. Our focus is on the integration of CORBA services, through a Business Objects Facility, to support the development of practical business applications, common business objects, and enterprise-level integrated systems.

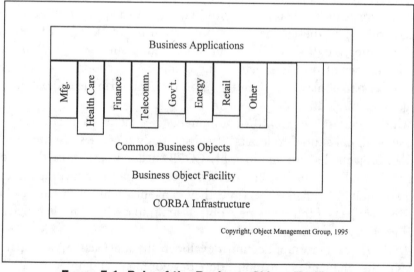

Copyright, Object Management Group, 1995

FIGURE 5.1. Role of the Business-Object Facility

We explore the BOF in greater detail and hope to provide a level of abstraction that greatly simplifies the development of applications for a distributed-object environment. The ideal is to allow application developers to work as if they were developing their application in a single process on a single computer and simply incorporate existing objects that represent the business concepts needed in their application. Problems of concurrency control, persistence, workload management, recoverability, heterogeneous languages, operating systems, and databases should be hidden from the application developer as much as possible. These problems should be solved in an appropriate manner by the BOF. Ultimately, the goal is to support the implementation of the Enterprise Computing Model architecture described in Chapter 2.

We begin by examining capabilities a BOF should provide to support business-application development. Next, we will discuss a particular approach to the solution of these problems as exemplified in the EDS BOF (EBOF) that accompanies this book. Finally, we will examine the implications of this facility to the development of current applications and the enterprise architecture.

5.1 BASIC BOF REQUIREMENTS

A BOF should address three basic objectives: (1) provide an application context, (2) support a business objects abstraction, and (3) provide and integrate needed support services. We discuss each of these in greater detail below.

5.1.1 Application Context

Conventional applications are typically developed for a functional area of a business. The database and the network environment bound the context of the application. As we move to true enterprise-level integration and beyond, the environment in which applications operate will no longer be bounded by the physical scope of the computing environment. When a query is issued, there will be logical rather than physical bounds to the scope of the query. When a report is printed, there may be many printers in widely distributed locations on which it could be printed. When an identifier is entered such as a project number or account number, these identifiers are often not universal, but must be interpreted in a particular context.

The primary basis for the context of an application is the identity and preferences of the current user. The user is employed by a particular organization and works in a particular location. The area of responsibility of the user may be defined as a further definition of context. These factors will be used in security controls. They also provide the basis for interpretation of external identifiers used to reference objects, for selection of I/O devices, and for selection of alternatives in modes or types of user interface facilities. The need for an application context creates the following requirements for a business-object facility and application environment:

- A **name service** must accommodate name contexts in determining the appropriate object referenced by an external identifier (e.g., a department within a division or a room within the building).
- A consistent set of **user preference attributes** must be defined and incorporated into the selection of devices, modes, and supporting facilities (i.e., specified printer or a display color preference).
- **Queries** must be logically bounded according to a context set by the user or implied from the user's business context or current operations (e.g., employees in a division or customers for a broker).

Of these requirements, the BOF must provide an appropriate integration of the naming service. The other requirements will be met by the definition of common business objects to represent user preferences and the user environment.

5.1.2 Business-Objects Abstraction

In the enterprise-computing model presented in Chapter 2, objects are actively shared by multiple applications so that all are operating on a consistent model of the business. The application developer should focus on the business concepts being represented and their interactions in the solution of business problems without being concerned about the computational mechanisms that allow these problems to be solved in a multi-user, heterogeneous, distributed computing environment. This means that a number of computational mechanisms (e.g., persistence) are incorporated into business objects with simplified or implicit interfaces presented to the application developer. This abstraction should make it possible for the application developer to build an application in much the same way as for a single-user, single-computer environment. The capabilities required for this abstraction are discussed briefly in the following sections.

5.1.2.1 Persistence

Persistence refers to the preservation of the state of objects if the computer system is shut down or fails, which generally means storing objects in databases. In the desired business-object abstraction, persistence should be a quality assigned to an object, and processing should be required to assure persistence will be performed without explicit action by the application programmer. The programmer should be able to program objects in the same way whether they are persistent or not. The programmer should have only indirect involvement with the persistence service through transaction management, a life cycle service, a naming service, and a query service. Whenever a transaction is committed, the new state of a persistent object should be automatically updated in the associated database(s). Figure 5.2 is an example of the level of abstraction that can be achieved in management of persistence.

The application developer created an instance of the Account class, which was defined elsewhere as persistent. The developer begins a transaction, obtains a factory reference to an appropriate address space, requests the factory to create an account instance, and commits the transaction if the instance was successfully created. Declaration of the Account class as persistent should cause the necessary code to be incorporated for the persistence functionality.

The database administrator determines how and where the object is to be stored and provides this information to the persistence facility. The generic factory object provides the linkage to the appropriate domain for instantiation of the object and the object is instantiated with appropriate linkage to the database. When the transaction commits, the object is written to the database. If the transaction rolls back, the object is not written to the database and, if it has been changed, its previous state is restored. These capabilities, of course,

```
Current thisTxn;
thisTxn.begin();
GenericLifeCycleObjectManager   theFactory;
CORBA::Object_ptr pObject =
     theFactory.create("Account");
Account_ptr pAccount = Account :: _narrow (pObject):
if (!CORBA:: is_nil (pAccount))
     thisTxn.commit();
else
     thisTxn. rollback();
```

FIGURE 5.2. Implicit Creation of a Persistent Object

require that the BOF have access to business-object meta-information and control over the implementation of certain operations on the business object. When a user references an existing object, the external identifier should be used to obtain the object reference through the naming service.

When objects are requested according to search criteria, their references should be obtained through a query service. Queries should be consistent for both persistent and transient (non-persistent) objects. The scope of queries should be determined not by the physical bounds of databases, but by logical bounds determined by object relationships and the application context and, possibly, other definitions of the relevant domain. In none of these cases are the objects involved necessarily persistent.

5.1.2.2 Concurrency

In a multi-application, multi-user environment, an object may be used by a number of applications and users. The business object facility should provide concurrency control to assure that the operations performed by competing processes do not compromise the integrity of the shared object. This will most likely be accomplished by *transaction serialization.*

Operations performed within the context of a transaction change the state of the system (the objects operated on) from one consistent state to a new consistent state. We refer to such a set of operations as "a *transaction.*" During the operation of a transaction, affected objects may be logically inconsistent for operations of other transactions. Serialization means controlling the interactions of multiple transactions such that the result is the same as if they were executed serially, one after another. Locking objects accessed in the context of a transaction and unlocking them when the transaction terminates can accomplish this. The application developer should be unaware of concurrency control. The locking and unlocking should be performed automatically. Concurrency should only be a performance concern when long-running transactions could delay other transactions.

5.1.2.3 Relationship Management

The business models implemented with objects include relationships between objects. Relationships may be one-to-one or one-to-many. Relationships may also depict an association between independent objects or containment where one object represents a general concept and contained objects represent components of the concept.

A mechanism is required by which relationships are implemented so that various operations on relationships can be performed in a consistent manner for all business objects. Applications must easily and consistently traverse relationships without violating encapsulation. They must also be able to represent a conceptual relationship whether the related objects are in the same computer or different computers. When the application developer programs changes to relationships, adding or deleting participants, the implementation mechanisms should assure that the representation is consistent for both participants. Furthermore, if the related objects are persistent, then the relationships must be persistent. The relationship mechanism will be an important element in other facilities discussed below.

The OMG Relationship Service specification does not fit well into this requirement for business objects. It is designed to address the need to relate objects on an ad hoc basis in a way that may not involve their participation. These relationships are particularly useful for system-management functions. For purposes of implementing the relationships defined in a business object model, they are overly complex, particularly for some forms of relationships. They are not designed to support business-object encapsulation. Consequently, the approach described will not incorporate the CORBA relationship service.

The relationships that exist in business models are usually *binary relationships*. Those that involve more than two classes can be broken into component binary relationships. Figure 5.3 illustrates a tertiary relationship resolved to two binary relationships. This can greatly simplify the implementation of relationships and can simplify the interfaces used by application developers as well. The complexity of higher-order relationships does not appear to be justified.

5.1.2.4 Life Cycle Services

Life cycle services are facilities for the creation, removal, copying, and moving of objects. These services must be integrated with the relationship and persistence facilities discussed above as well as with the transaction and referential integrity mechanisms discussed below. The creation, deletion, copying, and moving of objects must also be coordinated with the name service.

When a persistent object is created, it must be created in the database as well as in memory. The memory instance must be instantiated in a particular ORB domain and the database instance must be written to a particular database. When the object is removed, the active object as well as the corresponding database instance must be removed. However, database instance creation and deletion must actually occur only when the associated transaction commits.

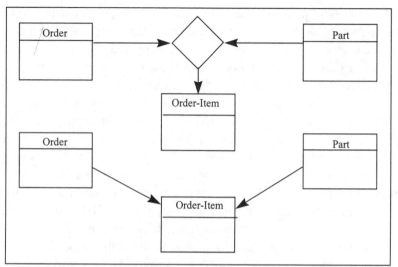

**Figure 5.3. A Typical Tertiary Relationship Resolved
to Two Binary Relationships**

Life cycle services must be supported by relationships. Depending on the nature of a relationship, it may be appropriate for the relationship to be traversed by *create, copy, move,* and *remove* operations. When an object is copied, the copy operation may propagate relationships to include closely associated objects. For example, an order object contains a collection of order items. If the order object is copied, its items should also be copied. Likewise, when an object is deleted, contained objects that depend on the containing object for their existence should be deleted as well. These operations should not, however, propagate through other relationships. For example, when an order object is copied or deleted, the related customer objects should not be copied or deleted. These semantics must be implemented in the code associated with relationships. The developer must determine when relationships should be traversed to implement the appropriate semantics. There will be situations where some implementations of an interface traverse the relationship and others do not. A BOF should provide the mechanism for implementation of traversals, but the determination of which operations traverse for a particular class of object should not be exposed in the interface.

5.1.2.5 Object Reference Management

In distributed systems, objects that exist in another ORB domain (e.g., a remote environment) are identified through an *object reference*. The object reference provides sufficient information to locate the object in another

ORB domain. When many processes are active and an object is related to many other objects, its object reference may be held many places. They may have obtained the reference directly or indirectly. CORBA does not define a way to determine if there are outstanding references to an object or where they are. This presents a problem for life cycle operations and garbage collection.

When an object is explicitly removed, an interested application may still hold a reference. Similarly, when an object is deactivated, i.e., removed from memory because it is inactive, any outstanding object references are no longer valid. An object may be dynamically moved to a different process to improve performance of an application or balance the workload. The moved object has a new object reference, but existing object references will remain unchanged. Some ORBs provide a mechanism for redirecting references to moved objects; however, this does not solve the problem in all cases. Finally, if a computer fails, then references to objects that were active on that computer are no longer valid. If they were persistent, then they may be re-activated in the same or another computer and thus have a new object reference. The challenge for life cycle operations is to resolve these *dangling references* in a way that is least disruptive to the applications.

The challenge for garbage collection, on the other hand, is to avoid creating dangling references when an object is still legitimately in use. Garbage collection is the reclamation of space occupied by objects that no longer need it. Garbage collection is important where applications do not explicitly remove an object, particularly when multiple applications share an object. This is a particular problem for transient objects since, once they are removed, there is no way to restore them. However, it is also a problem for deactivation of persistent objects since premature deactivation of persistent objects can cause significant performance degradation.

The BOF must implement mechanisms and strategies by which the occurrence of dangling references is minimized, attempts to access dangling references are handled gracefully, and the consumption of computer memory by unneeded objects is minimized. It should be possible for many applications developed independently to share objects with minimal concern about coordinating the removal of objects when they are no longer needed.

5.1.2.6 Active Adapters

Views and adapters were discussed in Chapter 2. The BOF should implement views and adapters so that access to objects can be properly controlled for security purposes by those responsible for the objects being viewed. Also, the viewed objects should be effectively incorporated and adapted into dependent applications. The BOF should implement these basic concepts with some important extensions. For example, when the state of the shared object changes, these changes should also be reflected in associated adapters so that applications are operating on globally consistent information. This requires an integration with the change-notification mechanism discussed later in this chapter.

It may be desirable for performance to cache state variable values of the shared object so that access to these variables does not require cross-domain messaging. Whenever a variable is changed in a adapter it must be changed in the shared object, and whenever a variable in the shared object is changed, it must be updated in all associated adapter objects. This coordination should be done implicitly, without any effort from the application developer. These changes must be coordinated with transaction and concurrency management to assure continued consistency of the business model.

5.1.2.7 Security

Application programmers should not be concerned about implementing security. In fact, since applications will often be executed in less secure environments, security controls for shared objects should be enforced independent of the application. Business applications should have restricted access to shared objects, particularly at the enterprise level. For example, an Employee object at the enterprise level may include considerable information and operations that should be restricted. Applications should have access restricted to a defined set of methods appropriate to the application functionality and the authority of the user. The implementation of views discussed in Chapter 2 provides a mechanism to accomplish this restriction of access. The general-purpose security facility should be used to determine the appropriate view used for a particular user and application. While an application may have access to objects of a particular class, a particular user may have access to only a subset of the instances of that class. The environment must provide mechanisms by which appropriate security controls will restrict the user to an authorized sub-set of the instances of a type.

5.1.2.8 Re-Enterable Business Objects

A business object frequently sends a message to another business object that will, directly or indirectly, send a message to the first business object, causing it to be re-entered. This may be the result of a recursive process, or simply

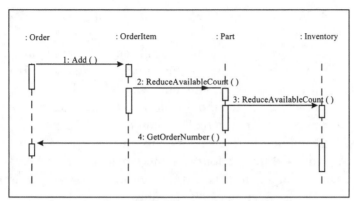

FIGURE 5.4. Re-Entrant Message Flow

a consequence of the modular structure of the object-oriented logic. Consider the example in Figure 5.4, where an order sends a message to the order item to add itself to the order. The order item in turn sends a message to the associated part to adjust its availability. The part then sends the inventory object a message to adjust the available quantity. The inventory object in turn asks the order object its order number to designate the allocation. If these objects are in different processes, such re-entrant message flow could cause the business objects to become locked in a deadly embrace. The BOF must allow for business objects to be re-entered under such circumstances, but not for others that could cause a concurrency conflict.

5.1.3 Support Services

The preceding section described a number of capabilities that must be provided by a BOF to support business-application development and the sharing of business objects by multiple applications. In addition, the BOF must incorporate several supporting services defined by OMG standards. The following sections describe the integration of these supporting services. In most cases, the required services are extensions to the defined CORBA services.

5.1.3.1 Transaction Service

In order to support recovery and concurrency control, actions to change the state of objects must be in the context of a transaction. Operations within the context of a transaction change a system from one consistent state to a new consistent state. The transaction service must provide a unique identity for a transaction as the basis of concurrency control, and it must perform commit or rollback operations when it is directed to terminate.

In order to perform the commit or rollback, the transaction must keep track of each object updated. At the same time, each updated object must be locked to control concurrency and unlocked when the transaction terminates. The transaction service should allow *nested transactions* where subordinate transactions will not actually commit until the master transaction commits. If a computer in the network fails during a transaction, the system should cause affected transactions to be terminated or rolled back. Later on when the failed component is reactivated, either on the same computer or a different one, the transaction can be resumed.

An application transaction in a distributed object system may involve a network of shared objects. Many independently developed applications may access and update these shared objects. The integrity of the shared objects cannot be left to be the lowest level of integrity of these independently developed applications. Controls need to be placed on the shared objects to validate changes and ensure the integrity of the shared information.

Each object should have a validation method that can determine if the state of the object is valid for completion of a transaction and update of its persistent state (the database). The point of control for this integrity validation is when an application transaction commits. This validation must be invoked when the transaction is committed and prior to any action to update the database.

This validation phase cannot be included in the normal *two-phase commit*. In a two-phase commit protocol, when a transaction is committed a prepare message is first sent to the resources involved in the transaction, one by one. This gives each resource an opportunity to participate in a voting process. However, the prepare phase stops when any resource votes for a rollback. A validate phase, on the other hand, would allow all resources to participate with the cumulative reporting of invalid conditions. This information can then be made available to the application for reporting to the user and possible resolution of the problems without rollback of the transaction. Once the validate phase is completed, the transaction service can proceed with the two-phase commit process.

However, within the two-phase commit, the BOF still requires a further extension. When prepare is sent to the business objects, they cause information to be passed to the persistence facility to update the database. When the persistence facility receives a prepare message, it will update the database pending receipt of the commit even though it might not have all of the update information from the affected business objects. For the persistence facility to optimize the database update, it must have all of the update information from the business objects before it receives its prepare message. This requires that the transaction service recognize a precedence of resources so that this optimization can take place. Figure 5.5 shows the object interactions for the validate phase combined with the staged, three-phase commit.

5.1.3.2 Rollback

Rollback restores objects to a prior state. One use of rollback is to provide a user the ability to undo some action. The most important application of rollback is to remove changes applied by an incomplete transaction. Rollback might be implemented by restoring the state of affected objects from a database. However, it is desirable that rollback be available independent of transactions and for non-persistent as well as persistent objects. A user making minor changes in a long-running transaction could undo an erroneous operation, or a trial and error solution mechanism could backtrack to try alternate paths. The rollback facility is an essential part of the transaction service.

5.1.3.3 Name Service

A name service provides a mechanism by which an external identifier, typically an identifier entered by a user, can be translated to a reference to an active object. The name service must provide a classification structure to correspond to the contexts in which names occur. For example, the context for

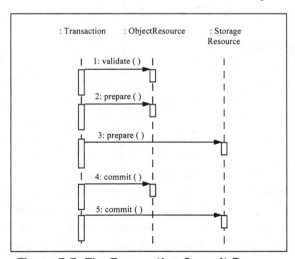

Figure 5.5. The Transaction Commit Process

Social Security numbers in the United States or the context for employees in a corporation, etc. It may be useful to structure name binding requests similar to the URL format used on the Internet for locating names in a global context such as \\rfs\detroit\employees\.

The name service must be linked to the life cycle service and persistence mechanism. When a request is received to resolve a name, the associated object may be a persistent object that is not active. The name service and the life cycle service together must assure that the desired object is appropriately activated before it is used.

The name service must be persistent so that the association of names to objects is preserved when the computer is turned off. The OMG name service specifications do not require persistence, although it is generally assumed that the bindings will be made persistent. This should be coordinated with the transaction service; this coordination is not defined by OMG specifications.

There is an assumption that when the naming service returns an object reference for an inactive object, the object will be activated when a message is sent to it. Activation is then the responsibility of the server, which contains the object it has bound to the name. This implicit activation will only work if the object was created, bound to the naming service, and stored in the database by the distributed-objects environment (as opposed to being created by a legacy application, for example), and if the process in which it was created is currently active or can be activated. Consequently, it becomes necessary to either extend the name service to resolve object references for inactive objects or provide some mechanism through the life cycle service to activate these objects implicitly when operations are performed on them.

5.1.3.4 Change Notification

Change notification provides a mechanism by which an interested object can be notified when a particular aspect of an object of interest changes. Change notification has a number of uses, including driving the update of user-interface displays, activation of constraints or rules, and support of active adapters. For example, if customer information is presented in a display, change notification provides the mechanism to update the display if any of the relevant aspects of the customer change. Only the particular customer object will generate notices. While change notification bears some similarity to the OMG event service specification, the requirements are quite different from those generally envisioned for the event service.

The event service specification defines events communicated from a source to a consumer and the possible use of an event channel to achieve independence of sources and consumers. It also defines push or pull modes. Change notification requires that a consumer be able to obtain push notices of change only after requested for one or more aspects of a specific instance of an object (receipt of events whenever they occur). In that respect it is similar to the direct, push connection of source and consumer in the OMG event service. However, the source object should be programmed for a generalized capability to accept requests for notification from one or more consumers but restricted to the consumer's interest in particular aspects. The event service does not define any mechanism for selective distribution of events to consumers nor does it specify the data about the event or the request it is satisfying.

Change notification also requires an optional level of service to guarantee delivery of a notice even though the source might be deactivated while the request is outstanding or the consumer is deactivated when the change occurs. This requires persistence of requests and notices. This could be addressed with some form of event channel to manage the persistence of both requests and change notices. However, this requires integration with the transaction service to coordinate persistent storage of requests and notices. It would demand that either event channels be designed for selective distribution of events or that an event channel be instantiated for each object that has change notification requests. Both these alternatives have performance implications.

Different applications will require different levels of service with respect to timeliness and persistence. The notification service should make such quality of service options available to the consumer when the notification request is made.

5.1.3.5 Workload Balancing

Traditionally, large-scale systems processing millions of transactions a day use large mainframe computers. In a distributed objects environment, the workload can be distributed over many smaller computers so that each computer handles only a fraction of the total work with a better price-performance ratio. The challenge is to manage this pool of smaller servers so that performance is optimized—servers should not receive more than their share of the work and provide poor performance. The BOF should provide dynamic balancing of the workload and enable incremental scaling up of the system capacity by the addition of new servers. In addition, the level of activity associated with each server will typically vary over time.

This workload management may be accomplished at different levels. For example, an algorithm may be used to allocate objects to processes when they are created, workload shifts may be implemented by dynamic allocation of objects to processes when the objects are retrieved from a database, or active objects may be moved to a process on a less active computer. The complexity of approach must be balanced against the ability of the system to respond to performance bottlenecks. The coordination of workload redistribution through the naming and life cycle services must allow dynamic adjustments without interrupting system operation.

5.2 THE BUSINESS OBJECTS FACILITY

This section describes a Business Objects Facility in greater detail. The basis of this discussion is an initial version of a BOF developed at EDS for building large-scale distributed business-object systems. The example application included in Appendix B was built with this BOF. It is written in C++ and requires the business objects to be coded in C++. It supports C++, OLE enabled, and Java clients; only C++ client support is included here. EBOF provides tools to support building of business objects, and a framework for a higher level abstraction for business objects. The package in Appendix B includes a complete suite of distributed object services necessary for the runtime environment, and tools to manage the runtime environment.

Figure 5.6 shows the boundaries of EBOF. The BOF is represented by the box in the center. Standards will soon be defined for analysis and design facilities and meta-object facilities that allow the output of analysis and

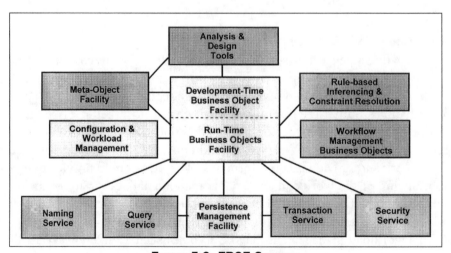

FIGURE 5.6. EBOF CONTEXT

design to be input to the development tools accompanying the EBOF. The two boxes on the right, rule-based and workflow facilities, are capabilities for extending the functionality supported by the BOF; these are anticipated as future OMG specifications. Across the bottom are services incorporated in business objects that should be transparent to the business-object developer. The Persistence Management Facility is distinguished, because it is significantly different from the current OMG Persistent Object Service specification. An RFP has been issued for a new Persistent State Service that will support future BOF implementations. Configuration and workload management are provided with the EBOF and are viewed as a future extension of system administration facilities.

Figure 5.7 illustrates the process followed by business-object developers using the EBOF. The analysis and design box represents preparatory work done outside the BOF. This will eventually be accepted directly from commercially available analysis and design tools. The programming facility is where the object specifications are entered. The tool will generate code and provide skeletons for operation methods where the developer is to insert the business logic. The configuration facility defines how object types are allocated to servers. Grouping of objects on servers is primarily a performance concern. The configuration facility creates the executable modules that are the run-time business object components. In the database administration

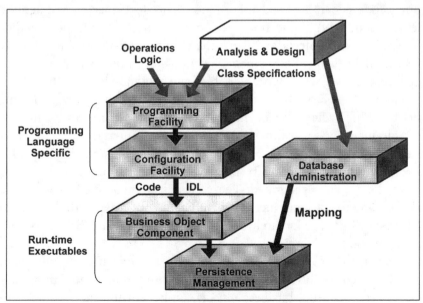

FIGURE 5.7. EBOF Components

box, the developer enters mappings of objects to database tables—only relational databases are currently supported. The database administration component generates the run-time persistence management facility. A Persistent State Service compliant with OMG specifications (currently under development) should replace the persistence management facility. The following sections describe the business-objects facility from a number of perspectives.

5.2.1 Business-Objects Representation

The EBOF supports abstract business objects, which incorporate a number of computational mechanisms. These mechanisms are implemented through inheritance from a common root class, `EBofBusinessObject_I` and through code generated by an external tool, Business Object Studio (BoStudio). As discussed earlier, to provide transaction management, concurrency control, transparent persistence, change notification, etc., the BOF must have access to business object meta-data and control over access to their instance variables. BoStudio achieves this by generating the object code and meta-information from business-object specifications.

While the application developer focuses on specifying the business objects using BoStudio, the BOF mechanisms are implemented automatically through code generation and inheritance. The developer supplements the generated code with application-specific code for the application methods. All business object interfaces inherit the common business-object interface from the IDL type EBofBusinessObject. Their implementations inherit shared business-object instance variables and methods for BOF functionality from the C++ class `EBofBusinessObject_i`. Similarly, every business object has a life cycle manager that provides life cycle services for the class. Life cycle managers also inherit from a common interface and a common implementation. In addition, a query manager is generated for every object with defined queries, and every object having persistent attributes has an associated store class generated. These classes are generated for the framework's use and the programmer is generally not concerned with them. Figure 5.8 shows the interface hierarchy for an Account object and Figure 5.9 shows the implementation hierarchy.

C++ does not provide run-time access to the object meta-information required for BOF facilities; code generation is used to make this information available. The resulting business objects implement instance variables in a collection of instance-variable components that contain information on

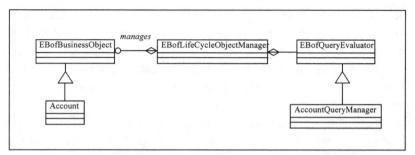

FIGURE 5.8. Interface Hierarchy for the Account Object

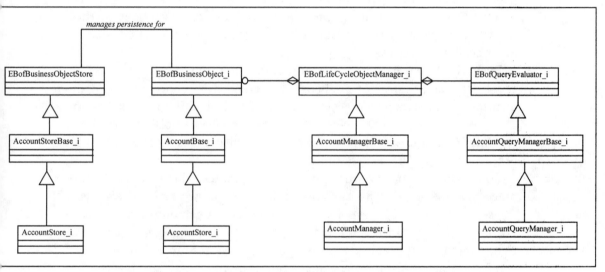

FIGURE 5.9. Implementation Hierarchy for the Account Object

attributes and relationships. The name, type, and value of each instance variable are accessible at run time and are managed by methods on EBofBusinessObject_i.

BoStudio generates accesser and mutator methods for the attributes and relationships. These methods conceal the code required to actually get or put instance variable values, and they incorporate other functionality, which will become apparent later in this discussion. Consequently, all access to business-object instance variables must be through these accesser methods, including references by methods on the same object. These methods are the implementation of the IDL interface for access to the instance variables.

BoStudio generates the code for business-object attributes and relationships, as well as methods for queries, stubs for the business operations, and IDL files. This effectively hides all aspects of distributed programming from the business-object developers. This makes programming much easier and assures the consistent implementation of the supporting mechanisms.

To facilitate management of business-object code, BoStudio generates two classes for each business object. The *base class* incorporates all the attributes and relationships along with their associated methods and any methods of the framework that may need to redefine each business object. The primary class in which the application developer programs the business logic methods inherits this. The developer is expected to leave the base class unmodified since it will be regenerated if there are changes to the business-object specification. The generated code for the primary class contains method shells that include code for business logic. The same scheme is followed for other generated classes.

Business objects are not created and destroyed through conventional C++ constructor and destructor methods. Create and delete operations are performed by the business-object manager object. BoStudio generates the EBofLifecycleObjectManager class for each business-object class. Each runtime environment will have one life cycle object manager instance for all of the instances of a business-object class.

For business objects with persistent attributes, the generated store objects completely encapsulate all interaction with the persistence service. These store objects are responsible for obtaining the appropriate database resource, externalizing or internalizing the state of the business object, and issuing appropriate requests against the database resource. The BoStudio generates operations /to encapsulate queries. Any business objects with queries have an additional interface and implementation generated for query management.

5.2.2 Object Sharing

In conventional systems data is generally shared through databases. The database-management system (DBMS) controls accesses and updates and resolves concurrency conflicts. The same is true of three-tiered, object-oriented applications. The state of objects is shared through the database and the concurrent activities of multiple users are resolved through assuring mutually exclusive access to the data of individual objects. An ORB-based environment may be used in a similar manner so that objects are created or retrieved from the database when an application needs them, perform certain functions in support of the application, record the results in persistence storage, and destroy the object instances in memory.

The goal of the EBOF is to allow objects to be shared dynamically in a distributed environment without requiring a database as a mediator. Consequently, multiple processes (or more specifically, multiple threads) could attempt to act on an object concurrently. At the same time, multiple applications are able to display or act upon the changing state of a shared object resulting in improved performance and support for cooperative work. As objects are changed, the database must be updated, but the objects can remain available for other applications without being retrieved from the database.

As an example, an application that models a stock exchange will have instances of stock objects in it. Multiple brokers may reference these stock objects. As brokers perform certain actions, the state of the stock changes, reflecting the market price and volume of the last transaction. Other brokers may want to be notified when the stock price changes so their displays should be automatically updated as the changes occur. This level of interactivity is difficult to achieve without active sharing of objects.

The requirement for concurrency control is addressed by transaction and concurrency services. Concurrency control achieves the serialization of transactions by providing locking of objects in use. Like the OMG transaction service a transaction is represented by an object. However, unlike the OMG concurrency service, concurrency control is implemented through locking mechanisms in the business objects. Use of a concurrency service would add overhead and restrict future flexibility in the design of object locking mechanisms.

Concurrency control methods are implemented on the `EBofBusinessObject_i` class and by code in the accesser methods, which call these concurrency control methods. A reference to the associated transaction is carried implicitly with all messages for that transaction. When a message accessing an instance variable is received by a business object, a check is made to determine if the object is locked, i.e., it is already in use. If the object is in use by another transaction, then the current transaction cannot proceed and is made to wait. If it is in use as a result of an earlier access by the same transaction, then it can proceed. This concurrency check is built into every business object. The business object also accepts a null transaction for read-only clients; these clients will access the still-current state of the object, which persists until the transaction commits.

A business object supports the rollback and commit transaction interfaces. When a transaction accesses an object, the object is locked on behalf of that transaction. A before copy of the instance variables is made and held local to the object. `EBofBusinessObject_i` also captures the identity of the current transaction it is participating in and uses this information to grant or deny future access requests as long as the transaction is active. The object is registered for the transaction so that when the transaction commits, the object can be notified to commit the changes, remove the lock and, if the object is persistent, to cause the database to be updated. If the transaction is rolled back, the lock is removed, and the before copy of the instance variables are used to restore the object to its prior state.

Figure 5.10 illustrates the sequence of operations in the EBOF when a business object manager creates a persistent Account business object within the context of a transaction. The application begins a transaction, creates a new business object, and then commits. The transaction commit will cause a validate message to be sent to the Account object to determine if its final state is valid. If the state is valid, the transaction will first send prepare messages followed by commit messages. All business objects receive prepare

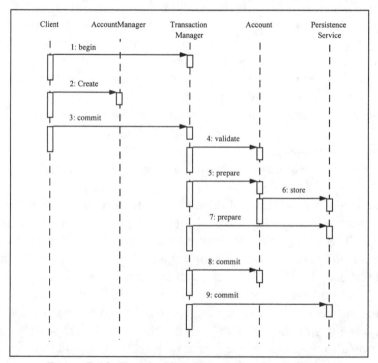

FIGURE 5.10. Transaction Processing for Create

messages before any persistence-management object, and all business objects receive commit messages before any persistence-management object. When the commit message is received, the business object commits its new values. When the database receives a commit, the database update is finalized.

Figure 5.11 illustrates the transaction process interactions for an update process. The application creates a transaction and issues a begin message. Figure 5.11 shows how application development is simplified by hiding the management of persistence and controlling database updates entirely in the transaction commit processing. All application operations, including business-object creation, occur within the context of a transaction. The identity of the transaction is carried implicitly with all operations and used to lock any object in which instance variables are accessed. When the transaction commits, commit messages are directed to each resource held by the transaction (i.e., each business object accessed) and the code inherited by the business object invokes the database mapping and update operations. The application developer is not aware of persistence. The database designer must provide the mapping and appropriate linkage to the database.

The EBOF transaction service extends the OMG transaction service in two ways. First it adds a validate phase to the two-phase commit protocol. This

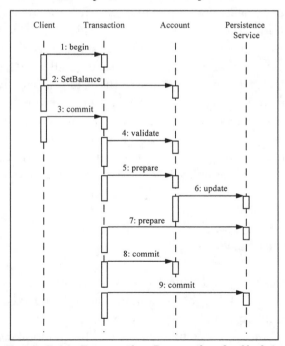

FIGURE 5.11. Transaction Processing for Update

```
interface EBofTransactionalResource :
  CosTransactions::Resource,
  CosTransactions::TransactionalObject{
void     validate() raises(EBofException);
};

interface EBofStorageResource :
 CosTransactions::Resource{
 };
```

FIGURE 5.12. Extended Transaction Interface

phase precedes the prepare phase. In addition, it stages database updates by sending prepare and commit messages to the database resources after all the non-database resources have been prepared or committed. Figure 5.12 shows the two specialized resources.

The EBofBusinessObject inherits from EBofTransactionalResource and its EBofBusinessObject_I implements the validate method. The database resources that are part of EBOF derive from EBofStorageResource. There are no additional operations to be supported here and the specialization is just to distinguish the interface.

The transaction service is linked to the persistence service for management of database connections. Each connection usually requires a license. Once a connection is established for a transaction, all activities for a particular database for that transaction utilize the same license for a particular database. At the same time, multiple databases can be involved in the same transaction. The reference to DBS is to a database server , which is an encapsulation of a particular persistent storage engine. The BOF internally ensures that same database connection is involved in the same transaction for the same database. The operation of the database server is discussed further later in this chapter.

5.2.3 Life Cycle Services

Life cycle services provide the mechanisms for creating, removing, copying, and moving objects in a distributed system. The distributed computing environment adds a dimension of complexity to these operations because a target object and other objects related to it may be in different domains. When a new instance is created, the life cycle service will determine which ORB domain it should be created in. It does so by requesting the workload management service to consider network activity to determine the most appropriate server to create an object of the desired type. When objects are removed they may contain references to dependent objects in the same or different ORB domains. The effects of removal must be propagated through the relationships by either deleting the relationship or propagating the object removal. Such propagating effects link the relationship service to the life cycle services.

We have extended the concept of life cycle services somewhat with two additional facilities: database retrieval and caching. An object may be instantiated as a completely new representation or it may be instantiated to activate an object whose state is stored in a database. In addition, objects not currently in use may be held in a cache to improve performance if they are used frequently. From a service standpoint, a request for a cached object should be the same as a request for an object that must be retrieved from a database. The life cycle object manager, introduced above, performs create and activate life cycle services on behalf of a business object. The business object itself implements the interface of the life cycle object to provide *remove, copy,* and *move* operations. A life cycle object manager exists for each class of business object. A separate instance of the life cycle object manager exists in each ORB domain that such an object can be instantiated to manage the class of objects in that domain.

A life cycle object manager is responsible for any instantiation of an object of the associated class within a particular environment. This includes objects new to the system and objects being read from a database and made active in the environment. When a new object is created, the business object manager creates the instance. If the object is persistent, then a database connection is established and the object is written to the database if and when the transaction that created it commits. The relationship of the life cycle object manager to the transaction service makes this possible without explicit programming by the application developer.

Existing objects may become activated in three different ways:

1. Through a request to resolve an external name.
2. Through propagation of relationships where an active object has a relationship to an inactive object.
3. Through execution of a query with specified selection criteria.

In the first two cases the identity of the object of interest is always an identifier that can be used to retrieve the object from the database; such requests always come through the naming service as a request to resolve an external name. Requests for objects that meet query criteria go directly to the business object manager. The naming service and query processing are discussed later in this chapter.

Because the reactivation is triggered as a result of receiving a request for an inactive object, the life cycle object manager may, based on some heuristics, decide to keep an object in memory when it is not in use or deactivate it to conserve resources. When a method invocation request is received through an object reference to an inactive object, the activation mechanism of the life cycle object manager is transparently invoked. This activation and deactivation management is transparent to the business object developer.

The current CORBA model defines workload management as an application responsibility. Mechanisms are needed to distribute the workload without application developer involvement. In the EBOF, when a new business object is to be created the life cycle service can create it in the server process that has the least number of objects to process. Once an object has been created, the name service continues to cause activation from the same business object manager, i.e., the same server process.

Sharing of objects means that a single server may have many objects, some of which may be of interest to multiple users. If these objects are all executed in a single-thread environment, actions pending on some objects will delay actions on other objects. For example, there might be 100 Account objects active in an environment with 100 users acting on them. If this is a single-threaded environment, while one Account object is responding to one user's request, all other requests to Account objects will be in a queue, waiting for a thread to become available. This can have a severe impact on system performance while underutilizing computing resources. If multiple threads are made available, there needs to be a limit to the number of active processes on a single computer. The EBOF supports multiple threads.

5.2.4 Relationship Service

The relationship service provides the mechanisms by which the relationships between business objects are managed. Application developers simply request information about relationships or request the addition or deletion of objects from relationships. The relationship service should take the necessary action to maintain the integrity of the relationships.

Relationships of persistent objects must be persistent as well. The EBOF provides persistent relationships. For simplicity, the prototype relationship service only provides binary relationships. This might sound limiting, but all *n*-ary relationships can be resolved into binary relationships.

Relationships are implemented at two levels. In memory, they are implemented as direct references or references via collections (for one-to-many relationships). For persistence, relationships are through foreign keys in the application database. The relationship service maintains the consistency of the collections and the database table.

If the application developer were required to write code for each relationship, the effort would be very tedious and subject to errors. BoStudio allows the developer to straightforwardly specify relationships and generates the necessary code to maintain the integrity of the relationships and support the life cycle services. These methods are generated in IDL as well as in the implementation files. These operations completely encapsulate the relationships and provide access to their collections through an iterator.

BoStudio generates IDL operations in the business object's interface and their implementation on its base implementation class for each relationship. For example, in Figure 5.13 an AccountBroker object in a one-to-many relationship with Client objects has the methods shown generated for it.

Figure 5.14 shows the methods on the Client object for the interface to update the relationship from the other end.

Notice the difference between the methods generated on either end of the relationship because of the different cardinality. On the one side you only need to set or get the member while on the many side, the get retrieves an iterator and set adds a new member to the collection representing the rela-

```
void Clients (out EBofQueryableIterator iterator)
   raises (EBofException);
unsigned long how_many_Clients ()
   raises (EBofException);
void add_Clients (in Client member)
   raises (EBofException);
void delete_Clients (in Client member)
   raises (EBofException);
boolean is_member_Clients (in Client member)
   raises (EBofException);
void private_add_Clients (in Client member)
   raises (EBofException);
void private_delete_Client (in Client member)
   raises (EBofException);
```

FIGURE 5.13. Relationship Methods on the Account Broker Object

```
void get_AccountBroker (out AccountBroker member)
   raises(EBofException);
void set_AccountBroker (in AccountBroker member)
   raises (EBofException);
void delete_AccountBroker (in AccountBroker member)
   raises (EBofException);
boolean is_member_AccountBroker
     (in AccountBroker member)
   raises (EBofException);
void private_set_AccountBroker
     (in AccountBroker member)
raises (EBofException);
void private_delete_AccountBroker
     (in AccountBroker member)
   raises (EBofException);
```

FIGURE 5.14. Relationship Methods on the Client Object

tionship. When a member is added to the relationship, the object on that side automatically informs the object on the other side of the change. The methods `private_add` and `private_delete` are not propagated to the other side of the relationship so the recursion stops.

5.2.5 Name Service

The EBOF contains an extended interface to the OMG name service, called EBofNameService. This interface allows querying the name service using a flat name syntax resembling the Internet URL format. This name syntax contains the type and identifier information along with all the context information. The naming service internally parses the name syntax into name contexts. Any identifiable object created with the EBOF is automatically registered with the naming service under its primary identifier upon successful commit of the transaction that created it. The application can also create other names for the same object. The object can later be retrieved through the name service using any of its names.

If the name service does not find an object's identifier in its registry, it then issues a request against the life cycle service to activate the object from the database. This is often the case when an object is being resolved that exists only in a database because it was created by a non-BOF based application. In this case, the name service issues a request against the life cycle service to activate the objects from the database. If this attempt fails, the object is deemed non-existent.

```
interface EBofNameService{
   void  Bind(in EBofName qualifiedName,
     in Object objectRef)
     raises(EBofException);
   Object Resolve(in EBofName qualifiedName)
     raises(EBofException);
   void  Unbind(in EBofName qualifiedName)
     raises(EBofException);
```

FIGURE **5.15. Simplified Interface to Naming Service**

For the primary identifier of an object, the EBofNameService constructs a unique context from the type name of the object of interest. Essentially, the type name becomes the context for identifiers of objects of that type. For an account object that uses the account number as the identifier, if the account number is xyz123 then the qualified name will be \\Account\xyz123. This name format is more intuitive and easier to work with. Figure 5.15 shows the simplified interface of the EBofNameService.

From the application-developer's standpoint, existing objects are always available through the naming service. However, this does not mean that all the objects bound to the naming service are also active. This would not be practical in most business systems because the number of such objects may be extremely large. As an example, a system that tracks a corporation's assets may have hundreds of thousands of asset items that could be bound to the naming service. All these asset objects cannot be activated when the system starts up, yet the applications inquiring about those assets should be able to request their references from the naming service.

The name service works closely with the life cycle service. When a user requests an object, the name service provides its reference. When the user sends a message to the object and the object is not currently active, the life cycle service quietly steps in and activates the object from the database. This is all transparent to the developer and happens for all business objects.

5.2.6 Persistence

Most business objects are persistent, i.e., they are preserved when the computer fails or is shut down. Persistence is achieved by saving the latest state of an object in an external database. The database is only updated when the state of objects being changed is consistent so that the database always contains a consistent representation of the business. Consequently, existing objects must be retrieved from the database when operations are to be performed on them and updated in the database when the operations are completed and the objects are in a new consistent state, i.e., when a transaction commits.

The BOF's objective is to make persistence as invisible as possible to the application developer. For the most part, it should only be necessary for the developer to designate if objects of a particular class are to be persistent or not. This level of transparency can be achieved with appropriate coordination of the transaction service, concurrency control, life cycle services, the naming service, and the persistence service.

The transaction service is the primary focus of this coordination by incorporating the standard two-phase commit protocol. When a transaction is active and a message is sent to an object that modifies its state, the object is automatically registered with the transaction service. Later on, when the transaction is committed, the database resources get involved during the prepare phase. If a business object has been changed, during the prepare phase it must pass its changed state to the persistence service and vote for commit. If the business object's state did not change during that transaction then it votes read-only. The transaction service also sends a prepare message to the database. After all the business objects and the database resources have voted unanimously to commit, the transaction service dispatches the commit messages to each resource, making the changes permanent.

When a business object receives a prepare message, it creates a local instance of the store object. The translation of object state between active object instances and persistent storage is then delegated to store objects. In each ORB domain, each class of persistent object has an associated store object to perform the necessary translations. The Account class has an associated AccountStore that knows how to perform persistence related operations on behalf of the Account class. All the store classes derive from the common base class `EBofBusinessObjectStore`. This class provides all persistence related operations, which include obtaining and the database resource and externalizing or internalizing the object's state as necessary. The store objects do not have IDL interfaces and are implemented as local C++ objects that interact with the business object and the persistence service.

The number of active database transactions is often limited by database license agreements, thus business object operations must perform database accesses within these restrictions. The EBOF represents available licenses as `EBofDBS` (database service) objects. A DBS provides service to a particular database as shown in Figure 5.16.

```
interface EBofDBS : EBofStorageResource,
   EBofQueryEvaluator {
      readonly attribute string datastoreType;
      void Initialize ( in string stringifiedPID);
      void Store ( inout EBofObjectIdentifier id,
         in EBofBusinessObjectData data,
         in EBofDataMap map)
         raises(EBofException);
      void Restore ( in EBofObjectIdentifier id,
         out EBofBusinessObjectData data,
          in EBofDataMap map)
         raises(EBofException);
      void Remove ( in EBofObjectIdentifier id
         in EBofDataMap map)
         raises(EBofException);
};
```

FIGURE 5.16. Interface for DBS Object

The EBofDBS object has only one attribute datastoreType, which defines the particular type DBMS to which access is provided. An environment may have several kinds of databases such as Oracle, Sybase, and Access. These names are used to obtain a particular kind of service. The stringifiedPID parameter identifies the particular database specified. The DBS object provides four basic operations: create, delete, update, and retrieve.

The basic unit of exchange between the EBofDBS and its clients is EBofBusinessObjectData. EBofBusinessObjectData is defined as an unbounded sequence of name value pairs where the name is the name of the attribute and value contains the attribute's value.

An EBofDBSManager provides overall management of the persistence facilities by managing a pool of EBofDBS objects. When an application needs access to persistent storage, EBofDBSManager allocates an EBofDBS object from the pool. The business object, through its store object, requests an instance of EBofDBS, identifying to it the persistence context and the current transaction. The EBofDBSManager ensures that if a database instance is currently initialized for that persistence context and is participating in the requested transaction, then that instance is reused. Otherwise it looks for a new one and initializes it for the desired persistence context and registers it with the transaction service. After the transaction terminates, EBofDBS informs EBofDBSManager that it is no longer participating in that transaction. The interface to the EBofDBSManager is specified in Figure 5.17.

```
interface EBofDBSManager {
  EBofDBS Connect(in string persistentContext,
    in CosTransactions::Coordinator coord)
    raises(EBofException);
  oneway void Disconnect(in EBofDBS dbs);
  void RegisterDBS(in string datastoreType,
    in EBofDBS dbs);
  oneway void UnRegisterDBS(in EBofDBS dbs);
```

FIGURE 5.17. Interface to EBofDBSManager Object

A persistence context is a logical representation of a database and contains all the necessary information to successfully connect to a database. Once a store object has obtained a EBofDBS reference, associated operations communicate directly with EBofDBS to perform database operations. The EBofDataMap provided to EBofDBS provides EBofDBS with the knowledge of how the business object is mapped to the underlying database. This enables the database to translate the state of the business object to the rows and columns in the database.

The EBOF currently interfaces to relational databases. The store object performs database operations by reading and writing EBofBusinessObjectData objects that provide an object-oriented representation of a row in a table. EBofDBS performs the necessary translation between a business object and the corresponding row. The EBOF allows a single business object to be mapped to multiple tables in a database

We have described persistence operations associated with a single, identified object. However, in addition to retrieving objects based on explicit external identifiers, it is also necessary to be able to retrieve objects or their data based on query criteria. Queries are used to obtain a subset of objects of a particular type or their data from which a unique object can be selected for further action and to collect objects of interest for compilation of reports.

In this version of EBOF, we have assumed that objects of interest for queries would be persistent and therefore the requirement could be satisfied by database queries. There are, of course, other situations where logical searches are needed because the objects may not all be persistent and the search logic might not be adequately expressed in a database query language. All queries return an iterator that can be further queried. This allows reducing the result subset incrementally.

```
interface AccountQueryManager : EBofQueryEvaluator {
// User-defined queries:
  EBofQueryableIterator GetAllAccounts()
    raises (EBofException);
};
```

FIGURE **5.18. A Query Manager Interface**

It is often desirable to retrieve some key pieces of information for a selected set of objects so that the information can be displayed to the user. The user then chooses some of the objects and does some more detailed work with them within transactions. For the EBOF, the developer defines methods on the query manager to define the appropriate queries to provide the display information.

EBOF currently supports queries that use SQL syntax. BoStudio supports query methods on business objects. EBOF queries are written in terms of business objects and their attributes but use SQL syntax. BoStudio allows the business object developer to define query methods and BoStudio then generates complete implementation of those query methods in the query manager. The IDL interface of the query manager is also generated. Figure 5.18 illustrates the interface for an account query manager that returns an iterator for a set of accounts. Figure 5.19 shows the C++ implementation code generated by BoStudio for the interface in Figure 5.18

5.2.8 Change Notification

Change notification provides a mechanism by which a target object can be requested to send a notification message to a specific recipient object whenever a specific state change occurs in the target object. The notification request is ad hoc. It is not explicitly anticipated in the implementation of the target object and the service is only provided when specifically requested and until the request is canceled. The change notification service consists of two interfaces. The first is called EBofNotificationConsumer and the second is EBofNotificationSupplier. Any object interested in changes to other objects must be derived from EBofNotificationConsumer to receive notices. Likewise, any object that is expected to be able to notify interested objects of its state changes must be derived from EBofNotificationSupplier.

```
EBofQueryableIterator_ptr
AccountQueryManagerBase_i::GetAllAccounts(Corba
  (Environment) &IT_env)
{
  EBofQueryableIterator_ptr iter =
    EBofQueryableIterator::_nil();
  EBofExceptionHandler exception;

  AccountStore *store = new AccountStore("RFS",
    exception, 0);
  EBofDataMap *map = store->GetDataMap();

  RWCString strQuery = "";
  strQuery += "select * from Account";

  if ( SetQueryEvaluator("RFS", exception) )
    iter = EBofQueryEvaluator_i::Evaluate(strQuery,
      QUERYLANG(SQL), 0, *map);
  else
    exception.Throw();

  return iter;
```

FIGURE 5.19. C++ Implementation Code for Query

These interfaces are specified in Figure 5.20. The EBOF supports the notification service through the base business object, which incorporates both the EBofNotificationSupplier and EBofNotificationConsumer interfaces.

A consumer who wants to be notified of a change in a target object's aspect (an attribute or relationship) requests notification by invoking the Notify operation on the supplier and passing the aspect identifier, a reference to itself, an opaque parameter value that is passed back to the consumer with notices, and the desired notification level. Whenever the target object aspect value changes, depending on the level of notification, the consumer object is notified appropriately. The consumer can later stop the notification service by invoking StopNotice. with the aspect identifier and a reference to itself (the consumer) This notification mechanism is very lightweight and avoids incurring any overhead if there are no objects to be notified.

A collection of all notification requests for a particular target object is

```
interface EBofNotificationSupplier{
  EBofBusinessObjectState Notify(
    in EBofAspects aspects,
    in EBofNotificationConsumer consumer,
    in octet consumer_parm,
    in EBofNotificationLevel level)
    raises(EBofException);
  voidStopNotice(in EBofAspects aspects,
    in EBofNotificationConsumer consumer,
    in octet consumer_parm)
    raises(EBofException);
  };

interface EBofNotificationConsumer{
  oneway void Notice(
    in EBofNotificationSupplier supplier,
    in octet consumer_parm,
    in EBofBusinessObjectState state);
  };
```

FIGURE 5.20. Interface for Change Notification

maintained by the target object. All business-object aspects are implemented as members of a collection defined on the common base business object class, EBofBusinessObject_i. This class contains methods that must be used for changing the aspect values. When an aspect value is changed, the change method will determine if there are notification requests for the particular aspect and send notification messages as appropriate.

5.3 APPLICATION OF THE BOF

The Business Objects Facility substantially reduces the amount of work developers must do to implement business applications in a distributed computing environment. It also provides key facilities to support implementation of the enterprise computing architecture of Chapter 2. The version of the BOF provided with this book does not include adapters and views. These will be required for full implementation of the enterprise model. The following sections describe the implications of the BOF to the three-tiered architecture and its support for the enterprise computing architecture.

5.3.1 The Three-Tiered Architecture

In the typical three-tiered architecture, the user interface is separated from the application objects and may run on a separate client computer. The application objects are retrieved from the database and the database is updated when a transaction is completed. The sharing of objects occurs through the database where multiple users and/or applications have mutually exclusive access to the objects at any point in time.

Using a BOF allows application objects to be actively shared and the workload supporting multiple users to be distributed over multiple server processes running on multiple computers. Objects of interest to a user are requested through the name service and activated on an appropriate server and computer. These objects may be viewed by multiple users concurrently. Transaction and concurrency facilities assure that actions by different users do not conflict.

The business-object abstraction conceals the details of database operations and the allocation of objects to server processes. The application may be interfaced to different databases without changes being required to the application code. Likewise, adjustments may be made to the allocation of objects to server processes so that the workload can be appropriately balanced. Change notification provides a mechanism by which the displays of one application can be updated when the objects being viewed are changed by another application. Validation methods provide assurance that all applications observe the applicable business rules that constrain the business model.

Views may be used to support the user interface and facilitate security. Each display may be supported by a view that provides access to the appropriate instance variables and operations on associated objects. The view may limit the visibility of the business objects to the client system. Consequently, information and operations for which the user is not authorized are never in the client computer, but are held in the more secure environment of the server computer(s).

5.3.2 The Enterprise Architecture

In the enterprise model, sharing of objects by applications occurs at the enterprise level. The enterprise objects are designed to comprehensively represent the elements of business concepts. Each application utilizes a local representation of these concepts, which is more appropriate and easier to understand in the particular application context. The key enabler for the enterprise architecture is the availability of adapters. Adapters provide reduced coupling from application to application and between applications and the enterprise objects. They also support the attachment of agents to provide adjunctive functionality. An adapter provides the local representation and is linked to the shared, enterprise representation so that multiple applications see a consistent state of the enterprise, although they may use somewhat different representations of the same concepts.

The mapping of adapters to the enterprise objects allows changes to occur in individual applications with minimal impact on the enterprise representation or other applications. Extensions to the enterprise representation to accommodate additional business information or new applications will have minimal impact on existing applications. The same is true for agents where adapters will reduce the coupling of agents and the enterprise or application objects upon which they depend. Furthermore, applications, with their adapters, may execute on local computers for performance. The enterprise objects are held in highly secure environments, with the adapters facilitating security restrictions on access to the enterprise representation.

In the enterprise model, applications become *plug and play components*. When an application is activated, its adapters are linked to the corresponding enterprise objects and it is immediately integrated into the business. When it applies changes to the enterprise objects through its adapters, other active applications will immediately see the effect. If the enterprise model changes, the ramifications to applications will be minimal because

1. new requirements can be added by simply adding new methods,
2. changes in data structures are concealed by the functional interface, and
3. the application adapters can be modified to insulate the application from the changes.

Adapters also facilitate the integration of legacy applications. Where the legacy application has a three-tiered architecture, adapters can replace application objects that correspond to enterprise objects and methods on the adapters can be used to adapt the application to the enterprise model. The enterprise layer essentially replaces the data storage layer of the three-tiered architecture. When the legacy application contains the enterprise business data, the legacy system is encapsulated in the enterprise layer. This may be through the use of multiple views to present a facade of a multiple object model, or it may be through using BOF facilities to interface to the legacy database.

Business-model rules might be implemented at both the enterprise level and the application level reflecting global and local restrictions. At the application level, business rules can be used to detect user errors based on context and application logic. At the enterprise level, they assure that no application can corrupt the business model.

When BOF standards are adopted by the OMG, applications can be built with consistent interfaces even though implemented with BOFs from different vendors. This will provide a new degree of freedom and compatibility in which an investment in common business objects will have a meaningful return, and more sophisticated solutions can be developed and shared to reduce the burden of development costs to individual users.

CHAPTER 6

Design Issues

Distributed-object systems represent a level of design complexity new to most application developers. Most are familiar with developing applications in a single, homogeneous environment with an associated database-management system and on-line terminals. Systems became more complex with the introduction of client-server architectures. Few developers have worked with distributed processing systems with client computers invoking supporting processes on multiple servers and multiple databases. While distributed-object systems are similar to other distributed-processing systems, there are significant differences.

These differences arise from several factors. First, the object paradigm provides encapsulation and polymorphism so that different objects on different servers may participate in an application at different times. Second, objects may be actively shared by different applications and/or users allowing them to work from the same, dynamic source of information. This is similar to shared databases, but much more dynamic. Third, these systems are expected to be heterogeneous: a mix of computers, databases, languages, and operating systems. While there are benefits to minimizing this diversity, it is desirable to preserve the openness. Fourth, objects may be identified and incorporated into a solution regardless of where they occur in the distributed environment. The naming service provides the connection between external names in various contexts and the associated object implementations. Fifth, distributed-object networks are virtually connectionless. Messages are communicated to objects anywhere in the network without the necessity for first establishing a connection. Logically, every message establishes an ad hoc, temporary connection until the message action is completed. Finally, the life cycle service and related functionality provides flexibility in the location of objects allowing for dynamic reallocation of processing for workload balancing and performance optimization.

We do not dwell on these differences because most systems developers are unfamiliar with distributed computing. There are many issues that should be considered regardless of whether or not they are related specifically to object technology. We examine the design issues that remain once the capabilities of a Business Object Facility (BOF (see Chapter 5) have been established. This provides a more complete and consistent view of the factors to be considered. We discuss these issues under the topics of active object sharing, levels of partitioning, object interface design, transaction scope, system integrity, internationalization, database-interface design, performance, reliability, and diversity of models.

6.1 Active Object Sharing

The distributed-object environment opens the door to the sharing of active objects by multiple users and applications. While this provides consistent information for all users, it also raises a number of design questions. The following sections consider various levels of sharing and their implications.

6.1.1 Data Passing

The traditional mode of sharing is by passing data from one process to another. This began with batch processing and evolved to databases. In these traditional systems the data is retrieved by a process, used, and updated as a result of the processing, then written back to the database for access by other processes. Only one process has a unit of data at a time; this unit may be a file, as in batch processing, one or more rows from various tables in a relational database, or some other collection of records.

This mode is used in the three-tiered architecture. It is a direct transformation of a Transaction Processing (TP) monitor style of computing, but uses objects for the application processing. In these applications, business objects are instantiated in memory when a user requests their service. As long as they are active, they remain dedicated to that user, once the user is finished with them, the data is updated in the persistent storage and the objects in memory are destroyed.

One reason this style of object-oriented computing is so popular is because it off-loads more difficult responsibilities such as concurrency control and buffering to the database manager. For example, in a banking application, if two users have a joint account and both users try to access the account at the same time, each will obtain a different instance of the Account object but not concurrently. The first user creates an Account instance and obtains current data from the database. The second user creates another instance, but will not be able to obtain data from the database until it is released by the first user when his transaction is completed. The serialization of these transactions to prevent concurrency conflict is managed solely by the database-management system.

6.1.2 Multi-User Objects

Distributed-object computing provides an environment in which objects can be actively shared by multiple users. If two different users try to access the same Account object, the system activates one object when the first user accesses it and when the second user requests it, the system provides a reference to the same object for the second user. The database no longer provides concurrency control, instead the object itself provides that control. This capability is provided in the BOF of Chapter 5.

Using the BOF, an Account object automatically inherits transaction and concurrency management. The Account object has an in-memory state that stays synchronized with its persistent state. When this Account object participates in a transaction and the transaction is committed, both the object's in-memory state and the persistent state are committed If the transaction aborts, the changes are rolled back. This provides the equivalent of row level locking; which is an advantage over some databases that control concurrency only at the table level. Sharing of objects can significantly reduce database retrievals. In addition, multiple users may have concurrent, read-only access to the same object so they can view changes as they occur. This can be used to support collaborative computing. Notification can be used to initiate dependent processes such as workflow management or exception alarms.

Dynamically sharing objects creates new application opportunities. The designer needs to learn how to take advantage of these capabilities. At the same time, sharing ties many applications to the same objects, potentially complicating application changes and creating common points of failure. Application designers must understand the importance of transactions in maintaining concurrency control and recoverability. All changes must be made to the shared objects within the scope of transactions. This is an important consideration if an application incorporates objects not managed by the BOF. Complementary functionality will need to be supported by the non-BOF components.

6.1.3 Client-Side Caching

Client-side caching refers to holding information once it is obtained rather than requesting it each time it is needed. When an object is shared, its users must access it over the network. Each time it is accessed, there is a delay. Cumulatively, these delays may have a significant performance impact. If a user caches attribute values obtained from the shared object, then the number of cross-domain requests will be reduced. Of course, the problem is that the principle object and the cache may get out of sync. Through the use of change notification, the cache object on the client side can be notified whenever a relevant value changes in the principle object. This keeps the two in sync. The designer must balance the additional development and maintenance effort for the cache object against the performance benefit. The stability of the principle object and the amount of messaging activity to be handled by the principle object must be considered.

For those objects whose data is expected to change frequently, caching may impose more of a burden than a benefit. The burden may also depend on the mode of change notification. Change notification should have different levels of service. If a notification is received each time an attribute aspect is changed it would be very expensive. However, if a notification occurs only after a transaction commits then notifications for multiple changes can be consolidated and the burden is reduced.

6.1.4 Sharing Granularity

Sharing of objects can occur at different levels. The concept of granularity was introduced in Chapter 1. We focused on the sharing of fine-grained objects: an Account object or a Customer object. The same general mechanisms apply to large-grained objects such as an engineering design or a word-processing document. Large-grained objects encapsulate a substantial amount of functionality. They appear to the rest of the system as a single object, but may be implemented as self-contained object-oriented applications.

Systems may be implemented as a number of subsystems that interoperate as large-grained objects. These subsystems are abstracted to a unit of functionality. Within the subsystem, there may be a large number of collaborating objects, together fulfilling the overall purpose of the subsystem. The entire subsystem may be viewed and modeled as an object whose interface provides access to the public functionality of the other objects contained in and collaborating with it. The subsystem interface object then delegates requests to the appropriate collaborating classes.

Concurrency control is then managed at the large-grained object level. When the object is in use, all elements are inaccessible by another transaction. This greatly simplifies the internal objects and avoids the overhead of concurrency control on each object. However, all elements of the large object will be inaccessible as long as it is in use by one transaction. This is very similar to service based architectures employed in non-object-oriented distributed systems.

This approach can result in a some optimization of network resources. In order to send a request to an object, the client needs to have a reference to the object. The large-grained object approach requires the client to have a reference to the object that represents the whole subsystem rather than having a reference for each object in that subsystem. Obtaining access to these finer-grained objects requires additional communications over the network. The application developers who interface to these subsystems may also find that interfacing to a number of different objects is more complex. At the same time, the developer of the large-grained object may have better control over the integrity of the model by filtering all requests through a single interface.

The key disadvantage of this approach is its lack of flexibility and scalability. It assumes that minimal external access is needed to the detail of the subsystem model and that the subsystem exists quite independent of other portions of the overall system. This is generally true of word-processing documents where there is little or no value in dynamic sharing of words or paragraphs in different documents or applications. However, it is not true for most of the information currently stored in many databases where the purpose of the database is to make the information sharable.

For example, a complex model such as an engineering design may be highly integrated and necessarily under the control of a single person, at least during a period of time. Others may be allowed to view the model, but not to change it. Typically, such models will be made available for viewing in versions that are complete and validated. It may be appropriate to implement these as large-grained objects.

At the same time, it is possible that such work products will become the subject of collaborative efforts. In these cases, participants should all have access to active views, which may provide different perspectives or visualizations of the model for different participants. Even though update control might remain with a single user, the collaborative views may be easier to implement if the application is designed for fine-grained sharing.

Large-grained objects provide less long-term flexibility. As the overall system, the business and the integration of services evolve, it is likely that other users will need access to elements of the subsystem. In addition to simple access to information, there will be functionality associated with this information. In order to preserve the large-grained encapsulation, the subsystem must then provide an increasingly complex interface. The external users will start building independent representations of the same concepts in order to encapsulate the data and functionality they are concerned about. The result is duplication of information and eventually duplication of functionality that must be independently maintained.

Later, if the large-grained object is opened up to provide fine-grained access or distributed processing, the conversion effort may be substantial. First, lower-level concurrency control must be added. To be consistent with the distributed system, the fine-grained objects should also be compliant with the naming and life cycle protocols. In addition, the interfaces to these lower-level objects may be less generalized and more vulnerable to errors than if the objects were designed for public access.

In general, we recommend that large-grained objects only be used to wrap existing legacy applications. All new applications should be broken into relatively fine-grained objects to enable greater sharing.

6.2 PARTITIONING

Systems may be partitioned at different levels. The different levels provide components for different purposes. The components may be source code modules, compiled modules, address spaces, or computer configurations.

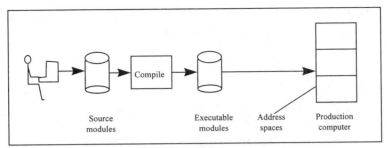

FIGURE 6.1. Levels of Partitioning

These are essentially different levels in a hierarchy. A computer may have several address spaces. An address space may incorporate several compiled modules and a compiled module may incorporate several source code modules. Components at each level may be shared, thus the same executable may be incorporated into different address spaces to support different applications, and the same source code may be incorporated into different executables. Figure 6.1 shows different levels of partitioning as software goes from programming to production. The partitioning at each level involves some design decisions. We consider each of these levels in the following sections.

6.2.1 Source-Code Modules

The definition of source-code modules will depend upon the language being used and the capabilities of the programming environment and/or configuration management tool available. The partitioning of source code serves two basic purposes: it defines a unit of work for a programmer and provides a unit of functionality for application configuration. These are the lowest levels at which components may be shared and applications configured. They are the lowest levels at which development and maintenance responsibility can be allocated.

6.2.2 Compiled Modules

Compiled modules are the lowest level of partitioning evident at run time (e.g., DLLs in the Windows environment or shared libraries in the UNIX environment). For some languages such as Smalltalk and Java, these may be byte code modules, but, generally, they will be composites of the source code modules for development and maintenance purposes. Compiled modules determine how applications can be configured at load time.

6.2.3 Address Spaces

An address space will be configured from compiled modules. The modules included will determine the capabilities of that address space. Address space partitioning may be affected by a number of factors:

- Capabilities of the address space may be limited to preserve resources or to limit access to proprietary functionality.
- The configuration may depend on the geographic locality to accommodate different languages and cultural preferences.
- Objects that interact frequently should be in the same address space. Some overhead is incurred if the interactions are with another address space on the same computer. Substantial delay may be incurred by communication over the network.
- Certain information and functionality may be restricted to address spaces in secure environments.
- An operating system might support only single-threaded address spaces and objects may need to be separated to reduce the bottleneck.
- Partitioning may be based on computer configuration boundaries of clients and servers for workload distribution.
- Certain functionality may be implemented in a particular language that requires separation from address spaces supporting other languages.
- Certain functionality may be owned by a particular organization and the partitioning supports billing and change control.

The language and ORB being used will affect the flexibility of address space configurations. For example, although not specified in the CORBA standard, Orbix allows objects to be co-located, i.e., assigned to logically separate address spaces but executed in the same address space. It often becomes necessary to change the way different object types are grouped together to form an address space in order to maintain acceptable performance when workloads change. A BOF should allow this reconfiguration without the need for program changes.

6.2.4 Computer Configurations

A computer may execute multiple address spaces. The principle boundaries for partitioning computer configurations are those between the layers of the Enterprise Computing Model presented in Chapter 2 and illustrated in Figure 6.2. The level of interaction of objects across these boundaries is generally lower than within a level. The level of interaction of objects between different user interfaces or between business objects of different applications is generally very low. Consequently, it is generally acceptable for different applications to run on different computers.

Objects within the enterprise objects layer may be clustered into cooperating groups since there will be low interaction boundaries within this level as well. Groupings of object classes as well as grouping of subsets of instances of the same class should be considered. For example, orders to be filled by a particular manufacturing plant need not be stored nor processed on the same computer as orders to be filled by another manufacturing plant. The proper location may also be affected by the life cycle such as orders being entered by a salesperson having different access requirements than orders being manufactured or delivered. The configuration of computers will determine the level of flexibility of workload balancing for performance. Configurations will also reflect restrictions in the location of objects for security purposes. These issues are discussed more later in the chapter.

6.2.5 Tightly Coupled Objects

In addition to looking for low interaction boundaries, we must look for clusters of objects that have high degrees of interaction. Often such objects may

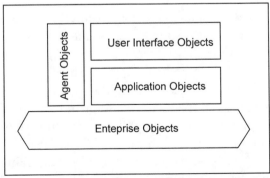

FIGURE 6.2. The Enterprise Computing Model

be described as containers and components such as an order and its associated items or a mechanical assembly and its associated components. The value of this perspective is in the use of implementation mechanisms to cause related objects to be instantiated in the same address space. Note that this is not the same as causing all orders and order items to be instantiated in one address space. The principle technique involves relationships. The algorithm for choosing a life cycle object manager, for example, might give preference to the same address space as a related object. When an object is copied or moved, the new instantiations of the related objects should occur in the same address space.

These are not simply containment issues, but are, instead, collaboration issues: the frequency with which the objects send messages to each other. Consequently, they are likely to be a function of the business processes supported and may change over time as new applications are developed or the business demands change.

6.3 OBJECT INTERFACE DESIGN

The detail of distributed-object interoperation is captured in the IDL. It is the formal expression of interfaces between objects, associated services, and address spaces. IDL defines what is accessible and, implicitly, what is not. It also determines the flexibility and adaptability of the system. The following sections discuss interface design with respect to legacy system interfaces, use of polymorphism, and exceptions.

6.3.1 Legacy-System Interfaces

Legacy systems may be wrapped in an object interface to appear in a distributed object environment as a single, large-grained object. IDL specifies the functional interfaces to the legacy system. If the legacy-system interface is sufficiently robust and the arguments and return values are elementary values, then this could be all that is needed. More typically, it will be necessary to build a wrapper program that performs some translation of arguments and return values. While it is possible to present a multiple-object interface to a legacy application, this undertaking is more complex, particularly if the underlying application is not object-oriented. With a multiple-object interface, the wrapper must be able to interpret and translate object references in the arguments and return values. These object references may include references to the actual objects of the legacy system.

For example, imagine an existing system written using a two-tiered model where the user interface and business layer are linked into one process with the database access through Microsoft's Open Database Connectivity (ODBC). Because of scalability and sharing requirements, the system is to be migrated to a CORBA-based environment. Assume the existing system had a number of C++ classes that captured the business domain fairly well and it is desirable not to disturb them.

In order to participate in the CORBA model, the interfaces of the classes to be accessed must be captured in IDL. However, CORBA requires the methods to include some implicit parameters such as the environment variable. In addition, these classes must be able to raise exceptions appropriate for distributed processing. It will probably be desirable to create separate interface implementation classes that will delegate incoming messages to the original application classes. Alternatively, if we take the subsystem based approach discussed earlier, we can capture the interface of the complete business subsystem in one interface type specification. We provide object implementation for that one interface, which will delegate the requests to the appropriate business classes within the application.

In order to understand these two choices further, consider an existing system used by a stock brokerage house to manage clients and execute trades on the floor of stock exchange on behalf of those clients. Assume further, that the existing system has C++ classes as described in the object model in Figure 6.3.

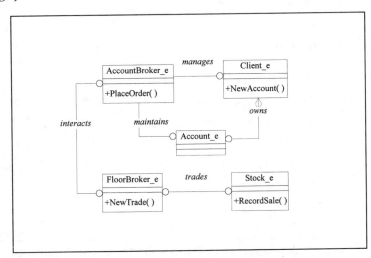

FIGURE 6.3. An Existing Legacy System

In the figure, "_e" has been appended to indicate that these are existing objects. To provide an IDL interface for each one of these classes but avoid any code modification to these existing classes, each one can be wrapped in another implementation class whose signatures will conform to the appropriate IDL bindings. This implementation class can then be used as the object implementation class in the normal sense.

Figure 6.4 shows this for the account object. The `AccountBroker_c` object is the reference obtained by a remote user, and has an IDL interface defined. This object delegates all the operation requests to its implementation class, represented by `AccountBroker_i`. `AccountBroker_i` in turn delegates the requests to `AccountBroker_e`, which is the unmodified class taken from the existing legacy application. The reason for the addition of two classes is discussed in Chapter 7. If it is not essential to leave the existing application code as it is, then `AccountBroker_e` should be modified to combine it with `AccountBroker_i`.

Figure 6.5 illustrates another approach where two large-grained objects may be defined, one representing the brokerage subsystem and the other representing the exchange subsystem. The IDL interfaces of objects representing these subsystems may represent the combined IDL interface of the objects in the subsystem that are accessible from outside. This approach then localizes the interaction between the objects in the same subsystem, hence improving the performance but it limits accessibility. Different situations may warrant either one of the two approaches and the application developers must weigh the tradeoffs.

6.3.2 Polymorphism

IDL interfaces should be defined with polymorphism in mind. The interface should avoid dictating the implementation so that different implementations

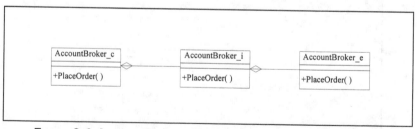

FIGURE 6.4. Legacy System Partitioned to Fine-grain Objects

may be interchangeable. An interface for a particular capability and protocol should be separated from other capabilities and protocols even if they currently occur on the same objects. This may be viewed as separating the roles of objects. The interface to support each role should be defined independently. The same interface can then be inherited by all types that participate in that role. This reserves flexibility in the future design of objects that may support some of those interfaces. The designer should note that the BOF may place some restrictions on interface inheritance through its use of inheritance.

As an example, consider Figure 6.6 where there is no implementation associated with the common interface captured in Broker. The protocol captured in Broker interface is separately implemented by AccountBroker and FloorBroker.

While IDL does not formally specify semantics, semantics should be defined in annotations. Take care that the same method names are not used

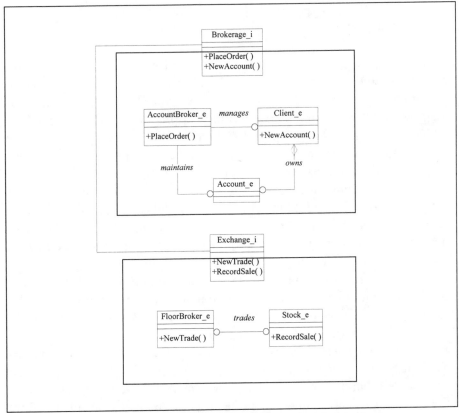

FIGURE 6.5. Legacy System Partitioned into Subsystems

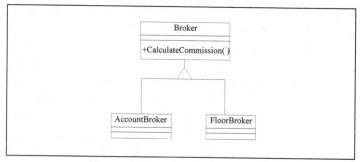

FIGURE 6.6. Interface Inheritance

with different semantics. While IDL allows it, this will create confusion. It may also present a problem in the future if interfaces with the same method name and different semantics are needed for the same object.

6.3.3 Exceptions

When an operation fails, the primary mechanism for communicating the exception condition to the caller is by returning an exception structure. Exception structures (or, more commonly, *exceptions*) are defined in IDL and mapped to different errors native to different programming languages (e.g., OMG IDL exceptions are mapped to native C++ exceptions).

Because exceptions are not objects, they have no methods and are not implemented with inheritance. The lack of inheritance makes it difficult to catch a whole family of exceptions in a graceful way. Imagine an operation that throws two different kinds of exception which, in turn, call some other functions that throw another four kinds of exceptions. The try block in C++ must now be programmed to catch these six exceptions, system exceptions, and other C++ exceptions.

We generally avoid specifying individual exceptions for different error conditions, but rather specify one exception for one module or interface that carries different error codes to further specify the particular error. Figure 6.7 shows code for a representative exception.

It is often insufficient to pass a single exception. A number of errors may occur during the course of performing a business operation. For example, when an order is submitted, a number of order items may have inconsistencies. All those inconsistencies should be reported back to the user who submitted the

```
enum EBofExceptionCategory { EnvironmentException,
   NormalException,DataEntryException,
RuleViolationException, IntegrityException,
ServiceError };
   struct EBofError{
      EBofExceptionCategory exceptionCategory;
      string exceptionSource;
      long exceptionCode;
      string exceptionReason;
};
   typedef sequence <EBofError> EBofErrors;
   exception EBofException{EBofErrors errors;
};
```

FIGURE 6.7. Code for a Representative Exception

order. Exception handling should be designed to make available an accumulation of exception information. The code in Figure 6.7 illustrates how exceptions are defined with in EBOF.

6.4 Transaction Scope

While a transaction is active, each object it accesses is locked to prevent access by other transactions. This will cause other transactions to be delayed and users may perceive this delay as a system performance problem. Consequently, it is important to consider the scope of transactions and avoid locking affected objects any longer than necessary.

6.4.1 Transaction Duration

There will be a minimal transaction duration based on the set of changes necessary to transition from one consistent state to another for any computer-based operation. Usually, this is the processing associated with a particular user request. In some cases it may be possible to break a business transaction into smaller application transactions each of which achieves a transition to a new consistent state. However, if another user intervenes between two of these sub-transactions, it may be possible that the result is not what the original user intended.

This also applies when a user is performing a series of operations to develop a complex solution. With each action the user assumes that the state of the affected objects is the result of his prior sequence of operations. If other users' actions can change the state of these objects while the first user is still working, the result may be consistent from an application perspective, but inconsistent with the user's intent. The first user is operating on the belief that the system is still in the state it was when his previous transaction was completed. Consequently, transactions are frequently defined as starting with the beginning of a user's activity and finishing when the user is ready to commit the final result. In some cases this may be a long time.

The designer must examine the nature of the work being done and the possibility that more than one user will attempt to update the same objects. These competing interests must be balanced to define a reasonable duration for user activity. If a user does not complete a business activity in an acceptable period of time, then it may be appropriate to alert the user, requesting that changes at that point or shortly thereafter be committed so that other users can gain access. Another refinement might be to alert a user when others are being delayed.

If other users only need read access, this can be allowed, even if the updating user has not committed. If the concurrency control implements functions like those described in Chapter 5, the read-only users will see a consistent set of information reflecting the state of the objects before the updating user started. The read-only user's displays may be updated, utilizing the change notification facility. When the active transaction is committed their displays will reflect the result. This is appropriate in almost all circumstances. However, remember that the viewing users are not seeing the current state of the business as reflected in the updating user's uncommitted transaction.

6.4.2 Risk of Lost Work

The operations performed within the scope of a transaction are generally not persistent until the transaction is committed. Unfortunately, for long transactions where the user has performed a number of related operations over a period of time, a system failure will cause all of the user's work to be lost. The designer should consider the risk of failure and the amount of work that could be lost and consider approaches to minimizing the loss.

One way is simply to break the user's activity into smaller transactions so that the user will only have to repeat the last, pending operation if there is a failure. However, a user may want to reserve judgment on the acceptability of the overall result. In other words, the user wants the intermediate results to be persistent, but not necessarily permanent. In addition, breaking the activity into smaller transactions allows other users to intervene, potentially introducing inconsistencies in the initial user's overall result. The ability to lock out updates by other users, preserve the original state of the affected objects, and, at the same time, preserve the intermediate states is needed.

6.4.3 Local Work Products

The most straightforward way to protect long update activities is with a logical *check-out, check-in* mechanism. When the user wants to perform a long transaction on a group of objects, the application marks the objects as checked out. If other users access those objects, they are warned that they are checked out; there are changes being applied. The updates, however, are not applied directly to the affected objects. A copy of these objects is created for the user to work on. The copy is isolated from the mainstream and becomes the user's local work product as shown in Figure 6.8. Each operation may then be treated as a transaction and be persistent. If the user decides the result is not desirable, then the copy may be discarded and the check-out status removed. The user might also create additional copies for alternative approaches or to reserve the opportunity to return to an interme-

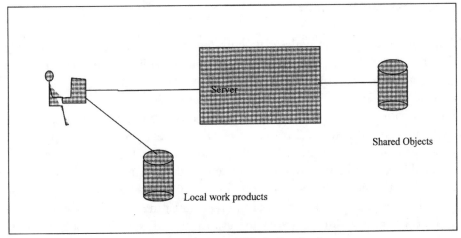

FIGURE 6.8. Local Work Products

diate solution. When the user decides a copy represents an acceptable solution, the check-in process either updates the original objects or replaces them with the copies. In some cases it may be desirable to provide a *versioning system* where the original and revised copy are both retained with different version numbers.

This check-out approach has the added advantage that the copy may be created in an environment closer to the user. This could provide improved performance, without creating a security risk to the master objects from which the copy was derived. Creation of object copies in an alternative environment is comprehended in the OMG life cycle services.

6.5 System Integrity

In many ways, concerns about system integrity are the same for distributed-object systems as for any other. However, the distribution of processing and data creates some additional concerns. In this section we review these concerns in five areas:

1. Data entry edits.
2. Relationships.
3. Business rules.
4. Accountability.
5. Access security.

6.5.1 Data Entry Edits

There are three levels at which data entry edits may occur: (1) data type validation, (2) range and possible-value checks, and (3) consistency checks. The issue for distributed-object systems is where these edits should occur, since the user interface tier may be on a different computer than the business objects and the application logic. The designer's inclination is to often put all of this editing in the user interface tier. We recommend against this approach in most cases.

The common assumption is that exchanges over the network must be avoided. It would be preferable to transfer the data from the user interface to the application after the user has filled in all of the fields. Then, in order to provide intermediate edits, the user interface must include all of the logic and supporting information necessary to perform the edits as the data is entered.

Generally, the rate at which users enter field values represents very little network activity. The designer should be very careful to leave logical edits to the application and not off-load them to the user interface. This tends to create a duplication of function and increases the complexity of both the application and the user interface to support the interface-level logic with relevant data. In the long term, the application will become more complex and inflexible.

We recommend that data-type edits occur in the user interface and edits for valid values and logical consistency be reserved to the application. As each field is entered it should be sent to the application. The application may then perform intermediate edits on possible values and alert the user if there is a problem. Some consistency checks may also be appropriate, but, in general, consistency should be checked when the user indicates that all the fields have been entered, i.e., when the user commits. In the previous chapter we talked about how the two-phase commit protocol should be expanded with a validation phase that precedes the preparation phase. With that extension, when the user commits, the transaction service will send a validate message to each involved resource, accumulating all reported inconsistencies.

6.5.2 Relationships

The distributed-objects environment introduces new design considerations for relationships because relationships may cross ORB domains. In addition, new BOF facilities that improve the business object abstraction make certain assumptions about the implementation of relationships. The most obvious concern with cross-domain relationships is system performance. Each traversal of such a relationship results in network activity. If the activity is high, the transaction will be delayed and the network load may impact other transactions. The answer is careful analysis of the placement of objects on servers when they are activated. If necessary, dynamic relocation of the objects having problem relationships brings them into the same computer or address space. There may also be opportunities to restructure methods by moving some operations out of the calling method to subordinate methods on the target object. Thus, more operations are performed local to the target object rather than being performed remotely by a calling method, i.e., delegation of functionality.

A related object may not be active when a relationship is traversed. This means an attempt to send the missing object a message will result in additional work to activate it. The object may be missing because it was idle and was deactivated to preserve resources, it might not have been activated, or the

ORB domain failed. If the ORB domain has failed, there should be an attempt to activate the object in a different domain. If this fails, then the transaction should be aborted. These actions can be built into the BOF so that programmers need not anticipate these exceptions for every relationship access.

6.5.3 Business Rules

Business-object attributes and relationships must be computationally correct (e.g., correct types and consistent relationship structures). They should also be validated for compliance with business rules. Here we are referring to any executable form that will test for compliance with requirements—these need not be rule expressions per se. Business rules may define the characteristics or numbers of objects that may participate in a relationship. They may define ranges or relationships between attributes. They may also define restrictions on the creation or deletion of objects. Since the states of objects may be inconsistent during the activity of a transaction, these checks must be made after the transaction is complete, but before it is committed and the database is updated.

The enterprise should not rely on each application to maintain the integrity of the enterprise model. The rules that apply at the enterprise level should be applied to the enterprise objects in a secure environment. These rules do not belong to any particular application. They are required to assure the integrity of the enterprise model and that the database always reflects a valid representation of the business.

The general approach should be to define rules on the enterprise objects that will ensure the integrity of the enterprise model and implement business policies that define constraints on relationships and creation or deletion of objects. In addition, there may be application-level policies that prevent user errors that might not violate enterprise rules. These should be implemented by rules in the application layer objects. In either case, the rules should be implemented as methods that will be invoked when a transaction commits and should also be available on demand to provide validation checks for feedback to the user.

6.5.4 Access Security

A distributed-object architecture creates new opportunities for violation of system security. The designer must assure that

1. a message received is from a properly authorized user,
2. the user is authorized to send the particular message,
3. an object is not moved to an environment with inadequate security, and
4. communication facilities do not allow unauthorized persons to intercept or sabotage information.

Distributed-object computing presents the possibility for greater accessibility to information and greater security risk. Messages can be sent from remote locations to update objects or initiate processes. Consequently, the distribution of objects must reflect the fact that messages cannot be accepted if they are sent over publicly accessible media without encryption or if they originate from sources that are not adequately controlled. Most security requirements will be met by a CORBA-compliant security facility and an ORB that utilizes the OMG Secure IIOP (Internet Inter-ORB Protocol). This ensures that the user is authorized and that no outsider will be able to intervene or impersonate an authorized user. However, the designer must still be sure that objects are only instantiated in adequately secure environments and that users are restricted to messages appropriate to their level of authority. For example, an employee object will have different modes of access. Managers may access salary information for their staff,while the staff may review all of their individual information but only change address and telephone information. The administration of security at the message-sending level could become a substantial burden.

We offer the following suggestions:

- Objects representing the primary source of business information or confidential information should always be restricted to a secure environment that assures high reliability and provides off-site backup and disaster recovery capabilities.
- Copies of objects may be allowed for authorized users, but changes to these objects will not affect their enterprise counterparts.
- Objects representing work products of multiple people, for example, departmental records and approved engineering designs, should be restricted to servers with security appropriate to the associated organizational function.
- Objects that represent end-user applications or work products are the responsibility of the individual end user, but the end user should have security facilities to support appropriate protections.

Views, as described in Chapter 2, provide valuable assistance in the administration of security. Views on an enterprise object can be created for each category of user that may be expected to access the enterprise object. Each view provides only the interface for which the user category is authorized. These views must be held in appropriately secure environments to prevent unauthorized access.

6.6 INTERNATIONALIZATION

Distributed-object systems offer the opportunity to integrate systems internationally. Activities all over the world may share enterprise objects, all see a consistent representation of the state of the business, and work collaboratively to accomplish their goals. The key to this global integration is to provide local specializations of the user interface designed for language, governmental, and cultural differences. The user interface should be supported by implementations of intelligent elementary values (see below).

Separation of the user interface and business objects is key to global integration. The user interface should contain no application logic so that the application is consistent for all localities and there is no replication of functionality in multiple interfaces to create a maintenance burden. The user interface should provide all displays, dialogs, messages, explanations, and help through application interface protocols that allow local sets of user interfaces to be interchanged.

6.7 Intelligent Elementary Values

Intelligent elementary values are objects that provide conversions to present their values as appropriate to different localities. The principle intelligent elementary values are measures, dates, and currencies. Measures can be implemented with a generic measure object that contains a current value and information on units of measure associated with the value [Metsker]. Methods on the object provide conversions from the intrinsic units to local units of measure for displays. Likewise, methods on a date object can present the date in the local language and according to local preferences. Appropriate contexts must be defined for external object identifiers. These context identifiers must be determined by the user interface so that the proper context will be passed to the naming service.

6.8 Database Interface

If the application uses an object-oriented database, there is a direct mapping of objects to the data storage structures, which requires minimal developer involvement. If the application uses a relational database, and many do, then the objects must be mapped to the relational tables. This is simpler if the database is created for the application, but most often the database already exists and the developer must resolve a variety of mapping problems. These problems have been faced in the development of three-tiered object-oriented applications, and commercially available tools have been developed to address this problem.

There remain four design issues needing special consideration in a distributed objects architecture: retrieval performance, lock management, distributed database commit, and object mobility.

6.8.1 Retrieval Performance

The retrieval-performance problem in a distributed-object environment is similar to that in the three-tiered architecture, but the solution may differ somewhat. The logical way to retrieve objects from a database is to retrieve the principle object based on its external key, then traverse relationships to retrieve related objects as the application encounters a need to access them. While this may minimize the working set of active objects, it can be devastating to performance due to the number of retrievals it generates. Most applications will need to retrieve a cluster of objects together. For relational databases, requesting information from several related tables together allows the database management system to optimize the query. For object-oriented databases, retrieval can be optimized by designing the database to physically cluster objects on the external storage media if they are frequently used together.

The primary mechanism for defining clustered access is the recognition of containment relationships. For example, an order object contains order item objects. Rather than retrieving the order and then each of the order items, all of the items can be retrieved in a single query and the objects activated. This achieves a substantial improvement, but there may still be objects being retrieved one at a time. Each of the order items may reference a part object containing additional information needed on a display or report, such as the part description and weight. It would be desirable to retrieve the associated part data in the same query, but the part objects are not "contained" in the order items.

Physical clustering can address this in object-oriented databases where the database-management system is able to satisfy multiple requests by buffering the data. However, for relational databases, optimization must be achieved by retrieving information for a number of objects in a single query and then instantiating all of the objects from the single result.

6.8.2 Lock Management

The business-objects facility described in Chapter 5 supports sharing of active objects. These objects incorporate concurrency control to prevent conflicting operations by multiple users. If the database is used exclusively by the BOF, there is no need to use the locking facilities of the database management system. However, if the database is shared, such as when the database belongs to a legacy application, then the database must still provide concurrency control.

In order to share a database with an external application, a BOF needs to include database locking operations. There are alternatives for when locking should occur. The retrieval process may always retrieve with locks and release the locks when the associated objects are deactivated. Alternatively, the objects may be retrieved without locks, and locks may be requested whenever the objects are accessed by an update transaction. This allows read-only processes in all applications sharing the database to have concurrent access but imposes additional locking overhead.

6.8.3 Distributed Database Commit

The problem of managing a commit to distributed databases is not new. If a transaction sends requests for commitment from multiple databases, there is the possibility that one or more of the databases will fail to commit. Others will succeed, leaving the overall system in an inconsistent state. This problem has been addressed by the *two-phase commit*.

In a distributed objects environment with multiple databases, the same problem exists. However, the solution should be extended to consider nested transactions. Applications may be developed to provide solutions to complex problems. Portions of these applications may be incorporated into another application so that the original transactions become subordinate to new transactions with greater scope involving other databases. Consequently, it is no longer adequate to implement the two-phase commit for the original transactions since it must extend to all of the databases touched by higher-level transactions. To address this, the transaction service commit protocol must comprehend the two-phase commit at all levels. This may be a particularly challenging problem when integrating a legacy application with an object-oriented wrapper.

6.8.4 Object Mobility

Different vendors will eventually implement business objects facilities in compliance with OMG specifications. This will make the business objects implemented in these BOFs interoperable—they will be able to interact even if they are implemented in different BOFs. The consistent use of a standard database interface such as the Persistent State Service currently being considered by OMG may provide another dimension of interoperability. If the BOF implementations have a consistent approach, then it should be possible to move objects into different BOF implementations while using the same persistent storage. In fact, it should be possible to instantiate a moved object in different language implementations. For performance as well as long-term technological flexibility, this is a desirable capability.

6.9 Performance

There are two key performance issues: workload distribution and query optimization. These are discussed in the following sections.

6.9.1 Workload Distribution

Good performance requires a network design with adequate capacities of computers and network links. It also requires an appropriate distribution of data storage, compute workload, and network activity. At the same time, the network configuration will be constrained by concerns about cost and security. While the cost of computing resources is a diminishing factor, it may be desirable to partition processing for shared services over two or more computers to optimize cost and performance. The equation can be expected to change over time as system utilization changes and the cost of hardware declines.

The cost and performance impact of communication bandwidth can be a significant factor in network design. Communication between computers will always introduce some delay. Communication over dial-up facilities is a major performance limitation, but provides high flexibility. Communication over alternative facilities may provide higher performance, but also may restricts flexibility both for shifts in utilization and for reconfiguration when a connection fails.

The Internet introduced a whole new dimension to communications. It offers the potential performance of leased facilities and the flexibility and dynamic reconfiguration capability of dial-up connections. The cost is very low, but the level of performance is often unpredictable, so reliance on such facilities must be approached cautiously.

In today's global corporation, systems often need to be deployed in many different countries. While there are high-speed computer lines available in the western world, there are many countries in which such high speed lines are very expensive or unavailable. The same application may be deployed in different configurations in different countries to accommodate these limitations.

The scope of sharing information is another important factor in network design and performance. If information is used only by a single user, then it ought to be stored close to that user. If it is used by many, widely dispersed users, then it must be accessible from many locations and the associated server must have appropriate capacity. In a distributed-object system, the shared objects may never be activated far from the persistent storage device. On the other hand, for long transactions, with complex computations and a definable working set of objects, it may be desirable to download the data and instantiate the objects close to the user. The scope of sharing is partitionable at intermediate levels. For example, the inventory for a corporation may be partitioned by plant or warehouse location so that this information is on servers near users at each location.

For data that seldom changes but is frequently accessed, it may be desirable to replicate the objects at many locations. The event service or change notification may be used to keep the replicated objects consistent with the master (see also the discussion of caching above).

Flexibility in the choice of different strategies for workload distribution is extremely desirable for distributed systems. It is quite common for some services to be used more than originally anticipated, which will require reconfiguration and allocation of additional computing resources to maintain acceptable performance. It is seldom easy to predict access patterns for object interfaces. After services are deployed the number of users of those services (other objects or end users) often increases; worse yet, the demand may change in periodic cycles. Also, as more applications are developed to use the services, the workload will increase.

A starting point for network configuration is to determine the level of computing appropriate at the end user interface. If the application is highly interactive or the user already has considerable computing capacity, it may be appropriate to perform much of the computing for applications at this level. On the other hand, if multiple users will interface to a shared application, or the cost of end user workstations is a concern, then computing at this level might be minimized.

Next, the computing capacity requirements for shared computers should be considered. Starting with an assumption that these computers will be centrally located, adjustments may be made to locate some server computers closer to users who will share some of the same objects. This may need to be balanced against ties to legacy systems, shared databases, and security. Once a basic strategy has been established, potential network links should be configured based on rough estimates of network traffic.

There are two levels from which this configuration may be approached. First, based on usage statistics, the object and network activity can be simulated to identify bottlenecks and evaluate alternative configurations. Second, bottlenecks can be identified and alternative configurations evaluated by changing the production system on a trial and error basis.

Unless the configuration is very simple or the application can be accommodated by existing facilities, simulation should be used during development so that reasonable performance is achieved when the system is installed. The simulation will require estimates of computing workload and network traffic associated with clients and servers. The level of sophistication required will depend on the costs and risks involved. If the costs or risks are high, it may be appropriate to obtain the assistance of an expert in network simulation. Once the system is operational and the complexity of interactions grows, it may be most effective to use the trial and error approach if tools for monitoring activity and performance are available and the configuration can be quickly changed.

6.9.2 Query Optimization

When the user has an external identifier for an object of interest, it will either already be bound to an object by the naming service or it can be retrieved by key from a database. Optimization of this sort was discussed earlier. When the user is interested in examining a group of objects based on some selection criteria, a query facility is required. In conventional systems the query facility is provided by the database. The scope of the query is the entire database and all objects of interest are assumed to be in the database. In a distributed-object architecture, the potential scope of the query could be multiple databases. In some cases the query might involve collection of objects that exist only in memory. One goal for the application developer is to perform the query without concern about persistence—whether or not the objects are in databases and which databases might be involved.

To achieve this goal queries must be based on searching collections. A collection defines a domain of objects, i.e., a search space. The OMG query service provides such a facility. For example, a query might be against all of the accounts of a broker to find a subset with a minimum level of investment. The Broker object may have a relationship to all of its Account objects so the Broker object would be the source of an appropriate collection. However, it may be that accounts are associated with clients rather than a broker directly so that the search would be a search of accounts within the broker's clients.

If the objects are persistent and must be retrieved from a database, then the search strategy and database retrieval mechanism could have a substantial impact on query performance. In the above example, if retrieval of a Client object causes the Account objects to be retrieved at the same time, then it would be appropriate to examine the Account objects one Client at a time. On the other hand, if accounts are not retrieved with the client, it would be useful, if possible, to first eliminate clients in which there could be no qualified accounts. This applies whenever search criteria traverse relationships: The criteria that traverse the fewest relationships (or none) should be applied first.

Such considerations should be built into predefined query specifications and might be used to optimize ad hoc query specifications submitted by users. The opportunities to optimize queries will be a function of the design of the BOF. The application developer needs to understand how the BOF executes queries, implements relationships, and provides results to optimize the application's performance.

In the long term, the scope of general queries must be logically constrained. Databases are traditionally developed to support particular organizations, thus the physical scope of the database defines the scope of queries. In the future, systems will be integrated and organizations may share or overlap in their use of databases. A casual query might examine many databases and millions of entries that are totally irrelevant to the user. Consequently, there is a need to define query domains to make sense to users. From a user's standpoint, there should be concentric circles of interest such that the smallest domain may be examined first, and if the result is not sufficient, domains of increasing scope can be examined. At this time, this is an application problem, but generalized, standard mechanisms should be developed in the future.

6.10 Reliability

In addition to the inherent reliability of the system components, there are three major factors to be considered by the system designer: failure containment, recovery, and change management. These are discussed below.

6.10.1 Failure Containment

As the scope of a distributed system expands to the enterprise level, there may be many interdependencies. A single failure could have propagating effects. The designer must examine the potential sources of failure and consider the consequences. To begin with, the impact of failure of each computing node and network link should be considered. This may suggest the need for redundant links or back-up computing capacity. The analysis should then expand to consider the consequences of groups of nodes and links failing as in a natural disaster or power outage. While such conditions may shut down operations in a geographical area, it would not be appropriate for the shutdown to take on global proportions.

The more complex analysis involves examining the impact of these failures on the execution of applications. If a failure causes an application to stall, it could hold resources that would stall other applications causing a chain reaction to lock up the system. Similar consequences may result if certain nodes or network links simply become overloaded causing a chain reaction of poor performance. If applications are accessing information from many nodes, they are more vulnerable to failure. It may be desirable to reduce the scope of transactions of some applications so that while some operations may be disabled by a failure, others remain operational.

Finally, the designer should examine any process, user application. or system service that can have a recursive effect in the event of a failure or exception. It may be appropriate to put certain checks into such processes to detect runaway conditions and take corrective action.

6.10.2 Recovery

Recovery will usually mean restoring operations from a database or databases. In the distributed environment, the normal failure should be limited to a single node or an geographical location, such as from a power failure. This should mean restart of a portion of the network. Applications operating within the scope of transactions should have straightforward recoveries. Any active transaction should fail and be backed out for objects still active on the operational nodes. When the transaction is later restarted, the appropriate state of objects on nodes that failed will be retrieved from the databases. The designer must assure that applications are consistent with this paradigm. If updates of any form are performed without transactional control, there may be a problem.

6.10.3 Change Management

Changes to a large, distributed system are a great source of risk. A single software change can affect many nodes. This is not new for system software—the installation of new operating systems or key software components has always been a source of considerable risk. However, we now face the possibility that changes to application software are just as risky. This is because the change may affect many shared objects that may impact many applications and users throughout the enterprise.

There are four key measures essential for control of the risk of change:

1. rigorous validation and testing,
2. the ability to back the change out and restore the system to a valid, prior state,
3. the ability to install a change with limited scope (i.e., it does not have to be installed everywhere at once, and
4. cautious adoption of shared components.

Changes must be carefully validated and controlled. They should be designed for limited-scope, phased implementation. If possible, before and after versions should be interchangeable and installation of a change should be reversible without other modifications or conversions. Changes with wide impact that cannot be phased in must be managed with particular caution. The potential impact of any change must be considered, and appropriate contingency plans identified. Particular attention must be given to components that will be widely shared.

The enterprise computing model discussed in Chapter 2 provides an important advantage. The most frequent changes and new developments should occur in the application layer, which has a limited scope of impact and can generally be phased in an organization at a time. Where there is a proven need for consistency of well-defined functionality, this functionality can be moved to the enterprise layer. Thus the enterprise layer should be changed most slowly and deliberately. The benefits can be significant, but they must be balanced against the risks. In the mean time, the most important role of the enterprise objects is to provide shared state and to provide controls to assure that the shared state is consistent and secure.

6.11 Summary

The adoption of a distributed-object architecture raises new design issues and adds new considerations to traditional design issues. The use of a business objects facility (BOF) introduces certain mechanisms and objectives that can also present design issues. While these issues present new challenges, they also present opportunities to achieve improved business system integration, flexibility, and responsiveness. As the implementations of business-objects facilities evolve, many of these design issues will be resolved with additional tools and supporting facilities.

REFERENCES

Metsker, Steven J. "Object Weights and Measures" *Object Magazine*, Vol. 6, No. 2, April, 1996.

CHAPTER 7

Programming CORBA Objects

This chapter examines the implications of programming objects for a distributed computing environment based on CORBA. While the program code will differ for other languages and ORB implementations, many of the issues discussed are independent of language and ORB. To be specific and provide meaningful examples, we focus on C++ programming for Orbix.

Chapters 5 and 6 discussed design problems, first those relating to the functionality needed to support distributed business objects, the Business Objects Facility (BOF), then the more general issues related to design and configuration of distributed systems. This chapter deals with more elementary issues of programming for distributed objects. We will build on the basic capabilities provided by the object request broker, without the abstraction and simplification provided by a Business Objects Facility.

The discussion in this chapter is not intended to teach C++ programming. It is assumed that the reader already knows how to program in C++. We focus on objects that are remotely accessible in a distributed computing environment, CORBA objects, and the issues that arise from interfacing to them through an ORB.

Not all objects in the design of business applications will be CORBA objects. User-interface objects and many local computational mechanisms should not be remotely accessible. However, in a business-objects model, we recommend that the business objects be designed and implemented in the anticipation of being remotely accessible. This is particularly relevant to objects intended for the enterprise layer introduced in Chapter 2. In most cases, business objects in the application layer should be implemented with the same approach. Long-term flexibility and development of the agent layer requires that they support remote access.

The following sections use Figure 7.1 as a framework for discussion. This is the same illustration of remote message-sending introduced in Chapter 1. We begin by examining the implications of having a reference to a remote object and sending it a message. The interface must be specified in IDL, and we discuss the restrictions IDL imposes on the interface specification. In the target address space, the message must be relayed to the target object. We examine the alternative ways of implementing this target-object interface and its implications to the implementation of the target C++ object. In a distributed computing environment there are no global variables to hold shared values. We discuss the use of context objects to provide a similar facility. Next, the programmer must be aware of the nature and role of some additional non-CORBA objects involved in the implementation of the distributed computing facilities; these are examined briefly. Finally, the impact of using a Business Objects Facility like that described in Chapter 5 is reviewed.

7.1 OBJECT REFERENCES

Figure 7.1 illustrates how a remote object is represented by a proxy object in the local address space. The proxy object receives messages and forwards them through the object request broker to the target object. This seems quite straightforward. When implemented in a C++ environment with strong typing and without memory management, it becomes a bit more involved. We examine the implications of referencing a remote object below. The implementation of the proxy object and references to it are covered first. Next, we examine the issue of identity comparisons, the special considerations for

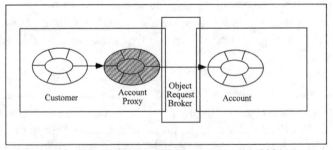

FIGURE 7.1. A Reference to a Remote Object

typecasting of remote object references, and the representation of null references. Finally, the implications of dangling references are explained.

7.1.1 Proxy References

A proxy object contains the object reference to a remote target object. It invokes the appropriate functionality on the ORB to cause messages to be sent to the remote object. Since all local references to a remote object are through a local proxy object, references in the code that send messages are in the same form as references to other local objects. The proxy object is always allocated from the C++ heap space and referenced through a pointer. The class name of the proxy object corresponds to that of the remote, primary object but with _ptr attached as a suffix.

For added programming convenience, another class is also generated with the _var as a suffix used to create an instance of the class as a local variable. This local variable object, usually created on the stack, contains a pointer to the proxy object. It adds to programming convenience by automatically managing memory associated with the proxy. If the _var form is used consistently throughout an application, the proxy will be returned to heap space when there are no longer any references (i.e., no more _var instances).

Figure 7.2 shows the Account_var instance, which is instantiated in the local stack, referencing the Account_ptr, proxy object. When a message is sent to the Account_var object it is delegated to the proxy object which, in turn, relays it through the object request broker to the target object. Each of these objects must be defined to support the same interface so they each can receive the same messages.

Syntactically, messages can be sent to either the _var or the _ptr object using the pointer syntax "->". An instance of either of these types can be freely assigned to a variable of the other type without any typecasts. This is

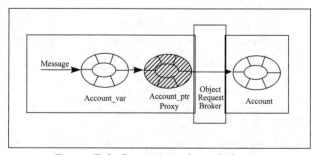

FIGURE 7.2. Proxy Interface Object

accomplished through the function overloading capability of C++.
Overloaded constructors create the appropriate instances and overloaded
conversion operators perform typecasting. As a result, the internal implementation of each of these types is transparent to the programmer. Below
are examples of code generated by the Orbix IDL compiler for the Account
interface.

```
#ifndef account_hh
#define account_hh

typedef Account * Account_ptr;

class Account : public virtual CORBA_Object{
    public:
            Account() : CORBA_Object(1) {}
    public:
            // a lot of stuff deleted.
};
class Account_var : public CORBA__var{
    public:
            // default constructor
            Account_var();
            // construct from a pointer
            Account_var(Account *);
            // copy constructor
            Account_var(const Account_var &);
            // destructor
            Account_var();
public:
            // assignment to a pointer
            Account_var & operator=(Account *);
            // assignment to another _var
            Account_var &operator=(const Account_var
                                   &);
            assignment to a _ptr.
            operator const Account * () const;
            operator Account *& ();

            // pointer operator
            Account * operator->();
};
```

FIGURE 7.3. Sample Code for the Account Classes

Several overloaded constructors allow the `Account_var` to be constructed either from a pointer or from another instance of the same type in the sample code. Whenever `Account_ptr` is either constructed from or assigned to `Account_var`, a shallow copy is made. When the `Account_var` goes out of scope, the copy is eliminated.

7.1.2 Identity Checks

In programming objects within a single address space, program logic can determine if two pointers refer to the same object by testing the pointers for equality. However, as seen in the forgoing discussion, there may be multiple instances of the intermediary object for a single proxy object. Furthermore, the CORBA standard does not guarantee that a remote object has only one proxy in the local address space. Neither does it guarantee that the object reference used by the ORB to locate the remote object will always be the same for a particular object. It is important for the programmer to understand that an equal identity check requires use of the `CORBA::is_equivalent` message. Sometimes this message will require communication over the network to make the appropriate determination.

7.1.3 Typecasting

When a C++ variable references an object, the variable type must correspond to the class of the object or one of its super classes. Similarly, when a variable references a proxy for a remote object, the type must correspond to the IDL type specification of the remote object, which is reflected in the local, proxy class.

A variable referencing a remote object as its interface type may be assigned to a variable designated as the same type or a super type of the source variable. This is referred to as *widening*; the new variable reference is to a less specific interface. If the new variable type is more specific than the sending variable type, then the _narrow method must be used to narrow the type. Consider the interface hierarchy shown in Figures 7.4(a), the corresponding C++ implementation code in Figure 7.4(b), and the code for narrowing and widening in Figure 7.4(c).

```
interface Broker{
 ...
};

interface AccountBroker : Broker{
 ...
};
```

FIGURE 7.4(A). Partial Interface Hierarchy for AccountBroker

```
class Broker : public virtual CORBA_Object{
    static Broker * _narrow(CORBA_Object *);
};

class AccountBroker : public Broker{
    public:
  static  AccountBroker * _narrow(CORBA_Object *);
};
```

FIGURE 7.4(B). Partial Code for Implementation Classes

```
AccountBroker_ptr   pBroker;
AccountBroker_ptr   pNarrowedBroker;
CORBA_Object_ptr pObject = pBroker;
                // implicit widening

pNarrowedBroker = AccountBroker::_narrow(pObject);

if ( CORBA::is_nil(pNarrowedBroker) ){
   // pObject was not of type AccountBroker
}
```

FIGURE 7.4(C). Widening and Narrowing a Reference

The CORBA specification does not require the use of inheritance by the C++ proxy implementation classes, but it does define the expected behavior. Whether or not inheritance is used, implicit widening—conversion of a derived interface to a less specific interface—is to be supported for the classes corresponding to the derived interface. This is simple if inheritance is used, as shown in Figure 7.4(c), because then implicit conversion is performed by the C++ compiler. Otherwise, conversion operators must be used to accomplish the conversion.

The more frequent conversion is when the base class, `CORBA_Object`, has to be converted to a derived class, called *narrowing*. As shown in Figure 7.4(c), each class supports a static method called `_narrow`. This method can take an instance of type `CORBA::Object` and return a properly cast object. Messages often contain references to objects passed as arguments or return values typed `CORBA::Object`. This designates any object with a CORBA interface. to send application messages to the object, it must first be narrowed and assigned to a variable for its particular interface. This is accomplished in Figure 7.4(c) by sending the `Account::_narrow` message.

The inheritance hierarchy of the target object class and the inheritance hierarchy of the IDL interface specifications may not be the same. Such cases may be somewhat confusing since a type casting that works for an implementation object reference locally may not work for the corresponding types in the remote address space. The target type, based on IDL inheritance, is not a specialization of the source type, based on C++ inheritance. When narrowing fails, a nil reference is returned

7.1.4 Null Pointers

The absence of an object can simply be indicated by a null pointer in a single address space. However, an object reference in a CORBA environment is to a proxy object representing a reference to a remote object. It is possible to have a valid proxy object for a reference, but the object reference in the proxy can be null, so that it does not reference any remote object. Each proxy class is required to provide a method nil that sets the remote object reference to a null reference. The CORBA interface defines the method `CORBA_is_nil`, which returns true if the object is a null reference and false if it is not. Figure 7.5 shows some ways in which null references can be generated and used.

`CORBA_is_nil` has somewhat loose semantics. Orbix considers an object nil if

a. the variable pointing to the proxy has a null value,
b. if the variable points to a properly allocated proxy object, but the proxy object itself has a null pointer, or
c. if there is an attempt to bind an object that has no implementation.

```
AccountFactory_ptr pAccountFactory;

try{
  pAccountFactory = AccountFactory::_bind();
}
catch(...){
  pAccountFactory = AccountFactory::_nil();
}

Account_ptr pAccount;

if ( !CORBA_is_nil(pAccountFactory) ){
  pAccount = pAccountFactory->create();
}
```

FIGURE 7.5. Operations on Null Objects

7.1.5 Dangling References

A process may continue to have a reference to an object in another process when the object no longer exists. We refer to such references as *dangling references* because they have lost their associated objects. This can occur because the remote process failed, but it can also occur under more normal circumstances. An object may be destroyed under the assumption that it is no longer in use or it might be explicitly deleted while some references to it remain active. CORBA does not define any mechanism by which the existence of outstanding references to an object can be determined. CORBA does define a forwarding facility to redirect references to moved objects. This facility only functions as long as the original address space is still active. Dangling references can also be created when objects are moved.

When a message is sent to a dangling reference, an exception will be raised. In response to such an exception, the message sender may attempt to locate the missing object. If it has been moved and it is registered with the naming service, then the naming service may have the new reference. If it is a persistent object, then it might be re-activated from the database and the message may be sent. While the OMG ORB specification defines an optional capability to return the new location of a moved object, the viability of these options depends on the particular situation. A Business Objects Facility should provide mechanisms to help resolve dangling references, but the application may still need to be programmed to handle them under some circumstances.

7.2 MESSAGE SENDING

There is a specific mapping of C++ to IDL that determines the way messages sent to or received from other languages are expressed in C++. Within an address space, a message sent to a remote object is fundamentally the same as a message sent to any other object. However, the information passed in the message and the information returned must be acceptable both for exchange over the network and for exchange with objects written in different languages.

The following paragraphs discuss the nature of this exchange and the restrictions it places on message arguments, return values and exception handling.

7.2.1 Arguments and Return Values

There are two significant factors to be considered about message arguments and return values: objects are passed by reference and arguments may be specified as "in-out" variables. Message arguments and return values pass objects by reference, not by value. This means an argument object local to the message sender will be remote to the message receiver, or possibly vice versa. Remote access can cause a significant performance impact. Elementary objects, data structures, sequences, and arrays are passed by value. Consequently, elementary values and sequences of name-value pairs are often used to provide local access to information that would otherwise require message sending to a remote object. Such techniques can improve performance, but can add to the complexity of the implementation. A specification is under consideration by OMG by which objects may be passed by value, but this will require cautious usage.

In-out parameters must be references to variables. The variables are used not only to provide input parameters but also to receive a result back to the caller. Out parameters are essentially the same as in-out except only the value returned is of primary interest. In-out parameters require exactly the same considerations as return values and follow the same rules of memory management. In other languages, such as Smalltalk, an out or in-out parameter may require a special expression to cause the variable to receive its resulting value.

7.2.2 Exceptions and Timeouts

While C++ exceptions can use the inheritance hierarchy, IDL exceptions follow the semantics of structures. They cannot be inherited from other exceptions and are passed by value from one address space to another. Programmatically, IDL exceptions in C++ are the same for distributed objects as for local C++ programming. The primary difference is that the application must anticipate failure in the communication network or the remote process. These result in either system exceptions or timeouts.

In distributed processing there can be many reasons for delays. A delay in completion of one transaction can have a snowball effect on delays to other transactions that share objects or other resources. It is important to place an upper limit on the time allowed for remote operations so that one delay does not impact the entire system. The programmer should give particular attention to the performance and reliability of the network carrying a request. Where the likelihood of failure is significant, an appropriate timeout should be set on the transaction to enable the process to try again or terminate in an orderly fashion.

7.3 INTERFACE DEFINITION

Objects that are to be accessible remotely must have interfaces defined in IDL. To preserve language independence, IDL does not allow all of the interface capabilities supported by C++. The fundamental restriction being that objects are only accessible through message-sending. The following sections discuss these constraints from a C++ perspective and issues related to the organization and management of interface specifications.

7.3.1 Overloading

OMG IDL does not allow multiple declarations with the same operation name such as where C++ would allow the same operation name to be used

```
interface AccountBroker{
  Client GetClient(in string clientName);
  Client GetClient(in long customerNumber); // Error.
```

FIGURE **7.6. Attempt to Function Overload**

with different argument specifications. In C++, this is called *function over-loading*. A method name can appear only once within the scope of an IDL interface. In Figure 7.6 the specification is invalid because the GetClient name is used more than once

7.3.2 Inheritance

Since IDL appears to be similar to C++, programmers may be misled into believing that inheritance should be addressed in the same way for IDL. However, IDL imposes additional inheritance restrictions. When one interface inherits from another, the derived interface gets all the identifiers (methods and attributes) of the inherited interfaces. It is illegal to inherit an operation or attribute name that is also defined on the derived interface. It is also illegal to inherit the same operation or attribute names from different parent interfaces (multiple inheritance). This can be rather frustrating when the semantics and the signature are the same for a method on two existing interfaces. The IDL compiler will not allow a new interface to be defined by inheritance of these two existing interfaces. In Figure 7.7, the inheritance of BrokerCustomer from Broker and Client is illegal because interfaces Broker and Client both define the operation OpenAccount. Hence BrokerCustomer gets two definitions of OpenAccount, which is illegal.

7.3.3 Abstract Interfaces

Abstract interfaces, like abstract classes, do not have corresponding implementations, but are used for inheritance of shared protocols. Abstract interfaces support polymorphism by providing a common interface definition for objects that may have different additional interface capabilities. By operating in terms of the shared interface, objects of different classes may participate in the same processes.

```
interface Broker{
       Account OpenAccount();

};

interface Client{
       Account OpenAccount()

};

interface BrokerCustomer : Broker, Client{
};
```

FIGURE **7.7. IDL Inheritance Violation**

Abstract interfaces should be carefully designed to support polymorphism. The behaviors used together should be on the same interface. Method names should be carefully chosen to be unique to avoid later conflicts when a new interface is defined by combining a unique set of abstract interfaces. Keep in mind that confusion may arise if the interface inheritance hierarchy is different from the implementation class hierarchy.

7.3.4 Organizing IDL Code

There may be hundreds of classes with different IDL interfaces in a typical system. The grouping of these interfaces into files is important for change control and management of the interfaces. It deserves a consistent strategy. In addition, grouping will also determine name spaces. Interfaces originating from different sources have a high probability of name conflicts in an enterprise wide computing environment. For example, how many systems do you know that use the name Object?

IDL defines the concept of *module* to address the issues of name spaces (C++ addresses the same issues with namespace). Objects relating to a common concept, subsystem, or source should be grouped into one module.

Since a module's name space has file scope, it seems that all interfaces for the same module should be in one file, which would lead to large header and skeleton files. It is usually desirable to have one IDL file for each interface and its related definitions. IDL allows most of C-preprocessor directives, an approach illustrated in Figures 7.8(a) and 7.8(b). This approach can be used

```
#ifndef exchange_idl
#define exchange_idl

#ifndef SecurityManagement_module
module SecurityManagement{
#define SecurityManagement_module
#define defined_security_module
#endif

#include "security.idl"

interface StockExchange{
  ...
};

#ifdef defined_security_module
}; // module SecurityManagement
#undef defined_security_module
#endif


#endif
```

FIGURE 7.8(A). StockExchange interface for SecurityManagement Module

```
#ifndef security_idl
#define security_idl

#ifndef SecurityManagement_module
module SecurityManagement_module{
#endif

interface Security{
  ...
};

#ifndef SecurityManagement_module
};
#endif

#endif
```

FIGURE 7.8(B). Security interface for SecurityManagement Module

to define each IDL interface in its own file and group them into modules to establish their name spaces. In the example system in Appendix B, the securities-management subsystem contains two primary interfaces, Security and Exchange. Each interface causes the other interfaces of the same module to be included with it.

7.4 OBJECT IMPLEMENTATION

C++ is a strongly typed language as is IDL. Both have multiple inheritance; however, interface types in C++ are class specifications (object implementations). While types in IDL are interface specifications independent of the implementation. This difference can cause difficulties.

7.4.1 Implementation Hierarchy

The implementation hierarchy is completely independent of the interface hierarchy. Figure 7.9 shows the interface hierarchy for AccountBroker, which is a specialized type of Broker. Figure 7.10 suggests a possible AccountBroker implementation class unrelated to any Broker class. Of course, it is possible and sometimes desirable to make use of inheritance for implementation purposes

```
interface Broker{
  void PlaceOrder();
};

interface AccountBroker : Broker{
  void OpenAccount();
};
```

FIGURE 7.9. Interface Hierarchy for AccountBroker

```
class AccountBroker_I{
  public:
    void PlaceOrder(CORBA::Environment &);
    Account_ptr OpenAccount(CORBA::Environment &);
};
```

FIGURE 7.10. Implementation Scheme for AccountBroker

too. A BOF may impose specific requirements on the implementation hierarchy.

Sometimes there is no implementation associated with an interface because it is meant to be an *abstract interface*—an interface not intended to be implemented only inherited. In such cases the implementation class for the specialized interface would implement the methods for both the abstract interface and the specialized interface.

The remote user of an object is only concerned about its IDL interface. The inheritance relationships of IDL interfaces suggest how that user might widen or narrow references to the remote object. While the remote object implementation must support all of the interfaces inherited by the IDL type, the implementation object may not have inherited its C++ interfaces from corresponding classes. It may have implemented the methods explicitly, or inherited them from other classes that implement subsets of the methods. Sometimes the methods are implementations through delegation to another object.

7.4.2 Interface Functionality

Objects implementing IDL interfaces must incorporate certain functionality to be capable of receiving messages from a remote domain. This functionality is provided by the Basic Object Adaptor (BOA). There are two ways of incorporating this functionality for application objects: inheritance and delegation.

CORBA 2.0 specifies the language bindings generally required by the client side. It is somewhat vague in specifying the BOA interface to the object implementations. Chapter 10 of the CORBA 2.0 specification indicates that OMG expects server code to be portable from one ORB implementation to another. It does not specify clearly what facilities all ORB's should provide to the server programmers. CORBA mentions two general approaches for implementing interfaces, but does not define the exact syntax of these approaches. While this gives vendors flexibility, it does not insure code portability. Orbix supports both approaches, but since the syntax is not standardized, this support is non-portable. Whichever approach used, it is transparent to the client program. We discuss these alternatives below.

7.4.2.1 Inheritance-Based Implementation

The Orbix IDL compiler can be invoked with a "-B" switch. When this switch is set, the compiler generates an additional class whose name is derived by appending BOAImpl to the interface name. Figures 7.10(b) and

7.10(c) illustrate the classes generated for the Account interface specified in Figure 7.10(a).

Note that the actual Account implementation class is `Account_i`. It inherits from `AccountBOAImpl`, thus incorporating the necessary methods to support the BOA interface. The declaration of these two separate classes allows the programmer to modify the `Account_i` implementation without involving the BOA support code.

7.4.2.2 Delegation-Based Implementation

The second approach described by the CORBA specification is to provide implementation through delegation. Orbix implements the delegation approach through several macros. This approach allows you to totally separate the implementation hierarchies from the interface hierarchy and then tie the two together through macros.

This approach provides a clean separation between the classes providing

```
interface Account{
};
```

FIGURE 7.10(A). Account Interface Declaration

```
class AccountBOAImpl : public virtual Account{
};
```

FIGURE 7.10(B). AccountBOAImpl Declaration

```
class Account_i : public AccountBOAImpl{
};

// Create an instance

Account_ptr pAccount = new Account_i;
```

FIGURE 7.10(C). Account_i Declaration

the actual implementation and those interfacing with the Basic Object Adapter. However, it does result in the creation of an additional TIE object as shown in Figure 7.11. TIE_Account holds a reference to its target object and delegates all function invocations to it. We prefer this approach because it makes it easier to wrap existing legacy code into a CORBA framework by avoiding multiple inheritance. It eliminates the need to use multiple inheritance to incorporate the BOAImpl functionality. The code in Figure 7.12 creates a TIE object, passing it a reference to the implementation class.

7.4.3 Attributes

IDL provides for the declaration of attributes and methods. The declaration of attributes is simply shorthand to define the accesser methods for those attributes. When an attribute is declared in the IDL, the IDL compiler generates signatures for get and set methods to get the current value or set a new value. If the declaration is preceded by the keyword readonly, only the get method will be defined.

An attribute is a value associated with an object. An attribute may be of any type. Attributes in the IDL can include values that define relationships. An attribute can be a reference to another object with an interface whose definition is visible to the IDL compiler; it may be an array or sequence of basic data types, or CORBA objects. The type specification does not determine the implementation of the attribute, only the value passed in the set method or returned by the get method. An attribute may be a value stored in the underlying implementation, it may be computed from attributes of related objects, or, for a readonly attribute, it may simply return a constant.

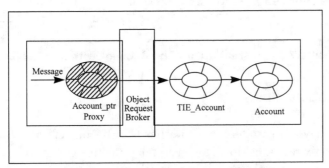

Figure 7.11. A Delegation Interface

```
#ifndef account_ih
#define account_ih

#include "account.hh"

class Account_i{
    public:
        virtual char * GetBalance (
            CORBA_Environment
        &IT_env=CORBA_default_environment) ;
};

// Define the TIE between Account and Account_i

// the macro below declares the programmers intent
                                        that the
// class Account_i will implement the interface of
// Account. This actually results in the definition
                                        of
// the class for the TIE object.

DEF_TIE_Account(Account_i)

#endif


// Create an instance of object implementation
    Account_i *ptrAccount = new Account_i;

// Create a TIE object for the Account class
    Account_var account = new
                TIE_Account(Account_i)(ptrAccount);
```

FIGURE 7.12. Instantiation of an Account with a TIE object

7.4.4 Relationships

Attributes may return references to other CORBA objects; i.e., they may be used to specify relationships. However, relationships generally involve functionality beyond simple get and set methods to maintain the integrity of complementary relationships and support other operations. For example, relationships must support appropriate traversal of object structures for *move, copy,* and *delete* operations. They may have implications to the creation of related objects. We recommend relationship methods be defined explicitly in the interface and attribute declarations be limited to accessing elementary data types or sequences and arrays of elementary data types. These mechanisms should be managed by a BOF, as discussed in Chapter 5.

7.4.5 Object Creation

Creating an object in a distributed environment is drastically different from creating one in a single-process environment. When creating a new object in a conventional C++ environment, memory is allocated for the object, either by declaring an instance in the local scope, or by allocating memory dynamically. In a distributed environment, it may be desirable or necessary to create the object in another process, possibly on a remote computer. Once the object is created, it will be referenced through a local proxy object. The creation process not only involves creation of the object in a remote environment, but the implicit creation of a local proxy object with an appropriate reference.

The usual method is to use a separate class of objects, normally called *factory objects*, to create the desired objects in the remote environment. To create an object in a remote environment, the programmer must identify an appropriate factory object in that environment and send it a message requesting creation of the object. This create request may carry specifications for the initialization of the requested object. The factory object creates the remote object with an initial state and returns its reference so a local proxy is created to access it. Figure 7.13 shows a simple scenario for object creation where the local `GenericFactory` returns a reference to a remote `AccountFactory` that creates the desired Account object. In the application in Appendix B, we call those factory objects, manager objects because they perform additional services defined for the BOF.

7.5 CONTEXTS

The OMG IDL provides a context clause to pass additional information to a server as part of an operation. Methods specified for an interface will carry arguments appropriate to the performance of the operation. It may be useful

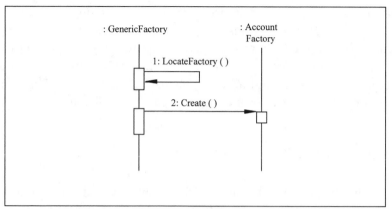

FIGURE 7.13. Object Creation

to pass additional information about the context of the activity without explicitly passing additional arguments. In a single-process application this is accomplished by setting global variables. To make this shared information available remotely, a context can be passed with a message.

Context objects are *pseudo objects*, meaning their interface is specified in the IDL, but they cannot be accessed remotely. Pseudo objects specified as arguments in a message are passed by value if such operations are valid for the particular object. The ORB is aware of pseudo objects and makes the necessary arrangements to pass them from one address space to another.

7.5.1 Context Structure

Context objects contain properties in name value pairs. They use NVList objects, another type of pseudo-object. An NVList can be viewed as an aggregation of instances of NamedValue objects. These, in turn, contain pairs of names and associated values. Figure 7.13(a) shows an interface with a GetBalance method that has no context specification.

A context clause can be used to further qualify the request to obtain the balance in a particular currency. The context might define information about the nationality of the requestor. This addition is shown in Figure 7.13(b). The interface in Figure 7.13(b) indicates to the ORB that the client may pass some context information to the server. It also indicates that one of the properties in the context will be the currency specifier. The context clause contains a comma separated list of the relevant property names. At run time, the client can build the context and add the named properties and values to the context.

```
interface Account{
  string GetBalance();
};
```

FIGURE 7.13(A). An Interface without a Context Specification

```
interface Account{
  string GetBalance() context("currency");
};
```

FIGURE 7.13(B). An Interface with Context Specification Added

Although contexts are mostly used for passing operation-related environment information from the client, an ORB may to also add to the list of properties. While the ORB can freely add properties to the context being passed, the client cannot send more properties than are specified in the context clause of the IDL specification.

7.5.2 Context Hierarchy

Contexts can be linked to form a hierarchy. When linked, `CORBA::Context.get_values` first searches in the context object passed for the invoked method. If it does not find the property, it goes up the chain to the parent context and looks for the required property. It keeps traveling up the context hierarchy until it either finds the required property or exhausts the context chain. This provides default values for required properties. Figure 7.14 shows how to create a child context from the default context. The child contexts obtained this way should be deleted when they are no longer needed by calling `CORBA_release`.

7.5.3 Adding Properties

Regardless of how a context object is created, to define context properties, the client program must add properties to the context. Context properties are

```
CORBA_Context_ptr defContex;

if ( !CORBA_Orbix.get_default_context(defContext)){
    cerr << "Error getting default context" << endl;
    defContext = CORBA_Context::_nil();
}
else{
    // code to add properties to the default
                                        context.
}

CORBA_Context_ptr cContext;

if ( CORBA_is_nil(defContext) ){
    // true if previously set to nil.
}
else{
    // create the child context.
    if(!defContext.create_child("contextname",
                            cContext)){
        cContext = CORBA_Context::_nil();
    }
}
```

FIGURE 7.14. Creating a Child Context

instances of NamedValue pairs accessed through an instance of NVList. The properties can be added one by one to the context by calling `CORBA::Context.set_one_value`. Alternatively, an NVList can set up all properties and then the property values are assigned by calling `CORBA::Context.set_value`. Figure 7.15 shows the code to set up context properties one at a time.

Setting multiple properties involves a bit more work. First, an NVList must be created, using the ORB interface, `CORBA::ORB.create_list`. Next, properties must be inserted in the list and the list must be provided to the `CORBA::Context.set_values` method. Figure 7.16 shows the steps involved.

7.5.4 Default Context

The default context can generally be used to pass the required properties to the server. Each process has a default context. This default context is initial-

```
CORBA_Context_ptr aContext;
CORBA_Any aValue;

aValue <<= "USDollars";

aContext.set_one_value("currency",aValue);
```

FIGURE 7.15. Setting Context Properties One at a Time

```
CORBA_NVList_ptr pList;
if ( !CORBA_Orbix.create_list(1,pList) ){
                              // create the list
cerr << "Error getting NVList" << endl;
return 1;
}

// add a named item in the list
CORBA_NamedValue_ptr pItem =
  pList->add_item("currency",CORBA_ARG_IN);

CORBA_Any *aValue = pItem->value();

*aValue <<= "USDollars";

context->set_values(pList);
```

FIGURE 7.16. Setting Context Values through NVList

ly empty in Orbix. A client can obtain this default context by invoking the method CORBA::ORB.get_default_context(). Figure 7.17 shows how to obtain the default context. When the client requests the default context, the ORB dynamically allocates it. It is the client's responsibility to eventually delete the context.

The appropriate way to delete the context is by calling CORBA_release (defaultContext). On the server side, a context is passed as an argument to the method. The ORB releases the context after the call returns. If the server wishes to retain the context, it should copy the context argument to one of its own variables. If the attempt to obtain a context fails, the context variable should be set to nil so that later on its nullness can be checked.

```
CORBA_Context_ptr defaultContex;

if ( !CORBA_Orbix.get_default_context(defaultContext))
    cerr << "Error getting default context" << endl;
else
    // code to add properties to the default con-
text.
if ( CORBA_is_nil(defaultContext) ){
    // true if previously set to nil.
}
```

FIGURE 7.17. Getting Default Context

7.6 OTHER RELATED COMPONENTS

Other data structures play an important role in the programming of CORBA objects. These include strings, sequences, and arrays. They are discussed briefly below.

7.6.1 Strings

The CORBA string data type maps to a C++ character array. CORBA provides functions to allocate and free memory needed for string variables that allow the ORB to perform memory management. CORBA::string_alloc should always be used to allocate memory for strings. CORBA::string_free must be used to release the memory. The class CORBA::String_var handles memory management related issues transparently in the same manner as other _var references.

7.6.2 Sequences and Arrays

Where lists of elements are involved, either primitive or user defined, the programmer uses arrays or sequences. Conceptually, CORBA arrays and sequences are the same. The fundamental difference is that arrays are of fixed size and can be multi-dimensional. An array is transferred from the client to the server and back in its entirety. If you define an array of size 100 and then use it to transfer one element, the data for the whole array is transferred. This can be very inefficient. Sequences, on the other hand, grow and shrink in size depending on the number of members, and are single-dimensional. When sequences are passed, only the required data is passed.

The use of sequences and arrays can lead to the transfer of large volumes of data over the network. Generally, processing of data should be close to its source. If large sets of data have to be transferred, keep communications protocol limitations in mind. For example, Windows 3.1 sockets 1.2 imposed a data size limit of 64 K bytes. If you try to return a sequence whose total size is larger than 64 K, Orbix will generate an exception.

7.6.3 Pseudo Objects

Pseudo objects are objects defined by CORBA standards that cannot be remotely accessed. In the implementation of the ORB and some CORBA services, there are certain objects that must be local to avoid functional or performance problems. These are implemented as pseudo objects. Their IDL specifications are not registered with the implementation repository because the IDL only provides documentation for the local interfaces.

The interface of pseudo objects is specified in an augmented form of IDL. Unlike all other CORBA objects, which derive from the base class CORBA::Object, they do not derive from CORBA::Object. In C++, pseudo objects are exactly like regular C++ objects. However, applications cannot define their own pseudo objects. CORBA recognizes nine pseudo objects: Environment, Request, Context, ORB, BOA, TypeCode, Principle, NamedValue, and NVList. Additional pseudo objects are defined by CORBA services like the security and the transaction services. Their implementation details are left to the ORB or defining service, but their mapping is clearly defined. Pseudo objects that qualify are passed by value in message arguments. Pseudo objects such as ORB and BOA cannot be used as arguments to remote objects.

7.7 BUSINESS OBJECTS FACILITY IMPLICATIONS

Chapter 5 described a Business Objects Facility (BOF). This facility supports a higher level business object abstraction that makes it easier to implement business objects in a distributed objects environment. The primary impact of the BOF is the integration of other CORBA services. Without a BOF, the programmer must implement an integration of these services before working on the solution to the business problem. The level of abstraction achieved by a BOF is best illustrated by walking thorough a scenario in which a programmer creates a small business-object application.

The application developer first specifies the business-object attributes, relationships, and methods to the code generation tool. The code-generation tool generates the interfaces and the skeleton code for the business-object implementations. This includes code for attributes and relationships that support transactions, concurrency control, notification, and database updates. The code generation tool also generates the database interface so that the business objects will be persistent. This may require the developer to map business object attributes to relational table fields.

The developer must still fill in the code for business-object methods. This code will implement the business functionality. It uses the appropriate accessor methods to reference attributes and relationships of business objects. This programming is considerably simplified by the BOF. However, the developer should still be aware of many of the issues discussed in this chapter to avoid pitfalls and resolve potential exception conditions.

The developer creates a user interface using an appropriate tool. This user interface may be in the same or a different language, and will typically be implemented to execute in a separate process. The user interface layer must be programmed to send messages to the business objects. The business objects, within their generated code, provide for ad hoc notification. The user interface can request notification when certain attributes or relationships change and the display will be updated accordingly. The user interface uses the name service to obtain object references to the business objects of interest. The developer must define configurations for executables, which will determine where business objects are executed and the databases in which they are stored.

Where the user wants to add information into the system, the programmer writes requests to the business-object manager to create business objects. The business-object manager will create those objects in the appropriate environments. The programmer obtains identifiers for these objects from the user, such as customer ID or part number, and binds these names to the object references using the name service. These objects can then be retrieved when the user wants to view or update them.

The programmer must define the scope of transactions. This will be based on the activities of the user and the points at which changes should be committed. In a simple case, a transaction starts when the user begins performing an activity and the results are committed or rolled back when the user selects the associated command.

The programmer is not concerned about concurrency conflicts because the BOF provides concurrency control in its generated code. Database reads or writes objects are activated (read from the database) when they are needed and the database is updated when the transaction is committed. The location of objects being executed is not a problem because the distribution is managed by BOF facilities and references to objects are provided by the name service. The programmer can add and delete objects from relationships. He or she is not concerned with maintaining the integrity of the relationships because that is handled by the BOF code.

The BOF provides concurrency control for business objects, but this control does not necessarily extend to other program variables and C++ objects. The programmer must take precautions to prevent concurrency conflicts when non-BOF code is re-entered.

The programmer needs to handle exceptions in a manner that is consistent with the BOF. BOFs should have a uniform mechanism for capturing and reporting exceptions. The programmer must program for the exception model, must accumulate exceptions, raise and catch them in the distributed environment. This must include the termination of transactions when appropriate.

Our discussion shows that the programming complexities are considerably reduced by the BOF. As the computing environment becomes more complex, with multiple databases, different languages, and additional computing platforms, the BOF code must be more sophisticated. The configuration of executables and equipment becomes more complex, but the tasks of the application developer remain relatively unchanged. The major challenge is designing business objects that use consistent names, capture the appropriate concepts, and provide appropriate attributes, relationships, and methods for sharing across the enterprise.

7.8 SUMMARY

The fundamental changes in programming for CORBA objects relates to CORBA interface specifications and associated restrictions, and concerns about interaction with objects in other processes. The CORBA interface brings restrictions on arguments, return values, typecasting, method naming, and inheritance. The interaction with remote objects raises issues about process failures, dangling references, context passing, life cycle operations, relationship management, and memory management. Many of these issues exist with or without a BOF.

The value of the BOF is in reducing some of the concerns about distributed computing and eliminating much of the programming necessary before the application developer can start work on the business problem.

The long-term value of the business-object facility, particularly if it complies with industry standards, is to provide flexibility in the configuration and extension of the computing environment and its applications. It also provides an important foundation for the development of business objects and plug-in applications as purchasable components. It achieves this by providing an application abstraction that makes applications independent of the topology of the distributed computing environment and by enabling business objects to be accessed, shared, and interoperate through standard protocols.

PART 3

Tools and Vendor Components

Part 1 dealt with concepts and Part 2 defined an implementation of distributed objects and related issues. A prototype implementation is included with this book. This implementation is based on the use of specific tools and components. In this part we examine these tools and components so that the reader better understands their role and functionality. These tools and components provide reasonable capabilities in support of our target architecture. Our selection of these tools and components was a function of their capabilities and availability for our use. Each enterprise has different infrastructure and business needs, and developers should make informed choices based on their requirements.

Our computing environment is a client-server configuration using Intel-based microcomputers. The clients are running Microsoft Windows '95, and the server is running Microsoft Windows NT. The primary programming language is C++ using the Microsoft Visual C++ compiler and programming tools. Visual Basic is an optional language for client-based presentation layer displays requiring minimal functionality. Our programming environments include tools and components for the design and implementation of graphical user interfaces. Microsoft SQL Server is used as the relational database. The application incorporates an interface that could be implemented for any relational database. This book will not dwell on describing most of these tools and components since there are many other sources of information.

There are several products that play very important roles in our example appli-
cation. The next two chapters describes these in detail. Chapter 8 covers the
Orbix object request broker from IONA Technologies and the features it provides.
Chapter 9 describes three C++ libraries from Rogue Wave.

The Orbix Object Request Broker

The Orbix object request broker from IONA Technologies was used in our BOF implementation and examples. Most object request brokers comply with OMG standards, but the implementation and certain extensions are unique to each product. Orbix supports the prototype and programming examples and provides an example of this type of product.

The first version of Orbix was released in June 1993 and has established a strong market position. Orbix is a complete implementation of the CORBA 2.0 standard, which provides the ability for object request brokers from different vendors to interoperate. Orbix is available on all major UNIX platforms, Windows 95/NT, MacOS, OS/2, VMS, MVS, and embedded real-time systems such as VxWorks. IONA also implemented the COM/CORBA mapping defined by OMG to provide a standard OLE automation interface. A detailed explanation of Orbix is outside the scope of this book. Refer to Orbix literature for additional documentation.

This chapter begins by discussing the criteria for selection of an ORB and provides a brief assessment of Orbix against each of these criteria. It provides an overview of the Orbix implementation and a discussion of some of the more significant extensions.

8.1 SELECTION CRITERIA

The object request broker may be the most important component for a distributed system. It should be given considerable attention. The following sections outline selection criteria. These are by no means complete, but highlight some of the important considerations.

8.1.1 Ease of Use

Distributed systems are complex by their very nature. The tools involved in building these systems usually have a steep learning curve. Ease of use needs special consideration because all ORBs are not the same. They may follow the same standard, but there are significant areas of difference between them. Based on our limited exposure to other ORB implementations, we believe Orbix is relatively easy to use. The best way to evaluate ease of use is to implement a simple prototype in each candidate's ORB. This may seem like a significant investment of time, but a careful evaluation is worthwhile. The effort can be an important learning experience.

8.1.2 Performance and Resource Requirements

Performance is relative. Some systems require performance in terms of milliseconds while others may be satisfied with a 30 second response time. Distributed-object systems incur delays and consume additional computing resources to exchange messages across domains. Delays occur due to the communication link, the processing to package and unpackage the information, and communication bottlenecks. The speed of the communication transport affects any ORB performance. The design and implementation of the specific ORB may introduce delays due to excessive computation or bottlenecks.

Orbix reduces the risk of bottlenecks by providing parallel connections to the server. The Orbix server daemon gets involved in establishing a connection between the client and the server, then backs out of the loop. Orbix also makes available a non-standard communication protocol for Orbix-to-Orbix communication, which imposes minimal overhead. A benchmark for this protocol showed its performance is 85% as good as the performance achieved through conventional remote procedure calls.

8.1.3 Compliance with Standards

One of the main purposes of development of the CORBA specification is to enable applications to communicate with each other in a heterogeneous environment. Interoperability is a key goal of CORBA that can only be achieved when ORBs comply with the standard. Vendors will always provide additional features to give them a competitive edge. Their compliance with standards will insure that alternative ORB implementations may be used for future applications or different programming languages.

The CORBA specification places few constraints on the implementation of an ORB. An ORB must provide certain services and present standard interfaces to these services. A CORBA compliant ORB has a standard interface for communicating with other ORBs over a network. All ORBs must support the Internet Inter-ORB Protocol (IIOP), although they may support other protocols too. Orbix complies with the CORBA 2.0 standard.

The CORBA specification concentrated more on the interface for the clients and left the interface for the servers somewhat open. Using a CORBA compliant ORB does not mean applications can be developed with the future option of plugging in a different ORB for the same application. Orbix provides a number of extensions that should be used with caution if compatibility with other ORBs is a concern. These are discussed later in the chapter.

8.1.4 Integration with Desktop Applications

CORBA is a technology to develop powerful enterprise-wide services and integrate applications. Microsoft dominates the desktop market. The integration of CORBA with Microsoft's COM/OLE is crucial for most environments that have adopted Microsoft's Windows environment. OMG has defined a COM/CORBA mapping, which IONA implemented in Orbix. Desktop applications can use the COM/CORBA protocol to interoperate with servers that interface using the CORBA standard. This is a key feature and is discussed later in this chapter.

8.1.5 Platforms and Language Bindings

CORBA IIOP allows ORBs from different vendors to interoperate. It is not necessary for all platforms used in an enterprise to be supported by the same

ORB vendor. However, since there are differences affecting developer productivity, it may be advantageous to minimize the number of different ORBs used. Orbix runs on most popular platforms and has bindings to the popular object-oriented languages.

8.1.6 Orbix Assessment Summary

The Orbix market position is supported by its capabilities. IONA is aggressively developing new capabilities. It is a strong participant in the development of new OMG standards that will establish availability of important features.

8.2 ORBIX IMPLEMENTATION

Figure 8.1 illustrates the standard CORBA architecture. Orbix implements this architecture. Since the CORBA specification defines interfaces, not implementation, there is more to understand about the Orbix implementation. For example, Orbix is implemented to utilize a POSIX operating system interface for portability across a wide variety of platforms. Several fundamental components of the ORB implementation are discussed below.

8.2.1 The Interoperation Mechanism

Interoperation of objects in a distributed environment requires the ability to reference objects in different address spaces, potentially on diverse com-

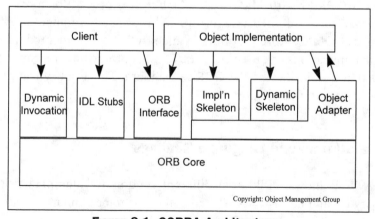

Copyright: Object Management Group

FIGURE 8.1. CORBA Architecture

puters in diverse languages. The ability to send messages to those remote objects and receive responses is also needed. This section describes the Orbix interoperability mechanism from the application developer's perspective. There are a number of pieces to put into place to establish this object interoperation.

The basic framework for interoperation was introduced in Chapter 2 and is shown in Figure 8.2. A remote object is represented locally by a proxy object that forwards messages through the ORB. This seems simple enough, but to achieve this as a practical matter is more complex. For example, if a reference to the proxy object is passed as an argument in a message to another remote object in a third environment, another proxy object needs to be created in that environment. This new proxy object should forward its messages to the same remote object as the first proxy object.

To send a message to an object, we must be able to identify that object. Sending a message to a remote object means identifying the environment as well as the object. Orbix provides multiple ways of obtaining an object reference. When the client invokes a method on a proxy object, the proxy object automatically blocks the client, marshals the parameters, makes a remote request, receives the result, and returns to the client with the result. The client program does not necessarily see the difference between the proxy object and the actual remote object implementation. Figure 8.2 illustrates the forwarding of a message by a proxy object (Account Proxy) to the remote object it represents (Account).

8.2.2 IDL Compiler

Another core component of Orbix is the IDL compiler, which compiles the IDL source code for the interface repository and generates source code for

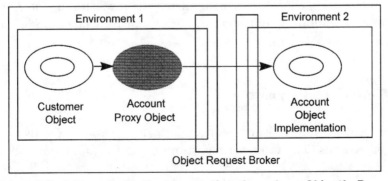

FIGURE 8.2. A Remote Method Invocation through an Object's Proxy

the application implementation. While Orbix supports bindings for a number of languages, we concentrate on the C++ bindings.

The IDL compiler generates C++ code for the client stubs and server skeletons. Client stubs are linked with the client code to support proxy objects. The server skeletons are linked with server code to provide the ORB mechanism for sending incoming messages to objects receiving messages from remote domains. The IDL compiler can also be used to generate skeletons for the implementation objects—the classes for the objects receiving messages through the ORB.

In the Windows platform, the IDL compiler can be instructed to either generate an OLE automation server or an OCX server for the client. In this case, the IDL compiler generates complete source code and a makefile for the appropriate native C++ compiler. The developer can then execute the makefile to build the OLE automation or OCX server. These servers register themselves with the Windows OLE registry when they are first started. Once implemented, they can be used from higher level development environments like Visual Basic.

8.2.3 Implementation Repository

As shown in Figure 8.1, the Basic Object Adapter (BOA) is responsible for dispatching incoming requests to an appropriate object implementation in a server process. Part of BOA's behavior is to start a server process, when it receives a request for an object. The BOA needs to know where the server implementations are in order to start them. This information is provided by the implementation repository.

OMG defines an implementation repository that stores the meta information about implementations. Orbix provides an implementation of this repository and some utilities to manipulate and browse through it. Any server whose execution is controlled by Orbix must be made known to the implementation repository.

8.2.4 Interface Repository

The implementation repository stores information required to activate object implementations. The interface repository contains information about the interfaces programmed in IDL. It is accessible on-line to support the dynamic binding facilities and requires persistent storage. OMG does not restrict how interface repository persistence can be implemented. Orbix uses a file system based storage mechanism that eliminates the need for a database system and simplifies portability to alternative environments.

The interface repository is itself an Orbix server. The clients needing to access the interface repository must include the preprocessor directive `#include <IR/IR.h>` and must link with the library Irclt.lib in addition to other libraries. Because the interface repository server is a regular Orbix server, it too must be defined in the implementation repository.

8.2.5 The Orbix Daemon Process

Orbix provides a daemon process, orbixdw.exe, which should always run in the background on all server machines. This daemon process is responsible for activating object implementations according to activation policies defined by the CORBA specification.

Orbixdw.exe does not participate in the normal communication that takes place between client and implementation objects. It

1. receives the incoming request to bind to an object implementation,
2. locates the object implementation through the implementation repository,
3. activates the server according to specified activation policy, and
4. establishes the connection between the client and the implementation, and backs out of the loop.

The client and the implementation then communicate with each other directly. Figure 8.3 shows the interaction diagram for the initial binding between two objects.

8.2.6 ORB Initialization

CORBA 2.0 requires an application to initialize an ORB by calling `ORB_init`. `ORB_init` returns a reference to a pseudo ORB object. The method `BOA_init` can then be invoked on it to obtain a reference to the BOA pseudo object. Once the ORB has been initialized methods like `resolve_ini-`

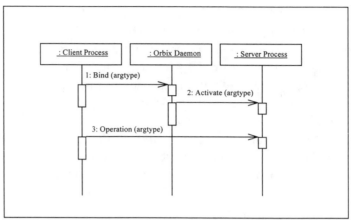

FIGURE 8.3. Interaction Diagram for Initial Binding

tial_references can be called to obtain references to common object services, like the name service and interface repository. This kind of initialization is extremely important in an environment with multiple ORB implementations and portable client and server programs using different ORBs.

Orbix, by default, does not require the programs to explicitly initialize the ORB and the BOA. They are initialized by the Orbix daemon as part of the activation of the server program or as part of the first bind by the client. These are generally considered to be responsibilities of the server implementation. In Orbix, impl_is_ready implicitly performs the ORB_init and BOA_Init. Orbix does provide support for these initialization operations by providing a separate library initsrv.lib on Windows NT, which has to be linked to get an implementation for these functions

As shown in Figure 8.1, the client environment uses the ORB interface to interface with the ORB. The server side uses the BOA interface to receive the operation requests. In Orbix, the operations defined on the BOA as well the ORB interface are provided by the object CORBA::Orbix.

8.3. COM/OLE INTERFACE

Orbix provides an integration with OLE automation that is CORBA compatible. In Windows, the Orbix IDL compiler can be instructed to generate all the required source code for an OLE automation server. One OLE automation server is generated for each interface definition. This behavior can be altered to generate one OLE automation server for multiple interfaces. An automation server acts as the automation server to the client and is also an

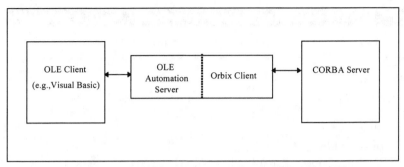

FIGURE 8.4. OLE CLIENT ACCESSING A CORBA SERVER

Orbix client to any CORBA 2.0 compliant object implementation. The mapping between the Microsoft IDL types and CORBA types for most basic data types is straightforward with a few exceptions. Table 8.1 shows how IDL data types are mapped to OLE data.

8.4 ORBIX EXTENSIONS

Orbix's capabilities go beyond the CORBA specification to improve the usability and performance of the ORB. It also addresses the special needs of some applications. We discuss these, both as possible future extensions to the standard and as examples of some of the technical problems we encountered. The following paragraphs describe some of these extensions.

8.4.1 Stream-Based Interface to DII

Most ORB-based applications use a static style of invoking methods. The client has prior knowledge of the kind of invocation it is going to make and links with and uses the proxy code for that object implementation. This style of invocation is too restrictive for applications that do not have prior knowledge of the object implementations they will be using e.g., debuggers or browsers. CORBA provides an alternate style of invocation for these applications, called dynamic invocation interface (DII). The client discovers the interface of the implementation at run-time and formats the requests at run-time by using the interface repository.

DII, as defined by CORBA, is fairly complex to use. Orbix extends DII by providing an intuitive interface to DII, using a stream-like protocol. In this

TABLE 8.1. Mapping of IDL Types to OLE Types

IDL Types	OLE Types
Float	float
Double	double
Long	long
Short	short
unsigned long	long
unsigned short	long
char	short
Boolean	short
octet	short
Enumeration	Translated to Visual Basic global constants
string	BSTR
object reference	OLE interface
Union	OLE interface
Structure	OLE interface
Sequences	OLE collection objects
Arrays	OLE collection objects
Exceptions	OLE interface
Any	OLE interface
Context	no mapping provided

extension, C++ stream insertion and extraction operators are overloaded for the request objects of different types. When the request has been created, the parameters can be inserted into the request using well known insertion operators and the result can be similarly extracted from the request stream.

8.4.2 Activation Modes

Orbix supports the four policies for implementation activation specified by the CORBA specification. They are

- **Shared activation:** The same server manages all objects with the same server name on a given machine.
- **Unshared activation:** Each server manages only one CORBA object and a new server is launched for each new object.

- **Per-method call activation:** A new server is launched for each method invocation.
- **Persistent activation:** In this mode, the server is launched manually. It then informs the ORB it is now active to receive method requests. Servers launched in this mode are assumed to be shared by multiple active objects.

In addition to these activation policies, Orbix offers further control on implementation activation policy by providing the following secondary activation modes:

- **Per-client:** A new server is launched for each new end-user. If a server is installed as a shared server with per-client mode, then the server will manage multiple objects for a particular user. A different server will be launched to manage objects for a different user.
- **Per-client-process:** A new server is launched for each new client process, even if those client processes are owned by the same end-user.
- **Multiple-client:** This is the default mode and allows different users to share multiple objects in the same process, in accordance with whichever fundamental activation mode is chosen.

8.4.3 Smart Proxies

When static invocation is being used, the IDL compiler generates the proxy code. The client links this proxy code and uses it to send messages to the object implementation. The object implementation developers may want to put some special intelligence on the client side for some sophisticated applications. For example, developers may want to provide caching of the object attributes on the client side to improve performance or the proxy code may need to transparently trap certain kinds of exceptions. Orbix provides smart proxies, which allow the server developer to include special intelligence on the client side, without the client developer knowing about it.

The smart proxies are developed one for each interface by the object implementation developer. The client links with the smart proxy code instead of the vanilla proxy code. Once linked, the client does not notice any difference between the smart proxy and vanilla proxy. The only limitation with the smart proxies is that they do not work with DII because DII does not involve the proxy code generated by the IDL compiler.

8.4.4 Collocation of Client and Server

Orbix allows an object's implementation to be collocated with the client object. In this case, the proxy object does not need to make a remote invocation and is referred directly to the in-core object implementation instance. This collocation allows developers greater flexibility to define IDL interfaces for all business logic, even if not all components of the application are initially distributed. Later on, they can selectively distribute the previously non-distributed components. Another important use of this capability is to ease the debugging of the object implementation. One can collocate the object implementation with the client, debug the object implementation logic, then distribute the implementation later.

When a client tries to bind to an object's implementation, Orbix always looks in the process' address space first for the desired implementation (unless a host is explicitly specified in the bind call). If the target object is found in that process' address space, then the subsequent operation invocation requests on that object result in local method calls rather then remote invocation.

Collocation can be further controlled by selectively turning it off or on through the method `CORBA::Orbix.collocated(CORBA::Boolean)`. When this method is passed as 1, Orbix looks in the process' address space only. If the object is not found in the process' address space, an exception is returned. Alternatively, passing 0 to this function turns on remote binding.

8.4.5 Filters

It is often desirable to execute some logic transparently before executing certain operations. Orbix allows execution of such logic through a mechanism called filters. Orbix provides two kinds of filters, discussed below.

8.4.5.1 Per-Process Filters

Process level filters allow eight monitoring points for requests coming in and replies going out of a process's address space. Figure 8.5 shows the per-process filter monitor points.

The outRequestPreMarshal and outRequestPostMarshal points provide an opportunity to execute code in the client's address space before and after marshaling (the parameters are added to the request buffer). The inRequestPreMarshal and inRequestPostMarshal execute code before and after marshaling the incoming request in the server's address space.

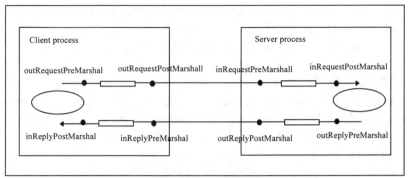

FIGURE 8.5. Per-Process Monitor Points
(from the *Orbix Programming Guide*; used with permission)

The other four points provide monitoring points for the outgoing reply in the server's address space and the incoming reply in the client's address space.

There are many possible uses for per-process filters. One use is to generate transparent trace information.It may be desired to monitor the usage of certain services in a distributed system. There are two reasons to do so: to study the usage patterns or for audit trail purposes. Per-process filters provide a mechanism to generate such information transparently. There are two special cases of per-process filters:

Authentication filter—For those environments where a security service is not available, the authentication filters can be used to pass authentication information from the client to a server.

Thread filter—Thread filters provide a way of creating lightweight threads when an operation request arrives in the server. This is available only for Orbix MT.

Per-process filters can also raise exceptions. However, they can raise only system exceptions. All such exceptions are propagated back to the client by Orbix, except for in ReplyPostMarshal. It is too late to do anything at this point. When an exception is raised by any of the four request filter points, the operation invocation request is not delivered to the target. If the server raises a user exception and any of the three reply filter points raise a system exception, then the system exception is raised with the client. The filter programmer should check for the presence of a user exception before raising any system exceptions.

Per-process filters can be created by deriving a class from CORBA::Filter and then declaring an instance of that class. A process can have multiple filters, all chained together. The constructor CORBA::Filter adds the object to the process' filter chain and they are all executed in sequence.

8.4.5.2 Per-Object Filters

The per-object filter facility provides two monitor points, pre- and post-execution. Per-object filters exist only in the server's address space. They provide the opportunity to execute code before a request is delivered to an object or after it has returned a reply to a request. Pre-filters are executed after all per-process in Request filters have been executed. Post-filters are executed before outReply per-process filters are executed. Per-object filters require the programmer to use the TIE approach (explained in section 8.5.2).

8.4.6 Loaders

When a remote client invokes a method on an object, Orbix passes the request on to the object's server process. Orbix maintains an object table in each process' address space, containing its object references. By default, if Orbix does not find the desired object in the current process' object table (an object fault), it returns an exception to the client process. Orbix provides a way to override this default behavior through a mechanism called loaders. If one or more loader processes are installed in a process, then when an object fault occurs, Orbix gives each of the installed loaders the opportunity to load the target object. If none of the loaders load the object, then an exception is raised with the client.

Object faults can also occur when either an object reference is passed to a process as an in parameter to a server or as an inout or out parameter to a client object. In these cases, if no loader creates the referenced object, then Orbix creates a proxy for it.

Loaders can be installed by deriving from the class CORBA::LoaderClass and then dynamically creating its instance. Orbix always provides a default loader that does nothing.

8.4.7 Locators

In a distributed environment, where object implementations are distributed over a LAN, and potentially a WAN, locating an implementation can be a problem. Orbix uses a set of classes that assist in locating a particular service in a network. When the client code invokes the _bind method, it uses the locator service by invoking the lookUp method on it. Orbix provides a default locator by creating an instance of the CORBA::locator of type CORBA::locatorClass. The lookUp method of the CORBA::locatorClass returns a sequence of strings containing the host names. Orbix then tries to connect to each host in the sequence, stopping at the first host that accepts the connection. The default locator class retrieves the list of hosts providing the desired service. The default locator randomizes the sequence of strings before returning it. This provides a very basic form of load balancing through random selection of factories.

The programmer can define a locator class by deriving a class from CORBA::locatorClass, creating its instance and then assigning the pointer CORBA::locator to point to it. The programmer could choose to use a locator for various reasons. The locator service can be specialized to use the underlying name service provided by a particular network environment. The locator service has little value when a CORBA name service is available. Although it could also be specialized to provide a more sophisticated form of load balancing.

8.4.8 Interface to the Orbix Daemon

Orbix is fundamentally a library-based ORB. However, it does require a daemon process, Orbixdw.exe, to support the activation modes of the BOA and to manage the implementation repository. Orbixdw.exe, does not participate in object-to-object communication but rather limits itself to the following tasks:

1. activating servers,
2. interfacing to the implementation repository, and
3. assisting the locators in searching the appropriate servers and managing their configuration files.

The interface of the Orbix daemon is specified in IT_daemon. Any client can connect to it and access its services.

8.4.9 Orbix Communications Protocol

Before the CORBA 2.0 standard, there was no transport level protocol defined by OMG. ORB implementors basically selected their own protocol. This original Orbix protocol is very lightweight and provides an optimized communication mechanism. In Orbix version 2.0, the OMG standard IIOP is implemented. Orbix also maintains its original protocol, which is used by default for backward compatibility and performance. Orbix can determine when it is communicating with another Orbix ORB and uses its own light-weight protocol. When it is communicating with a non-Orbix ORB, it uses the new IIOP for interoperability. Alternatively, Orbix can use another protocol such as multi-cast.

8.5 BUILDING AN ORBIX APPLICATION

The preceding sections detailed Orbix's capabilities and the mechanisms available to support distributed applications. We will illustrate how to put Orbix to work for a trivial application. This provides a starting point from which more complex problems can be addressed by incorporating additional options and capabilities.

8.5.1 Defining the Interface

The starting point of an Orbix application is a file containing the interface definition. This file has the extension idl and contains OMG IDL specifications for the interface.We use a time server for our example. As shown in Figure 8.6, the time server has a method called GetServerTime and returns the time of the server. We call the interface specification file timsrv.idl. The examples that follow assume Orbix has already been configured on your machine.

Figure 8.7 illustrates the process of generation of client and server stub code. When the IDL compiler is invoked without any parameters, it generates a header file with the declaration of the proxy class, some other classes, and two C++ files. The file <interface file name>C.cpp contains the marshaling and un-marshaling code that must to be linked by the client as well as the server code. The second file, <interface file name>S.cpp, contains the BOA related code the server requires. When the IDL compiler is invoked

```
interface TimeServer{
   string GetServerTime();
};
```

FIGURE 8.6. The Interface for TimerServer

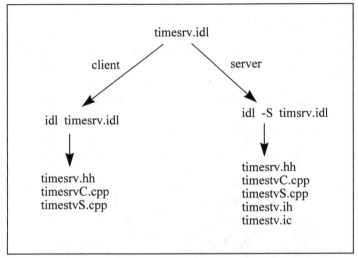

FIGURE 8.7. Files Produced by the IDL Compiler

with the -S flag, it generates the initial skeleton code for the object implementation. These declarations are in the file <interface file name>.ih and the stubs are in <interface file name>.ic. The names of the skeleton classes are generated using the convention <interface name>::==. The programmer then renames them and fills in the business logic for the implementation.

8.5.2 Object Implementations

The next step is to provide business logic for the object implementation. In our example, timesrv.idl was compiled and the IDL compiler produced files timesrv.ih and timesrv.ic. The generated name for the files and classes for the server stubs were generated by Orbix as a starting point for the server developer. We renamed timesrv.ih to timesrvi.h and timesrv.ic to timesrvi.cpp. We then renamed the class name from TimeServer::== to TimerServer_i to give it required file extensions and more meaningful class names. We use this

```
#ifndef timesrvi_h
#define timesrvi_h

#include "timesrv.hh"

class TimeServer_i{
 public:
   virtual char * GetServerTime (
    CORBA_Environment
              &IT_env=CORBA_default_environment) ;
};

// Define the TIE between TimeServer and TimeServer_i

DEF_TIE_TimeServer(TimeServer_i)

#endif
```

**FIGURE 8.8. An Implementation Class for TimeServer
using the TIE Approach**

naming convention throughout the book with _i appended to the interface
name for its implementation.

Orbix has two methods of defining an object's implementation. The first
requires deriving from the BOA class. When the IDL compiler is invoked
with the -B flag, it generates a file <interface name>BOAImpl. The implementation class, <interface name>_i, then derives from the <interface
name>BOAImpl class. Figure 8.9 shows the inheritance hierarchy for the
BOAImpl approach.

The second approach, the TIE approach, uses delegation instead of inheritance and provides a better separation of the business classes from the IDL
C++ classes. Figure 8.9 shows that the definition of an implementation class
using the TIE approach does not involve inheritance from the BOA class.
Figure 8.10 shows the classes involved in the TIE approach. We use the TIE
approach in the examples. It should be noted that the TIE mechanism is not
part of the CORBA 2.0 specification.

Using the TIE mechanism requires the use of some macros to tie a class
that implements an interface to the IDL C++ class. The macro DEF_TIE_<IDL
C++ class name>(<implementation class name>) defines a TIE class
that ties the IDL C++ class to the class that actually implements its interface.

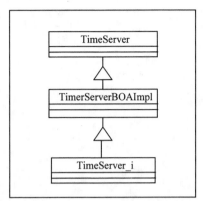

FIGURE 8.9. Class Hierarchy for BOAImpl Approach

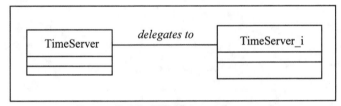

FIGURE 8.10. TIE Macros Approach

The business logic is provided in the timesrvi.cpp file. Since our interface only has one method to provide the current time, an implementation class object will get that time and return it. Figure 8.11 shows a possible implementation of `TimeServer_I::GetServerTime` operation.

8.5.3 The Server Main Program

Once the object implementation is built, we can write the main program for the server executable, so it can be made known to the implementation repository. The main server program must perform the following tasks:

- Create an instance of at least one object implementation to which the clients can bind. Alternatively, a loader can be declared to create that instance of the class. This loader instance then provides further references to object implementations.
- Invoke the method `impl_is_ready` on the `CORBA::BOA` class through its global static instance `CORBA::Orbix`. This tells Orbix this implementation is now ready to accept operation requests.

```
#include <time.h>
#include "timesrvi.h"

char *
TimeServer_i:: GetServerTime (CORBA_Environment
&IT_env)
{
  time_t ltime;

   time( &ltime );

  tm *time_detail = localtime(&ltime);

  char *ct;

  ct = ctime( &ltime );

  char *timeStr = CORBA_string_dupl(ct);

  delete ct;

  return timeStr;

}
```

FIGURE 8.11. Definition of GetServerTime

Figure 8.12 shows the C++ code for the main program for the time server.

8.5.4 The Client

An Orbix client needs an object reference before it can invoke an operation. The most fundamental way of obtaining an initial reference is to perform a _bind operation. This is a static operation on all IDL C++ classes and returns a properly typed object of type <interface name>_ptr, as defined by CORBA. This is not the recommended way of obtaining the object reference when a CORBA name service is available. Figure 8.13 shows the code for a sample client of our TimeServer.

```
#include <iostream.h>
#include "timesrvi.h"

main()
{

// Create an instance of object implementation
 TimeServer_i *ptrTimeServer = new TimeServer_i;

// Create a TIE object for the TimeServer class
 TimeServer_var timeServer = new
     TIE_TimeServer(TimeServer_i)(ptrTimeServer);

// cout << "Marker is " << timeServer->_marker() <<
endl;

// We are ready to start receiving the requests now.
   The impl_is_ready
// method informs Orbix to start sending method
   invocations to this server
// now.


 try{
  CORBA_Orbix.impl_is_ready("TimeSrv");
 }
 catch(CORBA_SystemException &se){
 cout << "Unexpected Exception: " << endl << &se;
 }

// This code will be reached when the impl_is_ready
   times out.

 return 1;
}
```

FIGURE 8.12. Main Server Code for TimeServer

8.5.5 Installing a Server

Before the client can invoke any kind of operation on a server, the server must be made known to Orbix by putting it in the implementation reposito-

```cpp
#include <iostream.h>
#include "timesrv.hh"

main(int argc,char *argv[])
{

// Declare an instance of the object reference.
// In CORBA 2.0 mapping,
// T_ptr class defines a pointer to the IDL C++
// class.

  TimeServer_ptr timeServer;

// _bind connects the client to the remote server.
// If the server is not active, then the BOA will
// activate according to the activation
// policy specified in the implementation
// repository.

try{
  timeServer = TimeServer::_bind(":TimeSrv");
}
catch(const CORBA_SystemException &se){
cout << "Unexpected exception: " << &se <<
  endl;

// In case of exception, set the proxy object
// to nil so we can test it later.
timeServer = TimeServer::_nil();
}

// If the proxy is not nil, then invoke method on //
    it.

if ( !CORBA_is_nil(timeServer) ){
try{
  CORBA_String_var serverTime =
  timeServer->GetServerTime();
  cout << "Server time is " <<
  serverTime << endl;

}
```
                                        (Continued)

FIGURE 8.13. Sample Client for TimeServer

```
catch(CORBA_SystemException &se){
 cerr << "Unexpected exception: " <<
 &se << endl;
}
CORBA_release(timeServer);
}
else
cerr << "No valid object found" << endl;
return 1;
}
```

FIGURE 8.13. Continued

ry. Orbix provides several commands to update and browse the implementation repository, which is pointed to by the environment variable IT_IMP_REP_PATH. We use the command putit to make this server known to Orbix and to specify its activation modes:

```
putit TimeSrv timesrv.exe
```

This command installs the executable timesrv.exe in the implementation repository with the server name being TimeSrv. Note that this is the name the client will provide to the _bind operation. Before the client can connect to the server, Orbixdw.exe must be started on the machine where the server is installed. Once that is done, the client can be invoked. When our example client is run, it produces the following output:

```
Server time is Wed Jan 07 11:12:42 1998
```

8.6 SUMMARY

Our choice of Orbix was influenced by several factors. It is fairly easy to use and a programmer of reasonable experience can be productive in a fairly short amount of time. Orbix is also a lightweight product, with different services packaged separately. It can be obtained and installed in a fairly minimal yet complete configuration. It also has some potentially valuable extensions. For many environments, one of the strongest reasons for choosing Orbix is its availability on virtually every hardware/software platform and its integration of the COM/OLE model.

CHAPTER 9

Application Component Libraries

Our discussion of application development would not be complete without a brief examination of the role of component libraries, especially those libraries providing basic application elements. In this chapter we discuss three libraries used in the development of the example application in the Appendix: Tools.h++, Orbstreams.h++, and DBTools.h++.

The three libraries are from Rogue Wave Software, Inc. We are not promoting a particular product, but these libraries exemplify the essential basic building blocks. It is important to understand the role of these building blocks to understand their value in application development and in the example implementation. It is also important to understand the value of using classes developed over time to incorporate a number of capabilities, such as internationalization and database I/O, needed in practical applications. In the following paragraphs, we discuss simple data types, collections, streams, and a relational-database interface.

9.1 SIMPLE DATA TYPES

Simple data types include integers, floating point numbers, and strings. The library provides arithmetic and string operations appropriate to these data types. In addition, the code is thread safe and supports streams, discussed later. The capabilities provided for strings are most important. Tools.h++ provides classes for several forms of strings and for operations on strings. These include RWCString, RWCTokenizer, RWDate and RWTime.

RWCString is an object-oriented representation of a C++ character string that performs automatic memory management and provides most of the operations generally used to manipulate character strings. These operations include being able to concatenate two strings together using intuitive overloaded operators and support for I/O operations.

RWCTokenizer provides the ability to parse a string that has certain delimiters. The RWLocale and RWLocaleSnapshot classes support internationalization by providing a mechanism for converting strings to and from dates, times, numbers, and currency It recognizes the formatting conventions of different localities. For example, currency can be formatted in US currency format using "$" or international format using "USD".

RWDate represents a date stored as a Julian date. Different member functions provide the ability to print a particular date in various formats and to apply mathematical operators to two dates just as one applies them to basic data types.

RWTime represents a time based on "0 hours January 1, 1901." Just like RWDate, RWTime can also be printed in several different formats and supports mathematical operations. RWZone can be used to set the particular time zone for date and time interpretations. Both RWDate and RWTime support streams.

9.2 COLLECTIONS

Tools.h++ provides a rich set of collection facilities. The collection classes are very similar to Smalltalk collections. The implementations of these classes support persistence. Collection templates incorporate C++ typing of the collection members. Collection classes and templates are discussed below.

9.2.1 Collection Classes

These classes are similar to Smalltalk's collection classes. They include simple linked lists, hash tables, and B-trees. All of these classes are derived from the common base class RWCollection and contain objects of type RWCollectable. RWCollectable is an abstract base class.

Any object stored in these collection classes must be derived from RWCollectable using either single or multiple inheritance. This abstract class contains virtual functions for identifying, hashing, comparing, storing, and retrieving collectable objects. There are types for most of the Tools.h++ basic data types, which can be used directly with the collection classes. These specialized types derive both from the basic data type and RWCollectable. For example, RWCString has a specialized type called RWCollectableString that derives from RWCollectable and RWCString to provide the appropriate functionality. Similarly there is RWCollectableDate, RWCollectableTime, and so on. The use of specialized types avoids the overhead associated with RWCollectable objects when they are not expected to participate in collections.

These collection classes provide various kinds of data structures. Perhaps the most commonly used are the single and double-linked lists. The single-linked lists are further extended to provide queue and stack classes. Another important group of collections is the key based structures ranging from simple tree structures to sophisticated B-trees. B-tree structures are further specialized to RWBTreeDictionary for key based retrieval and RWBTreeOnDisk, which is a file -based B-tree structure.

Accompanying each of these data structures is an iterator class. These iterator classes provide all the necessary methods to iterate over the elements stored in that data structure and always return elements of type RWCollectable.

An advantage of the Smalltalk-like collection classes is support for streams. As mentioned earlier, all elements being stored in the collection classes must derive from the abstract class RWCollectable. RWCollectable requires certain methods to be defined on its subclasses for them to participate in stream operations. These methods include computation of the size of the object and mechanisms for insertion and extraction of their data from a stream.

9.2.2 Template-Based Collections

In general, the Smalltalk-like classes provide a rich set of functionality but at the cost of type safety. A newer alternative is template-based classes which using the C++ template features. While the template-based classes provide type safety, they have two disadvantages: (1) they require the application developer to purchase a source code license for Tools.h++ because source code is required for compilation of the type-specific collections, and (2) streams are not supported by the template-based collections. If those two disadvantages are acceptable, then the template-based classes should be considered.

The template-based classes are divided between two general storage mechanisms: value-based and reference-based. Value-based collections store copies of the objects. When an object is inserted in a value-based collection, a copy is made of that object. This copy is made using the C++ constructor mechanism. If the elements being stored have embedded pointers, the copy constructors of the embedded objects are expected to make appropriate copies of the data being referenced. The objects being stored in the value-based collections are generally expected to have a default constructor and consistent copy, assignment, and equality semantics.

The reference-based data structures do not store the actual object, but rather a pointer to the object that is a member of the collection. This increases the risk that a member of the collection will be inadvertently destroyed while still referenced by the collection. On the other hand, these collections are very memory efficient because memory is not required for the replication of members. All the elements being stored in the reference-based template collections are expected to have well-defined equality semantics through the equality operator.

The more important template-based collections include single- and double-linked lists, and hash tables. The example application uses the single-linked lists and hash dictionaries. Hash dictionaries, RWTPtrHashDictionary maps keys to values using a hashing algorithm. This is an efficient mechanism for storing and retrieving objects based on an identifier.

9.3 STREAMS

The stream facility provides a mechanism for translating an object structure into a flattened stream of data that can later be parsed to recreate the original object structure. The storage and retrieval mechanism preserves the structure and relationships of the inserted objects, properly resolving structures with circularity or repeated elements. A stream may be an in-memory buffer on an external file. This is a straightforward facility for communication or storage of object structures. It is very useful for making objects persistent by storing them in disk files.

These flattened structures can also be passed by value through an ORB to a different address space and the objects can be reconstructed without any further programming work. CORBA provides a powerful mechanism for objects in different address spaces to communicate. However, this mechanism requires the object interfaces to be defined in IDL and restricts the objects to reference-based interactions. Unfortunately, there are many classes that do not merit network interfaces and do not function effectively through remote references. These are objects that should be passed by value from one address space to another.

For example, consider the class RWDate which, because it is not an elementary data type, would normally be passed by reference as a CORBA message argument or return value. Along with the RWDate class data are the methods that provide formatting options and data computations. It is inappropriate to incur the overhead of interacting remotely with a date object. The data of the RWDate class can be assigned to a structure defined in IDL and passed by value. The receiver can then reconstruct the RWDate object in the other address space. This adds to the complexity of the application and invites errors.

On the other hand, Orbix provides an extension that supports passing classes by value with an added IDL keyword: opaque. This keyword allows the classes to be passed by value without the need to either define an IDL interface for them or to convert their data to an IDL structure. However, the user must define marshaling and unmarshaling code invoked during the transfer to format the data for transfer and create the intended objects in the receiving address space. The benefit is that the marshaling and unmarshaling code is incorporated in the ORB instead of being scattered throughout the application.

RogueWave has enhanced the Orbix opaque feature with Orbstreams.h++. Orbstreams.h++ allows all RogueWave objects and user defined objects to be passed by value without defining IDL structures for them. This includes RogueWave's Smalltalk-like collection classes. For example, using Orbstreams.h++, it is possible to pass an object of type RWSlistCollectables (a single-linked list) by value, either as the return value of an IDL request or as an in-parameter. The feature makes custom marshaling and unmarshaling code unnecessary. Programming is further simplified for those classes that already derive from the RWCollectable abstract class. For these classes, otherwise tedious code is automatically generated through the use of macros provided by Orbstreams.h++.

Orbstreams.h++ provides an effective means to implement pass-by-value functionality in lieu of availability of the OMG pass-by-value specification currently under construction.

9.4 DATABASE ACCESS

Most business systems use relational databases. A database interface must address two fundamental problems: providing an object-oriented interface to the database manager and mapping objects to relational tables. It is always possible to develop a custom interface to encapsulate the underlying database-access mechanisms. For example, a layer can be developed on top of Sybase's Dblib to provide a higher level interface to the database engine. One advantage of this approach is that the functionality can be extended to include some mapping strategies right in the database-access mechanism. This approach also provides opportunities for some application-specific optimizations. For example, pre-compiled dynamic SQL queries can be used to cut down query execution times. Although this approach provides greater flexibility, it can become very costly and time-consuming to maintain the custom code. Any changes will require careful consideration by an experienced developer.

A less expensive and more adaptable approach with ongoing support can be obtained with third-party database-access libraries. Such libraries provide a consistent interface to heterogeneous databases on heterogeneous platforms. Using class libraries generally provides reasonably robust solutions and application portability across platforms. However, none of these libraries incorporate mapping mechanisms and may be difficult to extended to provide additional functionality. In our example application, we used the RogueWave database access class library, DBTools.h++, to implement the persistence service. It provides database and platform independence. Other products might be used in a similar manner. The following sections describe important capabilities of the DBTools.h++ library.

9.4.1 Basic Features

DBTools.h++ provides classes to work with relational databases in C++. It allows the application to be ported to different database management systems and encapsulates the SQL language. Thus shielding the application from vendor-specific variants of SQL while allowing the user to access the underlying libraries directly.

DBTools.h++ is completely compatible with Tools.h++. Besides supporting the basic data types of Tools.h++, DBTools.h++ provides additional storage data types like RWDBBlob for binary large objects, RWDBDate for date values, and RWDBDateTime for date and time values. These specialized data storage types provide for variations in representation between different database management systems.

In DBTools.h++, a database is represented by RWDBDatabase. An instance of RWDBDatabase represents a database server. Among other things, RWDBDatabase manages connections to the database. An instance of this class can only be obtained by invoking a static method on the class RWDBManager. A database connection is represented by an instance of RWDBConnection and is obtained on invoking the connection method on RWDBDatabase. Together, these classes manage the database sessions for the user.

DBTools.h++ provides classes to represent database table structures. RWDBTable provides a uniform representation of tables, whether they are database tables or tables representing the result of a join. RWDBColumn represents a database column, RWDBRow represents a database row, RWDBSchema represents the database schema, and RWDBStoredProc represents a store procedure in the database. A table object can be used to create and drop indexes on the table, grant or revoke privileges, and add and drop columns from the table. RWDBRow is mostly for internal use. RWDBSchema is an encapsulation of the database schema. A table object can be asked to provide its schema. If the underlying database supports stored procedures, then the RWDBStoredProc class can be used to build the parameter list for the stored procedure.

SQL commands can be programmatically constructed using objects to represent the elements of the command. RWDBSelector, RWDBUpdater, RWDBInserter, and RWDBDeleter represent the select, update, insert, and delete operations of SQL. An instance of RWDBSelector is used to establish a SELECT statement. Different clauses can be added to the select statement through intuitive overloading of various operators and through operations having names corresponding to the clause, e.g., the where operation adds the WHERE clause.

For those operations performing queries, DBTools.h++ assists in processing the results through RWDBResult, RWDBReader, and RWDBCursor. An instance of RWDBReader is used to process tabular data, row-by-row. Extraction operators can be used to extract result values from the current row in an RWDBReader. An RWDBResult is used when a database operation may produce multiple SQL table expressions. An RWDBReader object can be used to access rows of each table held in an RWDBResult.

DBTools.h++ provides access to the underlying database vendor-specific library through the class RWDBSystemHandle. RWDBSystemHandle is a base class from which a series of database-specific classes derive. The instance obtained can be type cast to the specific type, then all the implementation specific features are provided. This provides direct access to all the features of a specific database management system which, if exploited, can impair application portability.

DBTools.h++ provides error handling through the class RWDBStatus. Most DBTools.h++ classes that interact with the database provide a method to see if the operation just executed was valid and get an instance of status. The RWDBStatus object contains error codes and descriptive messages describing the error. The RWDBStatus class stores all the error messages provided by the vendor library and makes them accessible to the application. Furthermore, the application can install its own error handlers, which can throw C++ exceptions, and the application can then catch those exceptions.

9.4.2 DBTools.h++ Architecture

DBTools.h++ uses a design pattern commonly known as the Bridge pattern. This pattern separates an abstract interface from specialized implementations. For example, DBTools.h++ classes define a consistent interface for any

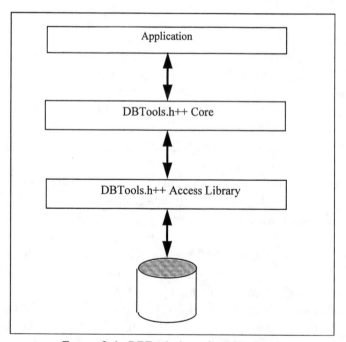

FIGURE 9.1. DBTools.h++ Architecture

database on any platform. These interface objects then delegate to implementation objects for the specific database-management system being used. This architecture is depicted in Figure 9.1 below.

Classes in the DBTools; core library describe the generic interfaces for database operations. The database-access implementation is provided the access library. Access libraries are database vendor specific. If you are using ODBC, you purchase access libraries for ODBC along with the database management system(s) you are using. It is possible to link multiple access libraries to a process so that an application can interface to databases using different database-management systems.

9.5 SUMMARY

Many of the components provided by these libraries may seem trivial. However, they include methods and appropriate structure for the integration of these elementary components in a variety of contexts involving database access, interoperability, exception handling, and persistence of application models. It is essential that applications are supported by a consistent set of such components or the development will take longer and risk failure and poor performance.

Running the Business-Objects Facility

EDS developed an initial version of BOF called EBOF (Enterprise Business Objects Facility) based on the concepts presented in this book. This initial version of the BOF is production grade software and is being used to build production applications. BOFs represent a new generation of development tools and we are witnessing the beginning of this era. These tools will evolve to support all the capabilities described earlier. This appendix describes the installation and setting up of the EBOF provided on the CD with this book.

The EBOF version accompanying this book is a demo version of EBOF and is limited in its capabilities. BoStudio, the interactive-development tool, allows only 10 objects to be defined in a repository file. The transaction server will not allow more than 10 transactions without having to restart it. No more than 10 objects can be created in any application server. The demo version gives a full flavor of the framework's capabilities, but is not useful for real systems. The application servers built with EBOF are expected to run on Windows NT 4.0. The database service provided will work with SQL Server, Sybase, and Oracle using ODBC to communicate with them. EBOF uses Orbix 2.2c (multithreaded), Visual C++ 5.0, and RogueWave's Tools.h++.

A.1 EBOF SETUP

EBOF creates an environment in which many services are integrated with an abstract business object. The package provided with the book consists of object services, tools to support EBOF operations, and libraries used to build and integrate business objects. EBOF includes eight primary services. These are naming service, life cycle service, database service, workload service, relationship service, query service, transaction service, and concurrency control. Some of these services are packaged as separate executables and others are library-based services. In almost all cases, the usage of these services is inherited by the business objects built using EBOF.

EBOF comes with an installation program that prompts the user for required options, installs the proper services, and sets the proper environment variables. There are a few things the user needs to know about the installation and set up process. First, install Orbix before installing EBOF, and the Orbix daemon should be running before the EBOF installation program starts up. During the installation, the setup tries to install the EBOF services in Orbix's implementation repository. If the Orbix daemon is not running, then the installation of services in the implementation repository will fail. If that happens, the services can still be registered with the implementation repository later on with appropriate options, as shown in the batch file created by the installation program.

EBOF requires certain environment variables to be defined. The installation program creates an autoexec.bat file rather than putting those variables in the NT registry in this release. These environment variables can be placed in the registry through the control panel if desired.

EBOF is a tool for building and managing distributed systems. Its own services can be configured to run in a distributed environment. We recommend that the database service be run on the same host as the DBMS. The database service consists of two components. The first component is the EBofDBSManager, which manages the pool of database connections. The second component is EBofDBS, which encapsulates a database. EBofDBS takes as arguments the number of connections and the type of database. Each instance of the EBofDBS process manages the number of database connections passed to it through the command line for the type of database indicated. For example, if you have 20 SQL server licenses, you can start four instances of EBofDBS, each managing five database connections, or you can start 20 instances of EBofDBS each managing a single connection. Internally, EBofDBS creates a thread for each database connection and all interactions for that connection are performed inside that thread. Since EBofDBS inter-acts heavily with the actual DBMS server we recommend that the EBofDBS be run on the same machine as the DBMS server. The EBofDBSManager does not have to run on the same host.

EBOF also includes a process not fully handled by the installation pro-gram. This process is called EBofWLAgent. The application servers built using EBOF can be configured to run in a highly distributed environment. The workload service manages the workload in a distributed environment and attempts to balance the load among the application servers. The work-load service is a central service. To facilitate the workload management, EBofWLAgent must be registered with Orbix's implementation repository on each machine where an EBOF-based application server may be running. Since this information is not available at installation time, EBofWLAgent is not registered with the implementation repository. Hence, you must register EBofWLAgent on the hosts where the application servers are running.

The final step after installation is to regenerate the IDL client stubs. After ensuring that Orbix is properly configured, go to the IDLInterfaces subdi-rectory under the EBOF installation directory and execute the makefile in that subdirectory with the following command:

```
nmake all -f makefile.iot
```

A.2 BUILDING APPLICATIONS WITH EBOF

When the user generates the source code for a component through BoStudio, a makefile is created compatible with the Visual C++ console-based applica-tion. The user should specify the paths for the necessary include files in Visual C++ for it to work properly. The recommended method for doing this is to select the Options item from the Tools menu. Select the Directories tab and specify the <ebof installation>\include and <ebof installation>\IDLInterfaces directories. Specify <ebof installation>\Lib for library paths.

EBOF includes two libraries, EBofInterfacesITD.lib and EBofInterfacesITR.lib. The EBofInterfacesITD.lib is a debug library that logs a significant amount of debug information. This information is placed in the subdirectory pointed to by the environment variable EBOF_LOG_AREA. Underneath this subdirec-tory, further subdirectories are created for each running process, which was been linked with EBofInterfacesITD.lib and contains a numbered log. These logs are truncated according to the size specified by the environment variable

EBOF_LOG_SIZE. EBofInterfacesITR.lib is the release version and does not log any information. EBofInterfacesITR.lib is much faster than EBofInterfacesITD.lib.

A developer license of multithreaded Orbix 2.2c is required to build applications with EBOF. A license of RogueWave's Tools.h++ is also required. To run EBOF-based applications, the runtime license of Orbix is required. RogueWave's DLLs can be freely distributed without any runtime charges. The installation program includes the necessary DLLs for RogueWave, but none of the header files are distributed;the same is true for Orbix.

Reliable Financial Services Business Application

This appendix presents the hypothetical business problem and the solution that is implemented as the example application. The application is a system to automate stock trading transactions at the Reliable Financial Services (RFS) brokerage company.

B.1 RFS OVERVIEW

RFS trades in all kinds of securities, including stocks, bonds, and mutual funds. RFS trades on all major stock exchanges and maintains sales offices in most major U.S. cities. The central office is located in New York City. RFS has account brokers in its sales offices and floor brokers in all the exchanges where it trades.

Account brokers interface directly with the clients. Account brokers provide financial advice to the clients and accept buy or sell orders. The account broker may be asked about current market price of certain securities. RFS receives the current market price through the consolidated ticker tape from NYSE. All client requests are logged whether they are executed or not. The account broker may contact the customer about the trade when he receives the trade disposition. Clients are usually sent a statement every month.

RFS clients can be individual investors or businesses. Each investor is required to maintain a cash or margin account with RFS. RFS clients may have multiple accounts. A primary broker is usually assigned to each customer. However, there is always a backup broker who can accept buy or sell orders for clients when their primary broker is unavailable. A client account may have a number of portfolios and each portfolio consists of a number of securities.

Clients call their account broker for a trade request. The account broker then communicates the client's request to the floor broker on the exchange where the security is traded. The floor broker executes the trade and confirms the execution back to the account broker. The account broker then notifies the client. RFS clients can place different types of orders.

A floor broker is responsible for executing the trade request. When a floor broker receives the trade request, he takes the request to the floor and tries to get the best price for the trade request. Floor brokers sometimes combine several different requests into one trade or may split a large request into several trades. It is the trade order that is taken to the floor. A trade order may be for one trade request or multiple ones. Once the order has been executed, the floor broker provides information on completion of the action to each account broker who generated a request.

The most common types of orders are the following:

- Market orders, which are executed immediately at the market price.
- Limit orders, which have a limit on the amount paid or received for securities.
- Stop orders, which usually have a stop price associated with them.
- Stop limit orders, which are a combination of the above two to minimize the risk and maximize the profit.

B.1.1 Trade Requests

When the client calls the account broker and places a trade request, a whole sequence of events starts. The trade request is recorded on a form, called an "order ticket." This ticket has the following information:

1. Client identification.
2. Account broker identification.
3. Description of trade (security symbol, number of shares, and whether it is a buy order or a sell order).

4. Order type—market order, etc.

5. Account identification—where the money is to be taken or put.

6. Miscellaneous—security instructions, payment instructions.

This ticket is then transmitted to the floor broker on the exchange where the security is traded. The floor broker can only combine requests for the same security with the same action. He cannot satisfy the request to sell 100 shares of XYZ with another request for purchase 100 shares of XYZ without first taking it to the exchange floor and offering it there. Once the floor broker has executed the trade, he sends a confirmation of the transaction to the office(s) where the request originated. This confirmation is recorded and commissions are calculated. The commission for each trade is split between the account broker, the floor broker and RFS. This commission is usually dispersed after the client has paid the net amount due. The confirmation report typically includes trade date and settlement date; relevant information from the original ticket; and all applicable prices, fees, commissions, taxes and net amounts.

B.2 PROTOTYPE SYSTEM REQUIREMENTS

RFS asked its IS department to build a portfolio of applications to support various business operations. The overall system is named Securities Management System (SMS). RFS analyzed its business processes and determined that the sequence of trading is susceptible to error at two points: communication of trade request between client and the account broker and the transmission of the trade request from account broker to the floor broker.

The account broker assistant is expected to help the account broker in both of the above areas. By providing electronic assistance to its brokers and other departments, RFS hoped to increase the reliability of its business processes, provide more timely information to its brokers, and conserve resources by providing electronic assistance to various other departments.

The prototype system is limited in scope as follows:

- Trading is only on the New York Stock Exchange.
- Only stocks traded are handled.
- Individual investors are the clients.
- Cash accounts are used.
- Market orders are the transactions handled.

All sales offices, the central office, and the floor brokers will be connected to each other through this computer system. The computer system includes five main applications: account broker assistant, floor broker assistant, controller office assistant, clearinghouse assistant, and system administrator assistant. These are outlined in the following sections.

B.2.1 Account Broker Assistant

The Account Broker Assistant allows the account broker to create/delete new accounts. This interface allows the account broker to accept buy or sell orders (create electronic tickets) which are transmitted to the floor broker. This interface receives all confirmations for trade requests generated by a broker. The account broker can obtain the current market value of a specified security from the consolidated ticker tape

The Account Broker Assistant gets a list of clients and current orders, which allows the account broker to follow up on certain activities. It also allows the account broker to look at the history of all transactions against an account. The account broker should also be able to get a listing of open trade orders and completed trades by day, week, month, and year.

The interface allows the account broker to get the value of client portfolios, look at the price history, unrealized gains, and so forth. It also allows the broker to create or update portfolios for the client, which aids in managing a client's portfolio.

B.2.2 Floor Broker Assistant

This interface allows the account broker to send a trade request to the floor broker, and to generate the order for the trade request. It also allows the floor broker to look for other trade requests for the same security. He can then possibly combine several trade requests or split them. It allows the floor broker to close a trade and send a notification to the account broker of the trade status.

B.2.3 Controller Office Assistant

This interface has the following components:

1. **Generate report:** The controller's office is responsible for generating different kinds of financial reports that need to be sent to different regulatory agencies.
2. **Generate statements:** This allows the controller's office to send monthly or quarterly statements to the clients describing the activities in their account for that period.

B.2.4 Clearinghouse Assistant

The clearinghouse is responsible for receiving and delivering securities and monies. This interface allows it to get information about trades at the end of the day. The certificates can then be sent to transfer agents to be transferred to the clients.

B.2.5 System Administrator Assistant

The system administrator allows the designated system administrator to view and update the list of allowed users of the system.

B.3 BOF SAMPLE

The following paragraphs describe the example implementation. The purpose of this example is to describe the process involved in building applications using EBOF. We built a small portion of the application described above. The application includes an Account broker assistant and a partially implemented stock exchange model.

The implementation includes a BoStudio repository file called RFS.bos, which can be opened by BoStudio. This file contains the specifications for all the business objects defined for this system, their relationships, and definitions of different components. The user is encouraged to generate some of the code again, which may be created in a separate directory, to get a feel of the kind of code EBOF generates. As described in Chapter 5, many files are generated for each business object. The programmer is primarily interested in the file with the same name as the business object with an _i appended to it. This will be of interest only if there were user-defined methods for that business object. The programmer may also be interested in providing an implementation of the Validate method.

In the example, the StockExchangeSrv component is able to instantiate Stock and FloorBroker objects, among others. The FloorBroker object is not implemented. The Stock Object does not have any specific business logic associated with it. It does have two query methods, GetStockBySymbol and GetAllStocks, which are completely generated by the system. No user code was written for the StockExchangeSrv component.

AccountBrokerSrv has several different examples where user code was written, AccountBroker has a method called AddPrimaryClient. The user interface layer provides all the data necessary to create a new client and pass the data to this method. This method is defined in AccountBrokeri.cpp.

The handwritten code in AccountBrokerSrv checks to see if a transaction is already active. If it is, fine, otherwise a new transaction is started. It then creates a new instance of the Client business object using the EbofGenericObjectManager. The client and the account broker have a one-to-many relationship. After the client object has been created, the account broker adds that instance to the appropriate relationship. If we started a transaction here, then it is committed, otherwise we can return. The only exposure of CORBA in this code is in the very last line where a "duplicate" is executed. According to CORBA rules, if an object is being returned and that object needs to exist after its reference has been returned, then its reference count has to be incremented with a call to the duplicate method. Other than that, we have effectively hidden all CORBA aspects from the user's view.

B.4 SETTING UP THE SAMPLE

The sample source code and the executable code are provided. The user can execute the application and get some understanding of EBOF capabilities, even without some of the other tools that are required. The first step is to install AccountBrokerSrv and StockExchangeSrv using the workload manager. Start the Orbix daemon and then start BoWorkloadManager. On the workload manager, first create a component called StockExchangeSrv and then AccountBrokerSrv. The StockExchangeSrv manages the business objects Stock and FloorBroker, while the AccountBrokerSrv manages Account, Client, AccountBroker and TradeRequestOrder. These must be provided as managed types when the component is being created in BoWorkloadManager. After the components have been created, create a single instance of each component. You have configured your application servers and Orbix's implementation repository has been modified.

Also included with the sample is an SQL file for SQL Server. This file can be used to create a database. The name of the database should be RFS and appropriate entries can be created in the ODBC manager. Execute PIDManager and make sure that the proper persistent context information is entered in the PID manager. After having created the database and a PID called RFS, you are all set to execute the client applications.

ExchangeManager is a GUI-based program that allows creation of new stock objects to be traded on the floor and also records their trades. The account broker assistant first prompts for the id of a broker. This means that the broker object should already exist. An additional program, called CreateBroker, is provided to create a single instance of a broker object. Once this has been done, the account broker assistant can be started.

The account broker assistant will present a list of all clients for this broker. It also allows creation of new clients. Any client can be selected and the assistant will present that client's summary information. A list of all the client's accounts can be obtained or a new account can be created.

The account broker assistant can also be used to examine all different stocks being traded on the floor and to monitor some stocks. If the prices of those stocks change, then EBOF will send notification to the account broker assistant for those stocks.

Have fun!

APPENDIX C

License

$\mathbf{B}$y opening the package containing the software and/or by using the software, you are agreeing to be bound by the following agreement.

Some of the software included with this product may be copyrighted, in which case all rights are reserved by the respective copyright holders. You are licensed to use the software on a single computer for educational purposes only and not for commercial purposes.

You many not redistribute the software. You may copy the software only for purposes of use in accordance with the terms of this License.

THE SOFTWARE IS PROVIDED AS IS, WHERE IS, WITHOUT WARRANTY OF ANY KIND, AND NO WARRANTY IS GIVEN THAT THE SOFTWARE IS ERROR-FREE OR THAT ITS USE WILL BE UNINTERRUPTED OR THAT IT WILL WORK IN CONNECTION WITH ANY OTHER SOFTWARE. ALL WARRANTIES, CONDITIONS, REPRESENTATIONS, INDEMNITIES AND GUARANTEES, WHETHER EXPRESS OR IMPLIED, ARISING BY LAW, CUSTOM, PRIOR ORAL OR WRITTEN STATEMENTS, (INCLUDING, BUT NOT LIMITED TO, ANY WARRANTY OF MERCHANTABILITY OR FITNESS FOR PARTICULAR PURPOSE OR OF ERROR-FREE AND UNINTERRUPTED USE OR ANY WARRANTY AGAINST INFRINGEMENT) ARE HEREBY OVERRIDDEN, EXCLUDED AND DISCLAIMED, EXCEPT AS OTHERWISE EXPRESSLY STATED IN THIS LICENSE.

Neither the Publisher nor its dealers or distributors assumes any liability for any alleged or actual damages arising from the use of the software.

You also agree to be bound by the terms of the EDS Software License Agreement set forth below.

EDS SOFTWARE LICENSE AGREEMENT

The product which you obtained may include software in which Electronic Data Systems, Corp. owns certain rights (the Software). By opening the package containing the Software and/or by using the Software, you are agreeing to be bound by the following legally binding and valid contract.

1. GRANT OF LICENSE: Electronic Data Systems, Corp. (EDS) grants to you the right to use one copy of the enclosed software on each of two and only two computers (each computer with a single CPU) for demonstration purposes and/or educational purposes only, and not for commercial purposes. You may not network the Software on more than two computers or otherwise use it on more than two computers or computer terminals at the same time. The terms of this EDS Software License Agreement (Agreement) shall be applicable to any upgrades, modified versions or updates of the Software.

2. INTELLECTUAL PROPERTY: The Software is owned by EDS or its suppliers and is protected by United States copyright laws and international treaty provisions. Therefore, you must treat the Software like any other copyrighted material (e.g., books, videos, or music CD's) except that you may either (a) make one copy of the Software solely for backup or archival purposes, or (b) transfer the Software to a single hard disk provided that you keep the original solely for backup or archival purposes. You may not make derivative works based upon the Software. You may not copy the written materials accompanying the Software. You may not download or transmit the Software electronically from one computer to another. You may not load the Software on a computer in any way that would allow the Software to be accessed, used, copied, modified, or examined through the Internet. The Software contains computer software technology including but not limited to methods, systems, algorithms, techniques, etc. (collectively, the "technology"), that is the property of EDS. Some or all of this technology may be protected by patents, trademarks, copyrights or other intellectual property rights (collectively, the "intellectual property."). EDS may have patents pending on certain aspects of the technology and may apply for patents on other aspects of the technology in the future. No license of any kind, either express or implied, is granted to any party as to any intellectual property except as expressly set forth herein

3. OTHER RESTRICTIONS: You may not rent, timeshare, lend, or lease the Software, but you may transfer the Software and accompanying written materials on a permanent basis provided that you retain no copies and that the recipient agrees to the terms of this EDS Software License Agreement. You may not reverse engineer, decompile, or disassemble the compiled Software as the Software contains trade secrets of EDS. You many not otherwise modify, alter, adapt, or merge the software. You many not remove or obscure EDS patent, trademark, or copyright notices. You agree that the Software will not be shipped, transferred or exported into any country or used in any manner prohibited by the United States Export Administration Act or any other export laws, restrictions or regulations.

4. NO WARRANTIES: THE SOFTWARE IS PROVIDED AS IS, WHERE IS, WITHOUT WARRANTY OF ANY KIND, AND NO WARRANTY IS GIVEN THAT THE SOFTWARE IS ERROR-FREE OR THAT ITS USE WILL BE UNINTERRUPTED OR THAT IT WILL WORK IN CONNECTION WITH ANY OTHER SOFTWARE. ALL WARRANTIES, CONDITIONS, REPRE-SENTATIONS, INDEMNITIES AND GUARANTEES, WHETHER EXPRESS OR IMPLIED, ARISING BY LAW, CUSTOM, PRIOR ORAL OR WRITTEN STATEMENTS, (INCLUDING, BUT NOT LIMITED TO, ANY WARRANTY OF MERCHANTABILITY OR FITNESS FOR PARTICULAR PURPOSE OR OF ERROR-FREE AND UNINTERRUPTED USE OR ANY WARRANTY AGAINST INFRINGEMENT) ARE HEREBY OVERRIDDEN, EXCLUDED AND DISCLAIMED, EXCEPT AS OTHERWISE EXPRESSLY STATED IN THIS LICENSE.

5. NO LIABILITY FOR CONSEQUENTIAL DAMAGES: In no event shall EDS or its suppliers be liable for any damages whatsoever (including, without limitation, damages for loss of business profits, business inter-ruption, loss of business information, or other pecuniary loss) arising out of the use of or inability to use the Software, even if EDS has been advised of the possibility of such damages. Because some states do not allow the exclusion or limitation of liability for consequential or incidental damages, the above limitation may not apply to you.

6. PURCHASER ASSUMES RISK OF DAMAGE: You bear the entire risk as to the quality and performance of the software. You assume risk to any hardware, software, data, or any other item as a result of the copying or use of the Software, including but not limited to the cost of any repairs or replacement of any item or any services.

7. CHOICE OF LAW: THIS AGREEMENT WILL BE INTERPRETED AND ENFORCED IN ACCORDANCE WITH THE LAWS OF THE STATE OF TEXAS APPLICABLE TO AGREEMENTS MADE ENTIRELY WITHIN THAT STATE BETWEEN PARTIES DOMICILED THEREIN. This Agreement will not be governed by the United Nations Convention on Contracts for the International Sale of Goods, the application of which is expressly excluded.

8. SEVERABILITY: If any provision of this Agreement is found void or unenforceable, it will not affect the validity of any other provision of this Agreement and those provisions shall remain valid and enforceable according to their terms.

9. UNITED STATES GOVERNMENT RESTRICTED RIGHTS: If this Software is acquired under the terms of a (1) GSA contract—Use, duplication, or disclosure shall be subject to the restrictions set forth in the applicable ADP Schedule contract; (2) US DoD Contract—Use duplication or disclosure by the U.S. Government shall be subject to restrictions as set forth in subparagraph (c)(1)(ii) of 252.227-7013; (3) Civilian Agency Contract—Use, reproduction, or disclosure is subject to 52.227-19(a) through (d) and restrictions set forth in the accompanying EDS Software License Agreement.

10. OTHER RIGHTS RESERVED: All rights not specifically granted in this Agreement are reserved by EDS.

11. TERMINATION: This Agreement shall terminate automatically if you fail to comply with any of the terms described herein. On termination, you agree to destroy all copies of the Software and any accompanying documentation or related publications.

ORBIX RUNTIME LICENSE AGREEMENT

READ THE TERMS OF THIS ORBIX LICENSE AGREEMENT (THE "AGREEMENT") CAREFULLY. BY OPENING THE PACKAGE CONTAINING THE SOFTWARE AND/OR BY

USING THE SOFTWARE, YOU (THE "CUSTOMER") ARE ACCEPTING AND AGREEING TO THE TERMS OF THIS AGREEMENT. IF YOU ARE NOT WILLING TO BE BOUND BY THE TERMS OF THIS AGREEMENT, THEN YOU SHOULD NOT USE THE SOFTWARE.

All right, title and interest in the Orbix Runtime Components (as defined in Section 1) provided to Licensee is owned by IONA Technologies Limited of 8-10 Lower Pembroke St., Dublin 2, Ireland. IONA has all rights necessary to enter into this Agreement. This Agreement does not grant Licensee any right, title or interest in the Orbix Runtime Components, other than the limited right to use and distribute such Orbix Runtime Components upon acceptance of and in accordance with the terms and conditions of this Agreement.

1. DEFINITIONS.
(a) The term "Software," as used herein, means the set of machine-readable material in object code form on magnetic media, or any upgrade thereof, provided to Licensee on this compact disc.

(b) The term "Orbix Runtime Components," as used herein, means any software program or components of Orbix which are included in the Software. The Orbix Runtime Components shall include, but not be limited to, the following:

   The Orbix libraries;
   The Orbix daemon;
   The Orbix utilities (e.g.: lsit, putit, killit, orbixcfg.exe, orbixdw.exe, rmit); and
   The Orbix Interface Repository.

2. GRANT OF LICENSE.
(a) IONA hereby grants to Licensee, subject to the conditions herein, a license to use the Orbix Runtime Components ("Orbix Runtime License"), but solely as (i) part of the Software (ii) and solely for personal non-commercial use. Licensee shall not have rights of onward distribution

(b) Licensee further agrees that the Orbix Runtime License granted here-in does not give Licensee or any other party any rights other than those specifically granted herein, and that such License specifically does not grant the Licensee or any other party the rights to:
execute the Orbix IDL compiler;
develop and link programs with the Orbix libraries; or
read and use the Orbix header files.

3. PROTECTION OF CONFIDENTIAL INFORMATION AND RESTRICTIONS.

(a) Licensee shall not remove any trademark, tradename, and copyright notice or other proprietary notice from the Orbix Runtime Components.

(b) Licensee may not modify, adapt, translate, decompile, disassemble or reverse engineer the Orbix Runtime Components or any part there-of in any form whatsoever. © Licensee may not copy the Orbix Runtime Components other than for back up or archive purposes.

4. LIMITED WARRANTY.

IONA DOES NOT WARRANT THAT THE FUNCTIONS CONTAINED IN THE ORBIX RUNTIME COMPONENTS OR THE RESULTS OF THEIR USE WILL MEET LICENSEE'S REQUIREMENTS, THAT THE OPERATION OF THE ORBIX RUNTIME COMPONENTS WILL BE UNINTERRUPTED OR ERROR FREE OR THAT ANY DEFECT IN THE ORBIX RUNTIME COM-PONENTS WILL BE CORRECTABLE. EXCEPT AS EXPRESSLY SET FORTH ABOVE, ORBIX RUNTIME COMPONENTS ARE PROVIDED TO LICENSEE "AS IS" WITHOUT WARRANTY OF ANY KIND, EITHER EXPRESS OR IMPLIED, INCLUDING BUT NOT LIMITED TO THE IMPLIED WARRANTIES OF MERCHANTABILITY AND FITNESS FOR A PARTICULAR PURPOSE. THE ENTIRE RISK AS TO THE SUITABILITY, QUALITY AND PERFORMANCE OF ORBIX RUNTIME COMPONENTS IS WITH LICENSEE AND NOT WITH THE IONA OR ITS DEALER. SOME JURISDICTIONS DO NOT ALLOW THE EXCLUSION OF IMPLIED WAR-RANTIES, SO THEIR EXCLUSION MAY NOT APPLY TO YOU.

5. LIMITED LIABILITY.

(a)   IONA'S CUMULATIVE LIABILITY TO LICENSEE OR ANY OTHER PARTY FOR ANY LOSS OR DAMAGES RESULTING FROM ANY CLAIMS, DEMANDS, OR ACTIONS ARISING OUT OF OR RELATING TO THIS AGREEMENT SHALL NOT EXCEED, IN ANY CASE, THE AMOUNT PAID BY LICENSEE TO IONA UNDER THE TERMS OF THIS AGREEMENT.

IN NO EVENT SHALL IONA OR ITS SUPPLIERS BE LIABLE FOR ANY INDIRECT, INCIDENTAL, CONSEQUENTIAL, SPECIAL, OR EXEMPLARY DAMAGES (INCLUDING, BUT NOT LIMITED TO, DAMAGES FOR LOSS OF BUSINESS PROFITS, BUSINESS INTERRUPTION, LOSS OF BUSINESS INFORMATION, DATA, GOODWILL OR OTHER PECUNIARY LOSS) ARISING OUT OF THE USE OF, OR INABILITY TO USE, THE SOFTWARE OR ORBIX RUNTIME COMPONENTS, EVEN IF IONA HAS BEEN ADVISED OF THE POSSIBILITY OF SUCH DAMAGES.

IN NO EVENT SHALL IONA BE RESPONSIBLE OR HELD LIABLE FOR ANY DAMAGES RESULTING FROM PHYSICAL DAMAGE TO TANGIBLE PROPERTY OR DEATH OR INJURY OF ANY PERSON WHETHER ARISING FROM IONA'S NEGLIGENCE OR OTHERWISE. BECAUSE SOME COUNTRIES DO NOT ALLOW CERTAIN OF THE ABOVE EXCLUSIONS OR LIMITATIONS OF LIABILITY, THE ABOVE LIMITATIONS MAY NOT APPLY TO YOU.

6. ASSIGNMENT.

The Orbix Runtime License granted hereunder to Licensee may not be assigned, sub-licensed or otherwise transferred by Licensee to any third party without the prior written consent of IONA. IONA may assign or transfer its rights and obligations under this Agreement without notice to or the consent of Licensee at any time.

7. TERMINATION.

(a)   This Agreement and the Orbix Runtime License granted hereunder may be terminated by IONA upon written notice to Licensee in the following situations:

     (i) in the event Licensee breaches any of the provisions of this Agreement; or

(b) Upon termination of this Agreement and of the Orbix Runtime License granted hereunder, Licensee shall cease any further use or distribution of the Orbix Runtime Components, and must return to IONA or destroy, as requested by IONA, all copies in any form of the Software incorporating any of the Orbix Runtime Components in the possession or control of Licensee.

(c) The provisions of Sections 3, 4, 5, and 7 of this Agreement shall survive the termination (for any reason) of this Agreement. IONA reserves the right to take any legal action necessary to recover any amounts payable by Licensee to IONA and any damages incurred by IONA.

8. AMENDMENT; WAIVER.

No modification or waiver of any provision of this Agreement shall be binding on either party unless specifically agreed upon in a writing signed by both parties hereto. Any failure or delay by IONA to exercise or enforce any of the rights or remedies granted hereunder will not operate as a waiver thereof. No waiver by IONA of any breach of this Agreement will operate as a waiver of any other or subsequent breach.

9. SEVERABILITY.

The unenforceability or invalidity of any of the provisions of this Agreement shall not affect the validity or enforceability of any other provision of this Agreement.

10. LAW AND JURISDICTION.

If this License is granted to a Licensee in the United States or Canada, this Agreement shall be governed by and construed in accordance with the laws of the State of Massachusetts and the parties hereby submit to the exclusive jurisdiction of the courts of the State of Massachusetts. If this License is granted to a Licensee in the rest of the world, this Agreement shall be governed by and construed in accordance with the laws of Ireland and the parties hereby submit to the exclusive jurisdiction of the courts of Ireland.

OrbixWeb (TM) V3.0 Evaluation Copy

Prior to installing the software you will need to obtain an evaluation license-key—keys can be obtained by filling out the order form on:

http://www.iona.com/OrbixWeb.html

OrbixWeb 3.0 is a fully self-contained environment and all of the necessary development and runtime components for building full Java-based CORBA client-server distributed applications are included in the release—an Orbix/C++ installation is not required.

Release notes are provided with this software—please read through these carefully.

You will also be required to agree to an OrbixWeb evaluation license agreement prior to installation.

Index

Whizz-Kidz
0171 233 6600